The Business Culture in Germany

The Business Culture in Germany
Portrait of a power house

Collin Randlesome

BUTTERWORTH
HEINEMANN

Butterworth-Heinemann Ltd
Linacre House, Jordan Hill, Oxford OX2 8DP

℞ A member of the Reed Elsevier group

OXFORD   LONDON   BOSTON
MUNICH   NEW DELHI   SINGAPORE   SYDNEY
TOKYO   TORONTO   WELLINGTON

First published 1994

British Library Cataloguing in Publication Data
Randlesome, Collin
  Business Culture in Germany
  I. Title
  338.60943

ISBN 0 7506 1833 7

Printed and bound in Great Britain by Clays, St Ives plc

Contents

Series preface   ix
Preface   xi
Acknowledgements   xv

1 Business and government   **1**
Introduction   1
Federal government in the west   1
Central government in the east   10
The Treuhandanstalt   13
State governments in west and east   15
Conclusion   17

2 Business and the economy   **19**
Introduction   19
Manufacturing   19
Services   31
Agriculture   33
Transport infrastructure   35
Conclusion   36

3 Business and the law   **38**
Introduction   38
The Grundgesetz (GG) or Basic Law   38
The administration of justice   39
The personnel of the law   42
Forms of business enterprise   45
The legal incorporation of eastern Germany   53
Conclusion   55

4 Business and finance   **56**
Introduction   56
The Bundesbank   56
The Big Three   62
Financial markets   68
Conclusion   72

5 Business and accountancy   **74**
   Introduction   74
   Background   74
   Statutory requirements   75
   Accounting principles   77
   Form and content of published accounts   77
   Accounting profession   87
   EC influence   89
   Conclusion   91

6 Business and the labour market   **93**
   Introduction   93
   Demographic trends   93
   Unemployment in the west   94
   Unemployment in the east   95
   Disadvantaged groups   98
   Conclusion   107

7 Business and trade unions   **108**
   Introduction   108
   Umbrella organizations   108
   Entrepreneurial activities   111
   Collective bargaining   112
   Industrial relations at the workplace   114
   Industrial democracy   115
   Industrial conflict   117
   Settlement procedures   117
   Industrial relations in general   118
   Trade-union activities in the east   123
   Medium-term concerns   125
   Conclusion   126

8 Business and employers' organizations   **128**
   Introduction   128
   Background   128
   Umbrella organizations   129
   The BDA   130
   Employers' associations and wage negotiations   132
   The BDI   135
   BDI branch activity   137
   The BDI in the east   138
   The DIHT   140
   The IHKs   140
   Conclusion   143

9 Business, education, training and development **144**
Introduction 144
School education in the west 145
Vocational training in the west 147
Higher vocational training in the west 149
Higher education in the west 151
Management development in the west 155
Lifelong learning 156
School education in the east 157
Vocational training in the east 158
Higher education in the east 159
Management development in the east 160
Reorganization of education and training in the east 162
Conclusion 163

10 Business and the environment **164**
Introduction 164
The origins of the problem 165
Environmental damage 166
The political response 168
Environmental agencies 169
Green police 172
The first successes in the west 173
Initial projects in the east 176
The reaction of business 177
Conclusion 181

11 Business and enterprise **182**
Introduction 182
The entrepreneur in the west 183
Medium-sized companies in the west 185
Finance for small companies 187
Start-ups in the west 189
Start-ups in the east 189
Small companies in the east 191
Management buyouts in the east 192
Conclusion 194

12 Business and business people **195**
Introduction 195
Male managers in the west 195
Female managers in the west 196
Male managers in the east 199
Female managers in the east 203

Engineers in west and east   203
Conclusion   207

13 Penetrating the German business culture   **208**
Introduction   208
Penetrating by marketing   208
Penetrating by acquiring   216
Conclusion   221

Sources and suggestions for further reading   223

Index   226

Series preface

The need for the present series of country books on business cultures arose from the success of *Business Cultures in Europe*, which was first published in 1990, reprinted in 1991, and went into a second edition in 1993. Thereafter, it was felt that the topic of business culture in the major countries in the European Community (EC) was deserving of a larger canvas than that afforded by a mere chapter. Hence a short series of country books is initially contemplated, beginning with Germany and continuing with further publications on Spain, France and the United Kingdom.

All the books in the series have a number of features in common, the most outstanding of which is probably the need to arrive at a tenable definition of 'business culture'.

If a country's 'culture' can be defined as 'the state of intellectual development among a people', then 'business culture' might be held to be 'the state of commercial development in a country'. But the concept of business culture surely embraces this and much more: it also takes in the beliefs, attitudes and values that underpin commercial activities and help to shape the behaviours of companies in a given country. These companies, in their turn, develop their own individual 'corporate cultures', which, put simply, manifest 'the way we do things round here'.

Implicit in the definition of a country's business culture provided above is the fact that there is no such thing as a single, homogeneous European business culture. Europe contains as many business cultures as it does countries. Although the similarities between the business cultures in Europe are legion, so are the differences.

What are the determinants of the business cultures of European countries? What are the factors affecting the similarities and differences between countries? It is self-evident that the relationship between business and government, the shape and orientation of the economy, the financial institutions, and the trade unions all exert a profound effect on the business cultures of all European countries. But is, for example, the attitude of business to green issues equally significant for the business cultures everywhere in Europe? Is, say, the practice of élitism sufficiently widespread to count as a determinant of business cultures in all European countries? The answer in both cases is 'no'.

In other words, the business culture in a particular country grows partly out of what could be called the 'current business environment' of that country. Yet business culture is a much broader concept because, alongside the impulses that are derived from the present business environment figure the historical experiences of the business community, such as the periods of hyper-inflation in Germany in 1923 and, in the west of the country, again after the Second World War. In Spain the legacy of Francoism is still a phenomenon the business community is striving to overcome. Of equal significance for the business culture are the future hopes and aspirations not only of business but also of society at large in a given country. How long, for example, should people work in any one week in the 1990s and beyond?

The books in the series focus on the business culture of the country concerned in the late 1970s, throughout the 1980s, and into the mid-1990s. The individual chapters in the books concentrate on those determinants of business culture that are held to be significant for the country under review. Some of the determinants are common to all the countries in the series; others are relevant for only one or two.

The authors of the books in the series have not hesitated to use foreign words and concepts in their works, because such expressions contribute much to the depiction of the nuances in the business culture of any country. They have, however, been at pains to provide a translation of the term in the foreign language on its first appearance in the book.

A conscious attempt has been made to use the common statistical base provided by the Organization for Economic Co-operation and Development (OECD) wherever possible, and especially with regard to major economic indicators such as growth rates and inflation, so that the reader can make meaningful comparisons between countries. Where common statistics are not available, reputable national sources have been used. Sources have been indicated for all figures and tables.

Towards the end of every book in the series a list of publications has been provided in the form of sources and suggestions for further reading. Here only standard works or publications have been included that might stimulate the reader to delve deeper into special aspects of the business culture in the country under review. These lists should not be regarded as exhaustive.

The authors trust that an appreciation of the business cultures in the major EC countries will lead to a better understanding of the structures and strategies of industries, markets and consumer preferences in the countries covered in the series. While it may not constitute the most important element of a practitioner's knowledge, cultural fluency in any one country could make that vital difference between actually gaining a contract or merely coming close.

Collin Randlesome

Preface

The business culture in Germany presents a fascinating picture in the mid-1990s. Attempts are still being made to introduce into eastern Germany the beliefs, attitudes and core values of the business culture that have been responsible for so much success and so much prosperity in the west. Among the values, strength and conservatism figure above all. They find their general expression in:

- A social market economy in Germany — not a free market economy. A social market economy implies as much market as possible, and as much state interventionism as necessary.
- An economy with a solid manufacturing base. Some 40 per cent of German Gross National Product (GNP) is still derived from manufacturing, including construction, in the third largest economy of the OECD countries.
- A strong research effort to underpin the German manufacturing economy, with approximately 2.9 per cent of GNP spent on Research and Development (R & D).
- A widespread concern for the physical environment, which, despite the high costs entailed, has resulted in western German companies becoming world leaders in products designed for environmental protection.
- The long-termism practised by most German companies, especially the larger ones. The major companies are not in business to make profits that will subsequently be distributed to shareholders as dividends; they are in business to generate surpluses in order to stay in business.
- Being in business is regarded as a worthy and worthwhile activity: selling out to the highest bidder is widely held to be an admission of failure, particularly for small and medium-sized companies.

The strength and conservatism of the German business culture are also reflected by the formal institutions affecting business:

- The legal system, which prescribes a dual board arrangement for major companies, thus separating shareholders' interests from man-

agement concerns, yet still succeeding in catering for employees' needs.
- The accountancy system, which tends to undervalue assets and understate profits.
- The banking system, at the head of which stands the independent and powerful **Deutsche Bundesbank** (German Federal Bank), but which also embraces the Big Three private commercial banks, with their long-term commitment to non-financial companies in the shape of lifeboat operations for firms in trouble and the long-term holding of large amounts of equity in thriving enterprises.
- The education, training and development system, which is considered to be a model to be aspired to by most countries in the developed world.

Strength and conservatism are even present in the less formal associations that developed in post-war western Germany, such as:

- The sixteen major trade unions, one per 'industry' – a major source of negotiating power.
- The employers' organizations, with their intricate web of interlinking structures, one of the consequences of which is that everyone at the top of German business knows everyone else, their staff, their products and their services.

Imagine, then, the problem of bringing together with the above the business culture in former East Germany, some of the characteristics of which were:

- A command economy, where the state, in the form of the East German Communist Party, exercised direct control over more than 96 per cent of GNP.
- An economy that was also strongly oriented towards manufacturing, but where the design and quality of its products were mostly inferior to those of its western counterpart.
- A manufacturing base that had been largely starved of investment in plant and equipment, except for certain prestige, and usually uneconomical, projects.
- An almost total neglect of any considerations for the protection of the environment.
- An education, training and development system, founded on Marxist ideology, which produced engineers with technological expertise some 20 years out of date, and middle managers who did not manage but merely functioned according to the whims of their directors general.

- A trade union structure that, like the economy, was dominated by the Communist Party.

All these contrasts and conflicts within Germany, and the attempts to resolve them, are portrayed in the following chapters, as indeed are the criticisms that have been voiced of certain aspects of the dominant western German business culture in the united country. These criticisms are founded on the consideration that western Germany flourished in the past through adopting a conservative approach but was successful in what could be called conditions of continuous change. However, with shorter product life-cycles, more volatile markets, and increased competition on a global scale — conditions of discontinuous change — concern is being expressed in certain quarters as to whether companies, even in the west of the country, are best equipped to face the challenges of the 1990s and beyond.

Criticism has focused particularly on the 'softer', less tangible, but equally revealing, aspects of the business culture, such as:

- A tendency for companies to be product-led rather than market-oriented.
- Manufacturing companies 'making nails with heads on', i.e. over-engineering their products, one of its latest manifestations being the Mercedes S-class, which has been called by German commentators 'a cathedral on wheels'.
- Risk aversion by major companies, with a preference for straightforward bank funding rather than complex share capital from the equity market.
- Publicity shyness, especially by small and certain medium-sized companies, which still cling to a legal status allowing them to remain extremely discreet even when they expand.
- A lack of a spirit of enterprise throughout western German business, and an accompanying split of vision between company 'owner-drivers' and their managers.

Perhaps, however, one of the most fascinating aspects of all, at this time of integration between the business cultures in former West and East Germany, is the reaction to the process by Germans in the united country. Here, too, the differing responses of citizens in both western and eastern Germany are depicted in detail.

Finally, the ways in which the German business culture might be penetrated by business people from other cultures are discussed.

Acknowledgements

I would like to thank Professor Charles Handy and Pitman Publishing for allowing me to use some of the material I originally wrote for *Making Managers*. Equally, I must thank Dr Paul Stonham, editor of *European Management Journal*, for permitting me to adapt, for the purposes of this book, some of the articles I first published in his journal.

I wish to extend my thanks to the editors of the Price Waterhouse *Guide to Doing Business in Germany* for permission to use extracts from this work, especially in the section on business and accountancy.

My thanks also go out to Dr Gerhard Wegen of Gleiss, Lutz, Hootz, Hirsch & Partners, Stuttgart, and to William B. Chambers of Lecham Partnership Limited, London, for authorization to refer to excerpts from their conference papers.

My gratitude is due to the OECD, whose publications are available through Her Majesty's Stationery Office (HMSO), for allowing me to replicate statistics relating to major economic indicators.

Finally, I am grateful to the Bundesministerium für Umweltschutz (BMU) (Federal Environment Ministry) for authorization to reproduce two diagrams that originally appeared in its publications.

1 Business and government

Introduction

The business culture in united Germany is informed by the attitudes and policies adopted by the federal government in Bonn, subsequently to be transferred in part to Berlin, and by the governments of the sixteen individual states. In addition, during the transition period after unification, the business culture was affected by the work of the **Treuhandanstalt** (Trust Agency), which was charged *inter alia* with the privatization of former state-owned companies in eastern Germany. However, the fact that not a single year goes by without important elections being held at the European, the federal or state level in Germany contributes to delays, compromises and even inconsistencies between industrial policy formulation and its actual implementation.

In general, the relationship between business and government in post-war western Germany was a reflection of the political tenets of the party in power and the economic circumstances prevailing at the time. In stark contrast, the relationship in the east was one of complete subjugation of business to the whims of the state. As a result, it is necessary to treat developments in the 1980s in the two former parts of Germany separately, before considering the activities of the Treuhandanstalt, the policies being pursued in selected individual states, and the general complexion of the relationship between business and government at the end of 1993.

Federal government in the west

The economic philosophy all post-war federal governments in western Germany claimed to espouse, to a greater or lesser degree, was that of the **soziale Marktwirtschaft** (social market economy). The philosophy became reality under Ludwig Erhard, initially in his capacity as Allies-appointed Director of Economic Affairs and later as Minister of Economics in the first four federal cabinets after the Second World War. Indeed, Konrad Adenauer, the first post-war Federal Chancellor, provided a significant definition of social market economy, which he called: 'A renunciation of planning and the direction of production, labour or sales, but within a comprehensive economic policy which also embraces social measures to ensure the welfare of the population as a whole, including provision for the needy'.

The Federal Chancellor for most of the 1980s was Helmut Kohl. He came to power in Bonn in October 1982, in a centre-right coalition led by the Christian Democrats (CDU) and their Bavarian sister-party, the Christian Socialists (CSU), with the Free Democrats (FDP) as junior partners. His accession to government marked the end of a thirteen-year period dominated by the Social Democrats (SPD) in centre-left coalitions with the FDP.

The new government under Helmut Kohl promised the people of western Germany the **wirtschaftliche Wende** (economic turnaround). What the country and business needed, according to Chancellor Kohl, was less state intervention and corporatism of the type that had become commonplace in the last thirteen years, and more market instead. From the very outset of his chancellorship, he pledged to put the 'market' back into the 'social market economy'. In addition, he stated that business had to rediscover the spirit of enterprise (see pp. 182–194) which had made possible the **Wirtschaftswunder** (economic miracle) of the 1950s and 1960s.

Indeed, the state of the economy at the end of 1982 facing Helmut Kohl's first government was anything but miraculous, with economic indicators showing:

- Growth at minus 1 per cent in real terms (only the third minus figure since 1950).
- Inflation above 5 per cent (a very high figure for western Germany).
- Current account in equilibrium.
- Unemployment at an annual average of 1.85 million per month, or 8.8 per cent of the working population.

In addition, investment was down by 5 per cent on the previous year and private consumption down by 2 per cent, both in real terms.

As the *1983–84 OECD Economic Survey on West Germany* observed:

> . . . the new federal government faced the difficult task of pursuing its medium-term goal of reducing government expenditure and inter-vention in order to achieve a durable improvement of growth and investment conditions, while at the same time supporting activity in the short run, the economy being in deep recession. In shaping the budget for 1983, it relied mainly on the retrenchment measures already proposed by its predecessor. But it raised the cuts in social expenditure to a total of DM 12 billion and placed limits on wage and salary increases of civil servants. In addition . . . it proposed

improved incentives for private investment which, however, were to be financed by tax increases.

An upturn in business activity began early in 1983 after a recession that had lasted for almost three years. The recovery was initially due to greater domestic demand but became increasingly sustained by external requirements for goods 'Made in Germany' (see pp. 25–26). In 1983 the rise in consumer prices fell to about 3 per cent per annum, the current account stayed in surplus, and even unemployment began to fall slightly.

Despite the favourable economic developments, the CDU party lost the state elections in Hesse in 1983. CDU delegates were criticized in their constituencies for the federal government's rigorous cost-cutting policies; employers' associations (see pp. 128–143) began to demand more positive policies to take advantage of the economic upswing, and *Bild*, the daily newspaper with the greatest circulation in western Germany, demanded in its largest banner headlines: 'Do something, please!'

Cuts in federal government subsidies, a clampdown on excessive bureaucracy, and a total overhaul of the tax system had already been promised, but in the autumn of 1983 Helmut Kohl launched a further initiative. In what has come to be known as his Marshall Plan Speech, he proclaimed to a meeting of the CDU/CSU parliamentary party the privatization of state holdings in certain companies. The sale of federal assets was initially intended to release the capital with which to subsidize future-oriented technologies. Shortly afterwards, Gerhard Stoltenberg, Federal Finance Minister at the time, announced the partial privatization of the federal holding in VEBA, a large conglomerate company. VEBA was to be only the first of several companies to be privatized. Others mentioned at the time were Volkswagen, Lufthansa (the national carrier), and Schenker (the very profitable subsidiary of the Deutsche Bundesbahn (DB) (German Federal Railways), specializing in freight-forwarding).

The tone had been set and the policies put in place, but the macro-economic results were at best mixed by the time of the federal elections in January 1987:

- Real growth averaged only 2 per cent over the period.
- Inflation was down to 2 per cent, thanks mainly to falling oil prices.
- The current account showed a surplus.
- Unemployment, however, had risen to over 2 million, or almost 9 per cent of the working population.

What had happened to industrial policy? As *The Economist* commented on 7 May 1988: 'In most other OECD countries, governments − conservative and socialist alike − have been deregulating, privatizing and cutting taxes'. They had been keeping the state out of business's decisions and letting markets, not governments, steer economic developments. In this respect '...Helmut Kohl's government has done little. Many of its subsidies to farmers, steelworkers, shipbuilders, coalminers and the rest have increased'. The cash subsidies alone were estimated to cost the western German taxpayer the equivalent of 2.2 per cent of GNP in 1988 (Table 1.1).

The statistics demonstrate the difficulties in terminating subsidies even in an economy as powerful as western Germany's. The level of subsidies rose almost without interruption, and by over 50 per cent, between the wirtschaftliche Wende and German unification, although Kohl's government repeatedly committed itself to reducing them. Some of the categories were not completely under western German but EC control, yet even the portion specifically designated for German farmers also rose (by some 250 per cent) over the period (see pp. 33−35).

The price for all this profligacy in the public sector was that corporate and personal taxation rates were still extremely high. Despite the promised 'tax reform of the century', pandering to special interest groups had delayed the much-needed legislation. In 1987 western German companies were confronted with a total tax of 70 per cent on retained earnings, e.g. double the rate in the United Kingdom. An unmarried employee with an annual income equivalent to $20,000 sacrificed 40 per cent of it in tax and social security contributions − between 10 and 20 per cent more than in any of the five largest OECD economies. The marginal rate for a citizen on a half-average income was 35 per cent, as against only 7 per cent in, for example, the United

Table 1.1   Western German federal subsidies in DM billions (1970−89)

Year	Total subsidies	Agriculture	Energy, mining	Manufacturing	Transport
1970	11.78	5.80	0.64	2.00	2.56
1975	20.39	6.21	1.52	3.49	7.45
1980	30.53	9.31	5.02	5.95	7.62
1985	37.81	12.99	4.49	8.41	8.05
1987	44.78	15.50	9.33	8.90	7.62
1988	47.67	17.54	8.06	9.04	8.18
1989	48.12	18.02	7.31	9.56	8.76

Source: Statistisches Bundesamt

States of America. Reform of the taxation system was completed in 1990, but even then the top rate of income tax was 53 per cent and corporation tax 50 per cent − still some of the highest rates in any of the OECD countries.

Similarly, the federal government's privatization programme had been very much a half-hearted affair up to 1987. A start was made in January 1984 with the sale of part of the government's holding in VEBA for DM 750 million, thus reducing ownership from 43.7 per cent to 30 per cent. Although the shares were sold, an attempt to revive the **Volkskapitalismus** (people's capitalism) of the 1960s by encouraging small investors to purchase VEBA shares failed. Proposals in 1984 and 1985 to privatize the government's 70 per cent holding in Lufthansa were vetoed by Franz Josef Strauss, who was afraid that a privatized Lufthansa would not buy aircraft from the European Airbus consortium, hence threatening western German jobs. Messerschmid-Bölkow-Blohm, a major Airbus partner, was based in Munich, the capital of Strauss's home state of Bavaria. The state of Bavaria also owned a strategic 'golden share' of 5 per cent of Lufthansa.

Gerhard Stoltenberg partially revived the privatization programme in June 1986. The federal government successfully reduced its stake in VIAG, a chemicals, energy and aluminium company, from 100 per cent, including the 12.65 per cent held by the government-owned Kreditanstalt für Wiederaufbau (KfW) (see p. 188), to 60 per cent. The partial privatization of VIAG raised DM 766 million. In October 1986 the government also reduced its stake in IVG from 100 per cent to 55 per cent, bringing in DM 163 million.

The partial privatization of IVG was the last in Kohl's first government, but so many of the jewels still remained in the crown. In addition to Lufthansa, nothing had been done about Volkswagen or Schenker.

As far as business interests were concerned, one of the most positive aspects of Helmut Kohl's Chancellorship up to 1987 was probably the redistribution of wealth it achieved. Taking into consideration taxes, social security contributions and the rate of inflation, the incomes of employees actually fell in the period from 1982 to 1985 by DM 17.5 billion, as calculated on the basis of 1985 figures. Over the same period the incomes of employers rose by DM 100 billion. In 1986 profits also rose much more steeply than wages. However, business failed to invest proportionately. Of the net increase in revenue enjoyed by business from 1982 to 1986, which amounted to DM 154 billion, only DM 22 billion was reinvested in capital goods and plant in western Germany. Outward investment flourished instead, especially towards the United States of America, and initial concern about **Industriestand-ort Deutschland** (western Germany as a location for industry) began to surface – a theme to which future reference will be made (see pp. 28–30).

Helmut Kohl enjoyed at least two strokes of good fortune in the period from October 1982 to the beginning of 1987. Only three months after he came to power, the recession ended and business activity began to pick up again. Then, in 1985, oil prices decreased dramatically – an extremely favourable development for an economy such as that of western Germany, which is so dependent on imported sources of energy (see pp. 20–21). He perhaps enjoyed a third slice of good luck over the same period in that the SPD, the main opposition party, was in massive disarray.

Nevertheless, in the federal elections held in January 1987 Helmut Kohl's CDU and its sister party, the CSU, recorded their worst performance since 1949, winning only 43.3 per cent of second votes cast. Fortunately for Chancellor Kohl, the SPD, with 37.0 per cent of second votes, also performed badly – its worst results since 1961. Kohl's coalition partners, the FDP, did well, with 9 per cent, while **Die Grünen** (the Greens) enjoyed their best federal elections ever, polling 8.3 per cent.

Despite the disappointing election results, the centre-right coalition returned to power in 1987 with the slogan **Weiter so** (more of the same). The policies remained very much as before, but so did the problems:

- An economy that, despite an impressive surge towards the end of the decade, had tended to grow slowly compared with other major OECD countries.
- High unemployment at around 2 million of the working population (see pp. 94–107).
- A state pensions scheme that was becoming increasingly hard to fund from current contributions on account of the rising dependency ratio.
- Disturbing demographic trends of an ageing and declining population, the influx of immigrants from eastern Europe notwithstanding (see pp. 93–94).

After Chancellor Kohl's victory in the federal elections, the privatization programme was set in motion again, this time with greater conviction. In March 1987 the government sold its remaining shares in VEBA for DM 2.5 billion. However, it had to suspend its plans to dispose of its stake in Volkswagen because of a foreign-exchange scandal at the company and on account of resistance from the state of Lower Saxony. One of the reasons for this resistance was that the company was the largest employer in the state, and the government there was reluctant to entrust the carmaker's fortunes to the whims of private shareholders. Lower Saxony still retains 20 per cent of Volkswagen, which is based in Wolfsburg.

In September 1987 the government decided to sell 48 per cent of its stake in the Deutsche Siedlungs- und Landesrentenbank (DSL Bank), an agricultural bank, for approximately DM 400 million. However, this plan was also postponed because of the world stockmarket crash in October 1987. The DSL Bank holding was floated by a consortium led by the Dresdner Bank in October 1989.

The first equity flotation, and, perhaps significantly, privatization after the crash was the sale of a 24.9 per cent stake in the Deutsche Verkehrs-Kredit-Bank (DVKB) in March 1988, which raised DM 58 million. Later in the same month the government finally sold its remaining shares in Volkswagen, representing 16 per cent of the company's total capital and 20 per cent of its votes, for DM 1.1 billion. In May 1988 the federal government also sold its remaining 60 per cent holding in VIAG for DM 1.46 billion. In September 1988 the government stakeholding in Lufthansa was reduced to 55 per cent when it declined to participate in a rights issue. The last major privatization before unification took place in October 1989, when the government sold Salzgitter, the state-owned steel company, to PREUSSAG, for more than DM 2 billion.

By the end of Chancellor Kohl's second government the federal state had, through major privatizations and the disposal of many smaller stakes, cut the number of companies in which it had direct or indirect holdings from the 808 it inherited in 1982 to 132. It raised DM 10 billion in the process.

In April 1989 Helmut Kohl had reshuffled his cabinet, changing three of the top four posts, together with five others. Gerhard Stoltenberg was removed as Finance Minister and replaced with Theo Waigel of the CSU; Hans Klein, also of the more conservative CSU, became minister spokesman responsible for the projection of the Chancellor's personal image. But neither changes in personalities, let alone refurbished images, were to provide the much-needed boost for the economy.

In the summer of 1989 western Germany looked back on too many years of economic underperformance (Table 1.2). Growth of just over 2 per cent per annum was too poor a performance to solve the underlying economic difficulties but too good to engender the kind of crisis atmosphere of 1982, when major changes had suddenly become possible. The OECD suggested that western Germany might be trapped in a vicious circle, where slow growth today leads to slow growth tomorrow. Average growth of just over 2 per cent throughout the 1980s was depressing business confidence and discouraging investment. If the low rate of investment had persisted, fiscal injections even of the modest variety envisaged in the tax reform could have resulted in major inflationary impulses. It was generally agreed that western

Table 1.2   *Western German growth rates (1979–93)*

Year	%
1979	4.0
1980	1.5
1981	0.0
1982	−1.0
1983	1.9
1984	3.3
1985	1.9
1986	2.3
1987	1.8
1988	3.4
1989	3.3
1990	4.5
1991	3.2
1992	0.8
1993	−1.9

Source: OECD

Germany's shortcomings lay not so much in the macroeconomic policies that had been pursued by Helmut Kohl's governments but in their failure to overcome constraints on the supply side of the economy, such as the over-regulation of services and labour-market rigidities (see pp. 31–33).

By September 1989, at the latest, business and government alike were occupied with matters even more weighty than the inadequacies of the economy. Much of eastern Europe, including eastern Germany, was in turmoil. On 28 November 1989, Chancellor Kohl wrong-footed the political opposition in the Federal Parliament with his presentation of a ten-point plan for overcoming the division of Germany. Though he had stated publicly only one year earlier that he would probably not see unification in his lifetime, Kohl and his CDU/CSU alliance seized the unity initiative from the outset.

The steps leading to unity are indicated later (see p. 11), but it is worth pausing here to consider the results of the first pan-German elections, held in December 1990. Helmut Kohl's CDU, together with its CSU allies, won only 43.8 per cent of the votes, fewer than they would have gained in any federal election in western Germany since 1949. The reluctance of Germans to vote overwhelmingly for the Unity Chancellor appeared superficially to indicate a lack of gratitude. After all, Helmut Kohl had demonstrated deft handling of most of the difficult problems surrounding unification since late 1989 and throughout 1990. Moreover, the economy in western Germany was continuing the surge begun two years earlier. Yet Germans, particularly in the west of the country, did not trust his pledge not to raise taxes to pay the unification levy.

The FDP, the second-largest party after the election in the centre-right government, had pursued a shrewd campaign, emphasizing the risk of a lurch to the right if the CDU/CSU achieved an absolute majority. The result was its best showing in a federal election since 1961, and more representation in the government coalition.

The SPD gained only 33.5 per cent of all votes cast, its worst outcome since 1957, mainly as a result of its initial lukewarm stance on German unity. Yet perhaps the biggest surprise of all was the demise of the Greens in the west — they fell below 5 per cent of the vote.

After the election in 1990 the burning question in the relationship between government and business became the one relating to the unity bill. On German Unity Day, 3 October 1990, Helmut Schlesinger, deputy president of the Deutsche Bundesbank at the time (see pp. 60–62), had proposed a radical solution to the cost of unification. He suggested a privatization programme far more comprehensive than western Germany had witnessed before, one that would even include the selling off of the German Federal Railways. He calculated, for example, that merely privatizing Deutsche Bundespost TELEKOM, the telephone company in western Germany, would raise at least DM 20 billion, twice as much as all the privatizations in Kohl's previous governments. However, in December 1990, the government ruled out even partial privatization on the grounds that it would be contrary to the **Grundgesetz** (GG) (Basic Law), since the entire company would have to be transferred from the civil service to become a private firm (see p. 32).

Instead, Chancellor Kohl was obliged to renege on his election promise not to raise taxes in order to fund unification. Amid continuing doubts concerning the real costs, measures were announced in February 1991 to raise over DM 22 billion, in roughly equal amounts, through higher unemployment contributions and the surcharge on income tax, which came into effect on 1 July 1991, the first anniversary of **Gemu** (German economic and monetary union). Additional petrol taxes were to raise DM 6 billion, with some DM 2 billion stemming from higher telephone charges and a tax on insurance premiums. According to Germany's **Bund der Steuerzahler** (BdST) (Taxpayers' Association), the increases added at least DM 1000 to the amount the average wage-earner hands over to the state every year. Moreover, it was announced that the standard rate of VAT would be increased from 14 to 15 per cent as from the beginning of 1993.

Even by the end of 1993 Germans in the west had still not forgiven Chancellor Kohl for what has gone down in the language as his **Steuerlüge** (tax lie).

Central government in the east

The former **Deutsche Demokratische Republik** (DDR) (German Democratic Republic), or East Germany, was recognized as economically the most successful of the Council for Mutual Economic Assistance (CMEA) countries. Indeed, it was held by many in both east and west to be the showcase of the eastern European economies. Its citizens enjoyed a higher standard of living than anywhere else in the Communist bloc, and its business institutions appeared to radiate success and stability.

Relations between government and business could hardly have been closer. The economy was overwhelmingly state-owned: in 1988, only 3.6 per cent of GNP originated from private enterprises, each of which, for example in the handicrafts field, was restricted by the state to employing a maximum of ten staff. It functioned in accordance with five-year plans, which were disaggregated into detailed one-year plans. These were put together by the State Planning Commission on the basis of priorities handed down to it by the **Sozialistische Einheitspartei Deutschlands** (SED) (Communist Party), and to a lesser extent, by proposals made from below by the almost 300 **Kombinate** (state-owned combines or conglomerates) in industry, construction and transport. The combines themselves were made up of some 8000 **volkseigene Betriebe** (VEBs) (nationally-owned enterprises), which were integrated, either vertically or horizontally, into the combines.

Thus the economy of former East Germany was, like many others in the eastern European bloc, a fairly self-sufficient one, where business was commanded to produce a range of goods and services, mainly for domestic consumption. The primary industrial sector (agriculture and mining) and the secondary sector (manufacturing) formed the backbone of the economy, accounting for 52 per cent of employment (see pp. 20–21).

External trade was limited and skewed towards the other countries in the CMEA, where eastern German manufactured goods were exchanged for fuel or raw materials. Eastern Germany thus exported mainly machinery, metals, chemicals and vehicles, precisely those products in which western Germany had become a world leader (see pp. 22–25) – a portent of one of the major post-unification problems, given superior western German quality and design. Exports to western countries, with former West Germany the main trading partner, were primarily intended to earn much-needed hard currency.

The unravelling of the eastern European bloc in 1989 started not only to threaten eastern German exports but also to frustrate citizens eager for the economic and political reforms sweeping the rest of eastern Europe. In the summer of 1989 East Germans began to flee their country through states whose borders were newly open to the west. In East Germany itself the fireworks display celebrating the fortieth anniversary of the foundation of the DDR turned out to be merely a harbinger of the end. Mass demonstrations favouring reform developed.

As defections and huge protests in Leipzig, Dresden and East Berlin partially paralyzed the country, Erich Honecker, the aged East German leader, resigned in favour of Egon Krenz, his protégé in the SED. Yet Honecker's resignation could neither prevent the government's subsequent demise nor delay the event that would symbolize the end of the division of Germany, the fall of the Berlin Wall, on 9 November 1989.

Soon after, Hans Modrow became head of a caretaker government that began to negotiate with West Germany on the basis of the issues raised by Chancellor Kohl's ten-point plan for German unification. The first free, democratic elections in East Germany were scheduled for May 1990, as the five East German states prepared to join the eleven in West Germany. Yet so intense was the pressure for change that the elections were brought forward to March 1990, thus encouraging East German political parties to lean heavily on the support of their West German counterparts. East Germany's Christian Democrats won the elections, with promises to establish a favourable exchange rate and protect savings during negotiations for German economic and monetary union.

Gemu took place on 1 July 1990, and further references to the process are made in a subsequent chapter (see pp. 59–60). Political unification followed on 3 October 1990. As of this date, the German Democratic Republic acceded to the Federal Republic. The five **neue Bundesländer** (new federal states) – a term detested by most former East Germans, because it ignores the rich traditions of certain eastern states – of Brandenburg, Mecklenburg-Western Pomerania, Saxony, Saxony-Anhalt and Thuringia, as well as East Berlin, which was reunited with West Berlin, became constituent parts of the enlarged Federal Republic of Germany with equal rights. On their accession the former citizens of the DDR automatically joined the EC, with the same rights and duties as people in all other parts of the Community, though certain transitional measures applied until the end of 1992.

The pan-German elections of 2 December 1990 rendered official unification complete. Helmut Kohl's Christian Democrats emerged as the winners, partly as a result of his promise to turn eastern Germany into a '**blühende Landschaft**' ('blossoming landscape'), under western German management, within four years – by the time of the next pan-German elections in December 1994.

The conversion of a former planned economy into a social market economy — as much 'market' as possible: as much 'state' as necessary — could not be completed in one stage. In addition to the passing of laws, to which subsequent reference will be made (see pp. 53—55), far-reaching steps towards restructuring and modernizing the economy were launched throughout eastern Germany. Intensive efforts were begun to reform rigid practices and streamline outdated production facilities.

The initial macroeconomic effects of this conversion process are reflected in an acute fall in growth rates in eastern Germany. Since reliable economic statistics are not available on pre-unification outturns, the statistics in Table 1.3 should be treated with caution.

Incentive programmes offered by the federal, state, and local governments are, however, promoting investment, which is aimed at boosting growth. This is being done by renewing production potential, increasing productivity, and creating much-needed jobs in competitive industries (see pp. 26—27). In 1991 federal investment in eastern Germany amounted to approximately DM 65 billion. Some 80 per cent of the total investment was spent on developing the road, rail and telecommunications infrastructure (see pp. 35—36). In 1992 total net transfers to eastern Germany rose to a staggering DM 180 billion. The federal government was responsible for DM 74 billion of these transfers, thus accounting significantly for the first of its twin deficits — the public-sector budget deficit (see pp. 17—18).

By mid-1992 prospects in eastern Germany were beginning to look rosier, and references to **Aufschwung Ost** (upturn in the east), which began as a new federal government package of interventionist measures in 1991, were heard with greater frequency. Unfortunately, talk of an upturn proved to be too optimistic: a more accurate term would have been 'reduced downturn', as whole industrial sectors were still coming to terms with the effects of restructuring (see pp. 26—27). At the same time western Germany had entered a recession. As a result, prospects for business in the east still looked bleak at the end of 1993.

Table 1.3   *Eastern German growth rates (1990—93)*

Year	%
1990	−13
1991	−15
1992	−10
1993	6.3

Source: Statistisches Bundesamt

The Treuhandanstalt

To facilitate the transition from a command economy to a social market economy, the last former East German government set up the Treuhandanstalt. In June 1990, title to the 8000 VEBs, banks, former state farms and co-operatives, shops and restaurants was transferred to the Treuhandanstalt, thus making it the largest holding company in the world, employing nearly all eastern Germany's 9 million workers.

The statutory duties of this body are defined in the **Treuhandgesetz** (Trust Agency Law) of 17 June 1990, and can be summarized as follows:

- Privatization – rapid and comprehensive reduction of the state's role as entrepreneur.
- Structural adjustment:
  (*a*) restoration of competitiveness,
  (*b*) reconstruction of companies,
  (*c*) promotion and development of effective company structures,
  (*d*) asset management,
  (*e*) application of state assets according to the principles of the social market economy.
- Securing and creating employment opportunities.
- Relief and support of public finances.

Further detail on the Trust Agency Law can be found on pp. 53–54.

The Treuhandanstalt set up its headquarters in Berlin and acquired, in addition, fifteen regional offices throughout eastern Germany. Its direct employees eventually numbered 3000. When first established, it was staffed mainly by former East German functionaries, some of whom were products of the **Seilschaften** (Communist old-boy networks, placing former comrades in influential jobs), who were less than enthusiastic about privatization. In an attempt to add weight to its commitment to privatization, and to maximize efficiency, the German government soon placed executives from the west in the top posts. However, the first of these, Rainer Gohlke, resigned in August 1990 after just one month in the job, using the word 'chaos' to describe the state of the economy in eastern Germany. He was replaced as head of the Treuhandanstalt by Detlev Rohwedder, who was brutally murdered by terrorists on 1 April 1991. The third president was Birgit Breuel.

At first it was calculated that one-third of the original 8000 VEBs would survive in the social market economy without undue problems; one-third would make the transition but only with substantial external investment; and a further third were beyond redemption. In the course of the privatization process in the east the original 8000 companies swelled in number to 12,672 as the larger combines were broken down into smaller and more saleable units.

On 1 March 1993 some 11,000 companies, banks, farms, shops and restaurants had been sold or closed down by the Treuhandanstalt. By far the largest number of acquisitions in eastern Germany were made by companies with their headquarters in western Germany. The 'bank grab' in the east by the Deutsche Bank and the Dresdner Bank has now gone down in legend (see p. 67), and other major western German companies were not slow to seize opportunities there either (see pp. 23–25). These acquisitions have also been accompanied by a limited number of management buyouts (see pp. 192–194).

Fewer than 500 companies in eastern Germany were bought by foreign firms. Top of the league of foreign acquirers were British companies, followed by the Swiss, French, Austrians and Dutch. Among the foreign investors figured British Gas, Asea Brown Boveri, Lafarge Coppée and Unilever N.V. But Coca-Cola made the largest single foreign investment of all, totalling DM 660 million. Problems facing potential foreign buyers ranged from company valuation difficulties (see p. 89) and uncertainty over the ownership of land (see p. 54), to the heavily-polluted state of certain factory sites (see pp. 166–168). Many were also struck by the thought: 'If it's any good, why haven't the western Germans bought it first?'

The privatization of former East German companies represented only one aspect of the Treuhandanstalt's work; it was also obliged to close down companies it deemed to be beyond rescue. By March 1993 over 1000 companies had been liquidated, among them Pentacon, the Dresden manufacturer of Praktica cameras, perhaps former East Germany's most famous product. Interflug, the ex-state airline, suffered a similar fate.

Moreover, most western German companies looking to acquire companies in eastern Germany were only prepared to make major investments at the cost of large-scale redundancies. Robotron, an electronics company now owned by Siemens, was obliged to reduce its staff from 68,000 to 15,000. Carl Zeiss Oberkochen, buying its namesake in Jena, insisted on redundancies on a similar scale. Wholesale company closures and the reduction of workforces inevitably led to huge rises in unemployment in eastern Germany, a theme which will be treated in a subsequent chapter (see pp. 94–98).

The Treuhandanstalt is scheduled to cease its activity by the end of 1994. Its work, however, is likely to be unfinished by that date. With approximately one and a half years of the mandate still to run, it was left with a rump of 1258 companies on its hands. The problem was that many of the remaining companies were large firms in basic industries. They were too unattractive to sell and too big to close down, accounting for approximately one-fifth of eastern Germany's industrial workforce.

The federal government set strict limits to preserving an 'industrial core'. Only firms with a good chance of competing in the market place were to receive federal aid, and for a limited period only. The burden of preserving companies with regional significance thus fell on the states in the east.

State governments in west and east

Germany's decentralized political organization means that individual state governments have more power than such governments in comparable countries. Although the official federal government policy is one of non-intervention in business, in the states the regional politicians are enthusiastic interventionists on behalf of business interests in their particular domains.

The result is that often state policies clash openly with Federal policies. As we have noted (see p. 5), Franz Josef Strauss, the late Minister President of Bavaria, torpedoed the planned sale of the federal government's stake in Lufthansa in 1984 and 1985. Similarly, the sale of the federal government's 20 per cent stake in Volkswagen was announced in 1983, confirmed in 1985, but did not finally take place until March 1988, partly on account of resistance from Lower Saxony (see pp. 6–7).

Perhaps, however, the leading proponent of state interventionism before unification was Lothar Späth, the former Minister President of Baden-Württemberg. He persuaded many high-technology businesses to settle in his state by establishing centres of excellence for research into biotechnology and information technology at the universities of Stuttgart and Ulm. He also saw to it that, by 1991, the state sported thirty-six science parks, which collectively give it the highest ratio of scientists per head in Europe. With seventy-five patent applications per 100,000 inhabitants, Baden-Württemberg also prides itself on producing more innovations than any other state in Germany. Public funding for research is extremely generous: in 1992, the state spent 3.5 per cent of its Gross Domestic Product (GDP) on research and development, compared with 2.9 per cent nationally (see p. 30).

In addition, Lothar Späth inevitably came to prominence in the spectacular series of takeovers by Daimler-Benz in the 1980s (AEG, Dornier, MTU and MBB), since the car company has its headquarters in the state capital of Stuttgart. He was especially active during the Dornier acquisition, because the aerospace company is based at Friedrichshafen, in the south of Baden-Württemberg. In the course of protracted negotiations Lothar Späth smoothed the way for the strife-ridden Dornier family and Daimler-Benz to finalize the transaction, which duly occurred when the car company purchased 66 per cent of the shares. Baden-Württemburg itself acquired 4 per cent.

If the states in the east are seeking a model of technology transfer to emulate, then they can do no better than to study the case of Baden-Württemberg. Unfortunately, their economic problems are of a more basic nature. Even Saxony, Baden-Württemberg's 'twin state' in the east, and probably the one with the best chances of economic success, was still fighting against massive. problems in 1993. The state's unemployment rate was 11 per cent in that year, when more jobs were still being destroyed than created.

In the autumn of 1992 the Treuhandanstalt launched its Atlas programme in Saxony, where the trust agency initially agreed to place forty companies in the scheme. It was to modernize and subsidize these companies for one year, after which it would assess their fitness for the market. Yet the state itself was already beginning to offer similar subsidies. Saxony's government rescued Edelstahlwerke Fretal by agreeing to pay DM 150 million to a western-German acquirer in order to sweeten the deal.

The fear in federal government circles is that eastern Germany is becoming a 'dual economy' of capital-intensive enterprise alongside failing, subsidized smokestack industries. Such was certainly not the intention when, after unification, the federal government attempted to change the former state-dependent business culture by exporting former western politicians eastwards and placing them in key government positions. In 1993, three of the five states had western minister presidents, among them Saxony with the most dynamic of all, Kurt Biedenkopf.

This policy represented a calculated risk at galvanizing the eastern states. The danger was that the new men from the west might further aggravate opinion in the east, which is often bitter about the way in which westerners have imposed the market economy on their failed Communist system. The benefit was that such experienced politicians could provide new leadership to Christian Democrats in the east, who have so far not produced outstanding personalities capable of engendering co-operation between tainted former Communists and zealous young reformers with little experience of political office. Reactions to such appointments have varied between accusations of typical **Wessi** (western German) arrogance towards the east in foisting such personalities on the regional party and frank admissions from **Ossis** (eastern Germans) that they do not trust anyone from their own land.

Indeed Volker Rühe, general secretary of the Christian Democratic Union at the time, spoke of 'two societies in one country', though he did express the hope that the two would be better mixed by the end of 1994, the date of the second pan-German elections. Others are not so optimistic. Robert Leicht, deputy editor of the weekly *Die Zeit*, has stated: 'If you put an east German and a west German together, you will find that they are more different than a German is from a British person... The traditions and habits of these people are impregnated more than they realize'. Hans-Wolfgang Pfeifer, chief executive of the daily *Frankfurter Allgemeine*, goes further: 'You have to realize that these people have been living in a completely different world... A not inconsiderable part of our newspaper is incomprehensible to them'.

Perhaps a more auspicious and discreet form of west−east assistance than exporting western politicians is to be found in the 'state-twinning' system. Here North-Rhine Westphalia has sent over 2000 officials and advisers to Brandenburg, its adopted 'twin' state in the east. Lower Saxony has lent personnel to its eastern neighbour, Saxony-Anhalt; while Baden-Württemberg is helping Saxony, and so on.

Only if such initiatives are successful will western Germans' fears that their prosperity has been shackled to an economic corpse be assuaged (such fears found their expression in the scurrilous television series, *Motzki*, where Ossis were protrayed as lazy, whingeing free-loaders). And only then will eastern German bitterness be overcome, and they will stop complaining that they are being ruled over by a bunch of **Bessis** (besserwissende Wessis) (know-all westerners).

Conclusion

Such social tensions notwithstanding, the relations between business and government in 1993 were fraught. Industrial production was down by some 12 per cent on the previous year, manufacturing orders had fallen by more than 13 per cent, and retail sales in western Germany were below even the depressed levels of 1992. Moreover, the pace of decline led business people throughout the country to fear Germany's worst post-war recession.

The somewhat belated government response was to secure agreement by all the country's parties and states in April 1993 to a **Solidarpakt** (solidarity pact), a drastic austerity package to fend off a deepening recession and raise money for rebuilding the east. The agreement embraced DM 110 billion a year for direct transfers to the five eastern German states and for financing the DM 400 billion in debts left behind by the former East German government. The money was to come from a general rise of 7.5 per cent in income tax, starting in 1995.

This still left Germany with twin deficits to confront. The first foresaw public-sector budget deficits of DM 145 billion in 1993 and DM 140 billion in 1994, the equivalent of some 4.1 and 3.9 per cent of GNP respectively. Both these figures were outside the deficit limit of 3 per cent defined by the Maastricht treaty as a precondition for European Monetary Union (EMU). The second prophesied a rising current account deficit of 2 per cent of GNP in 1993, 3 per cent in 1994, and 4 per cent in 1995 (see pp. 36–37). In 1993 the twin deficits were putting downward pressure on the exchange rate and upward pressure on inflation. The Bundesbank's policy of keeping money supply tight (see p. 58) was exerting dampening effects on the real economy and boosting un-employment (see pp. 94–95).

According to an Allensbach opinion poll held in August 1991, 64 per cent of business people, politicians and civil servants in western Germany were confident that the country as a whole would experience a **zweites Wirtschaftswunder** (second economic miracle) in the next three years – before the second pan-German elections in December 1994. Some 55 per cent of their counterparts in eastern Germany were of the same opinion. Yet among ordinary Germans only 24 per cent of westerners and 25 per cent of easterners were confident of a dramatic economic performance by the united country by the end of 1994. Given the parlous state of the economy in the east and the fact that the west was still in recession in 1993, the sagacity of ordinary Germans can only be admired.

2 Business and the economy

Introduction

The business culture in Germany as a whole is dominated by consider-ations of manufacturing and the wealth creation associated with it. This is partly because Germans in both west and east share a passion for **Technik** (the art and science of manufacturing useful artefacts, see also pp. 203−204). Indeed the **Wohlstandsgesellschaft** (affluent society) in present-day western Germany, and towards which aspirations are turned in the east, depends to a very large extent on the high-quality output of the country's manufacturing industries. High-value-added products, high technology, and technical innovation are fundamental to maintaining this affluence in the west and achieving it in the east. The united country devotes a considerable proportion of national resources to **Forschung und Entwicklung** (Research and Development or R & D), and some individual companies based in the west invest up to 10 per cent of turnover on R & D in order to retain their competitive edge.

Unfortunately, Germany's manufacturing industries were experi-encing more than their fair share of problems in the early 1990s, when they were accused of being too fat, too heavy and too dear. Nor were they being supported by a dynamic services sector, partly on account of the supply-side rigidities already noted (see p. 8). In addition, agriculture continued to represent a problem sector in both west and east.

Manufacturing

The main sector components of western Germany's GNP, before the effects of unification came to be felt, are illustrated in Table 2.1. Indus-try, including construction, clearly dominates, and during the 1980s there was no significant change in GNP sector composition towards the service industries − a development that Germans in general have interpreted as the slippery slope to nowhere whenever they have observed the phenomenon in other economies. Most Germans are

Table 2.1   *Sector components of GNP in western Germany in 1984 and 1989*

	Percent of GNP	
Sector	1984	1989
Industry	40.6	39.7
Commerce and transport	15.3	14.2
Other services	26.2	27.7
State, private households, etc.	13.3	12.7
Agriculture	2.0	1.6

Source: Economist Intelligence Unit, *West Germany: Country Profile, 1990−91*

convinced that a healthy industrial base is the foundation on which all sound economies are built. They have thus ignored siren voices from both inside, but especially from outside, the country urging them actively to promote services as a substitute for manufacturing.

Efforts to relate eastern German economic statistics to western Germany's before 1990 have met with little success. But despite the inherent statistical problems, the figures on labour distribution suggest that the sector composition of eastern Germany was similar to that in the west (Table 2.2). The salient point here is that manufacturing in the two separate parts of Germany accounted for a large percentage of GNP, and in the case of western Germany significantly more than in any of the major OECD countries.

Even by the late 1960s manufacturing was by far the most important sector of the economy in western Germany, the contribution of agriculture having diminished steadily since the Second World War. The traditional smokestack industries were severely affected by the oil crises of 1973 and 1979, although almost all have since staged impress-

Table 2.2   *Distribution of persons employed*

Sector	Western Germany %	Eastern Germany %
Industry/crafts	33.6	40.5
Construction	6.6	6.6
Commerce and transport	18.6	16.2
State (western Germany)	16.0	
'Non-productive' (eastern Germany)		21.4
Agriculture/forestry	4.9	10.8

Source: Economist Intelligence Unit, *West Germany: Country Profile, 1990−91*

ive recoveries. Before the first oil shock, western Germany had to import some 55 per cent of its energy requirements, but nationwide conservation measures cut energy consumption by roughly 6 per cent from 1973 to 1983. West Germany is fortunate in possessing large coal deposits, so it also shifted away from oil-fired power stations towards coal-fired and nuclear ones, until the Greens came to prominence (see p. 168).

As *The Economist* of 26 November 1988 recalled, energy-conservation policies could not fully protect the manufacturing sector from the two oil crises. In addition, western Germany's goods' producers had to discard energy-intensive capital equipment and dismiss workers. Manufacturers of chemicals, pharmaceuticals, cars and aircraft all emerged from the oil-exacerbated downturn by installing more energy-efficient plant and reducing their workforces. Even after the collapse in the world price of oil in the mid-1980s, manufacturing industry did not turn again to oil as a primary source of energy.

Unfortunately, similar measures were not taken in eastern Germany. While much of the area of the five states in the east is an old industrial region where manufacturing enjoys a long tradition, energy continued to be provided mainly by inefficient, highly-polluting, lignite-burning power stations. Moreover, as in other Communist countries, unemployment was an unacceptable phenomenon, so overmanning was rife in virtually all sectors of the economy. In addition, there was little state investment in much-needed new plant and machinery.

According to a study by the **Institut der Weltwirtschaft** (IWW) (Institute of International Economics) in Kiel, at least 21 per cent of industrial machinery and equipment in the area of former East Germany was more than twenty years old in 1990, compared with only 5 per cent in former West Germany. Only 27 per cent of new plant was commissioned there in the five years between 1985 and 1990 (40 per cent in the west).

Little wonder, then, that immediately post-unification there were frequent references throughout the country to what Joseph Alois Schumpeter, the celebrated Austrian-born economist, called in a different context 'creative destruction'. The west's modern manufacturing industries initially experienced the creation, and the east's run-down factories the destruction!

Manufacturing industry remains the backbone of the German economy. In western Germany alone there were some 46,700 goods-producing companies in 1992. Only about 2 per cent of them are large companies with more than 1000 employees, while roughly a half are small firms with fewer than fifty staff on the payroll. Thus the great majority are of medium size (see pp. 185–187).

The significance of Germany's large manufacturing companies as a source of employment is in inverse proportion to their percentage of all companies. In the west approximately half of all those in manufacturing industry are employed by large companies, which also account for about 50 per cent of industrial output. Many of these companies are internationally known and maintain either subsidiaries or research facilities abroad. Nearly all of them take the form of joint-stock corporations (see pp. 50−53), and are extremely important for the existence of the **Mittelstand** (small and medium-sized companies), which frequently act as suppliers to them (Table 2.3).

Germany's major manufacturing branches are now considered.

Table 2.3   *The largest manufacturing companies in Germany (1991)*

Company, domicile	Sector	Turnover (DM m.)	Workforce
1 Daimler-Benz AG, Stuttgart	automotive, electrical engineering, aerospace	94,660	375,300
2 Volkswagen AG, Wolfsburg	automotive	77,000	266,000
3 Siemens AG, Munich	electrical engineering	73,000	402,000
4 Veba AG, Düsseldorf	energy, chemicals	60,000	116,500
5 RWE AG, Essen	energy, building	49,900	102,200
6 Hoechst AG, Frankfurt	chemicals, pharmaceuticals	47,200	179,300
7 BASF AG, Ludwigshafen	chemicals, energy	46,600	129,400
8 Bundespost Telekom, Bonn	telecommunications	43,200	250,000
9 Bayer AG, Leverkusen	chemicals, pharmaceuticals	42,400	164,200
10 Thyssen AG, Duisburg	steel, machinery	36,600	148,400
11 Bosch GmbH, Stuttgart	electrical engineering	33,600	148,600
12 Bayerische Motorenwerke Munich	automotive	29,800	74,200

Source: *Facts about Germany*, 1992

Automobiles

Germany is the largest producer of cars in the world after Japan and the United States of America. In 1991 the western German automobile industry, with a workforce of some 800,000, registered a turnover in the region of DM 217 billion. It produced 4,680,000 cars, of which 2.2 million were exported.

The automobile industry in eastern Germany has a long tradition, but the models produced under the Communist regime (Trabant and Wartburg) stood no chance of success when faced with international competition once the country was united. Their production has been phased out. In 1990 Volkswagen began to establish a new car-production facility in Mosel, near Zwickau, with manufacturing due to start in 1994. Adam Opel joined with Automobilwerk Eisenach, which was formerly part of the IFA combine, to found a new plant west of Eisenach. Finally, Mercedes-Benz was building a new facility for the production of light and medium-sized trucks at Ludwigsfelde, south of Berlin. Western Germany's carmakers intended to invest about DM 10 billion in the east of the country by 1994. Once production is in full swing in the mid-1990s as many as 500,000 cars will leave the production lines each year − twice as many as in former East Germany.

Mechanical engineering

This section of manufacturing industry embraces over 3600 companies in western Germany and some 930 in the eastern states. It is thus Germany's largest branch of industry. Small firms have always predominated, and it is thanks to their flexibility and technological expertise that Germany is among the leaders in this field. Only 3 per cent of companies have more than 1000 employees on the payroll. These are mainly companies that mass-produce or design and manufacture large, complex items of equipment. Over 90 per cent of the companies in this branch are small or medium-sized, with less than 300 employees. They are specialists who play a key role as suppliers of high-quality plant and production equipment to industry at home and abroad. They manufacture some 17,000 different products, from computer consoles to printing machines, agricultural machinery to machine tools. In 1991 this branch of industry, with a total workforce of just under 1.2 million, produced a turnover of some DM 240 billion. Some 60 per cent of the goods produced were exported. Germany thus accounted for one-fifth of total exports of plant and machinery by western industrialized countries.

Calculations by the **Verein Deutscher Maschinenbau-Anstalten** (VDMA) (Association of German Machinery and Plant Manufacturers) in Frankfurt-am-Main pointed to a doubling of the production value of eastern Germany's mechanical engineering industries by the end of 1994. This was to be achieved mainly from joint ventures with companies based in western Germany.

Chemicals

The chemical industry is the most important branch of basic materials and production goods in Germany. Its state-of-the-art technology in the west has put it among the world's best. This applies in particular to the three principal companies, Hoechst, BASF and Bayer. There are also a large number of significant medium-sized companies forming part of this branch. The total workforce is about 594,000, and turnover in western Germany in 1990 was DM 165.9 billion. Roughly 50 per cent of output was exported. The chemical industry in the west is making considerable efforts to improve environmental protection and has in some areas assumed a pioneering role (see pp. 175–180).

Although chemical production enjoys a long tradition in the east, it is unable to compete in many fields, because most of the chemical plants are not up to date. According to information from the **Verband der Chemischen Industrie** (VCI) (Association of the Chemical Industry) in Frankfurt-am-Main, the situation in the east in 1990 was characterized by production of a high percentage of basic and standard chemicals in old facilities with low productivity. The aim is to retain the core of the main chemical companies in the east, and the two largest facilities there, Leuna AG and Buna AG, have begun to implement modernization programmes. This has not been accomplished without considerable assistance from the large companies in the west.

Electrical engineering

With a turnover of DM 207 billion in 1991 in western Germany and more than 1 million employees, electrical engineering is among the country's most significant branches of industry. Siemens is the flagship of the branch, Europe's largest and the world's fourth-largest company in electrical and electronic products. In 1990, Siemens had 42,000 R & D staff and a research budget of some DM 8 billion.

Siemens was probably the greatest commercial beneficiary from unification. The company won at almost every stage in the process of rebuilding eastern Germany. The reconstruction began with the refurbishment of the telecommunications network, continued with energy generation and distribution, and ended with the building of the transport infrastructure. Addressing a news conference in July 1992, Karl-Heinz Kaske, the outgoing chairman of the Siemens management 'board, said: 'Without unification, Germany would have suffered two years of recession. And I ask myself whether the extra gross national product generated does not partially compensate for the costs of unification'.

Eastern Germany also has a significant electrical industry, and although production and turnover fell considerably after unification, the situation has improved since 1991. Siemens is one of the major investors in the east.

Food, beverages and tobacco

In 1991 in western Germany a workforce of approximately 493,000 produced a turnover of DM 197.2 billion. This branch of industry was also one of the most important in the east but, according to the **Deutsches Institut für Wirtschaftsforschung** (DIW) (German Institute of Economic Research) in Berlin, it is also one that is faced with the harshest structural changes. Compared with its equivalent in the west, the branch offers an inadequate range of goods, and product quality is also problematical.

All these branches of industry, and especially those in the west, have achieved success on account of German fascination with Technik and painstaking attention to the detail of the product – to such a degree in fact that manufacturing companies large, medium sized and small have been criticized for being product-oriented, even systems-oriented, rather than market-led (see p. 206). Yet these branches in the west could not have been so successful, for so many years with so many products, without heeding the message of the markets. Nor has success been confined to the domestic market or even to Europe, though approximately 55 per cent of Germany's foreign trade since 1990 has been conducted with EC countries.

From 1952 to 1991 the value of exports always exceeded imports in the west, and this in spite of several DM revaluations. Throughout the 1980s the export surplus rose constantly, reaching DM 134.5 billion in 1989. There was a slight net deficit in 1991, followed by larger ones in 1992 and 1993 as the huge pent-up demand in the east boosted united Germany's imports. Nearly one in three gainfully-employed persons in Germany works directly for export, and even in the early 1990s Germans exported more per capita than the citizens of any other country.

As could be expected from a predominantly industrial economy, manufactured goods constituted the major component of the country's exports. In 1989 western Germany accounted for 17.4 per cent of world trade in manufactured capital goods, the largest share for any of the

OECD countries. Regarding advanced technology (14.4 per cent), the country came third after the United States of America and Japan, and in terms of sophisticated technology (21.6 per cent), second behind Japan. In the former category German industry was successful in such fields as pharmaceutical products, new organic chemicals and synthetics, plant-protection agents, and advanced optical and measuring instruments. One area where Germany dominates world trade is in the export of environmental protection technology (see p. 177).

It cannot be denied, however, that manufacturing industry in both west and east was experiencing its share of problems in the early 1990s. While it is not possible to embrace the criticisms of an American commentator – that Germany is only skilled at making nineteenth-century products, and could soon become the new Sick Man of Europe because it is deficient in information technology and biotechnology – the industries that, it is alleged, are about to dominate the twenty-first century – certain shortcomings do give cause for concern. Nor is it possible to concur fully with a German commentator who claims that Europe in general and Germany in particular are falling behind in the global race towards the information technology age. Nevertheless, some aspects of the manufacturing economy are disturbing.

One problem that came into sharper focus in the west in the 1980s was that of the **Nord-Süd Gefälle** (north–south divide). During the time of the Wirtschaftswunder the states in the north were the boom areas, the base for the smokestack, or heavy, industries. The south was economically less developed. But even then western Germany's north–south divide was small compared with the United Kingdom's or Italy's. As the *Financial Times* noted on 28 October 1987, 'Though it is true that the north contains the problem industries like steel and shipbuilding, while the south has a larger share of the high-technology businesses, German industry is regionally so diversified that there is no shortage of examples to counter the cliché'.

The embryonic north–south divide had been promoted by the interventionist activities of politicians at the state level in the south (see pp. 15–16). The policies of former Minister Presidents Lothar Späth in Baden-Württemberg and Franz Josef Strauss in Bavaria attracted new sunrise, or high-technology, companies to the southern states. Their efforts were undoubtedly aided by the proximity of such celebrated holiday areas as the Black Forest and the Alps, since ever more Germans in the west are beginning to favour the **Freizeitgesellschaft** (leisure society) over the erstwhile **Leistungsgesellschaft** (high-performance society) – themes to which further reference will be made (pp. 119–120 and 165).

In the 1990s the north–south divide was replaced as a subject of concern by the **Ost–West Gefälle** (east–west divide). Wholesale company closures and the reduction of workforces in the east led to de-industrialization on a massive scale there. In January 1991 there were some 2,076,000 employees in industry and mining in the eastern states, but by August 1992 this number had declined to 896,000. The effects on employment in the individual states in the east are evident from Table 2.4.

Despite the heavy investment in the east by the federal government and the individual states, and despite the efforts of the Treuhandanstalt, more investment is needed from western-based firms. In 1991 such companies invested DM 9.5 billion in the east, and in 1992 the figure rose to some DM 18.7 billion. VEBA, the multinational energy and chemicals firm, was by far the largest investor, with over DM 1 billion. By 1996 it plans to have invested DM 7 billion in its subsidiaries there. The next largest investors were Volkswagen (DM 5 billion by the end of 1995) and Daimler-Benz (DM 2.5 billion). Yet whether such pledges will actually be honoured in full, let alone be matched by other companies, was open to question at the end of 1993 as the country's major companies especially were suffering from the recession (see p. 29).

If the economy in the east is to experience full recovery over the medium and long term, the citizens there cannot rely solely on their fellow countrymen in the west; they will also have to learn to help themselves. But signs of an enterprise culture were beginning to emerge in the 1990s. In 1988 there were only 182,000 self-employed persons in the workforce in the east, including family members helping in the businesses (2.1 per cent of the workforce, compared with 12.6 per cent in former West Germany). In 1990 alone, however, 350,000 applications to establish businesses in the east were received by the appropriate authorities (see pp. 189–190).

Table 2.4 *De-industrialization in the eastern states (1991–92)*

State	% loss of employment in industry and mining
Thuringia	65
East Berlin	58
Saxony	57
Saxony-Anhalt	55
Mecklenburg-West Pomerania	51
Brandenburg	49

Source: Globus

Equally as disturbing as the east—west divide are the worries being expressed in certain quarters on the topic of Industriestandort Deutschland. Critics point to a surge of German investments abroad, a dearth of foreign inward investment, and a failure of German companies to invest within their own borders.

Over the period from 1985 to 1987 foreign direct investment by western German companies totalled DM 51 billion, almost double the DM 27 billion for the three preceding years. Between 1988 and 1990 this sum had increased to DM 84 billion. Taking just 1986 as an example, the following major acquisitions were made:

- Hoechst bought Celanese for DM 5.7 billion.
- Bertelsmann, the publishing company, purchased Doubleday and RCA for 1.2 billion.
- Volkswagen paid DM 1.1 billion for Seat.
- Allianz, the insurance company, spent DM 1 billion on Cornhill.

Indeed, by early 1992, the United Kingdom had become the most favoured location for foreign direct German investment in Europe, lying second worldwide only to the United States of America. Direct German investment in the United Kingdom totalled DM 23.5 billion in 1992, most of it by manufacturing industry. By mid-1993 the British government was running advertising campaigns in German newspapers, claiming that over 1000 German companies had located there.

The scale and location of these investments need not necessarily be interpreted as evidence of a deterioration in Germany's attractiveness as an industrial site; it could also be regarded as proof of stronger integration into the world economy. Indeed it might be held that it is only natural for companies to secure their export-built market shares abroad by investing on the spot. A company whose sales in another country reach a certain level may find it advantageous to invest there in order to move closer to the foreign market by shifting production facilities. This would reduce transport and distribution costs or avoid existing or impending protectionist legislation.

But Germany has lost some of its appeal as a target for foreign direct investment. Tracking the same years as above, from 1985 to 1987, direct investment from abroad totalled a paltry DM 10 billion, and from 1988 to 1990, DM 19 billion. Though GoldStar, the Korean electronics company, and Alps, another electronics firm but from Japan, set up in western Germany in 1988, the Japanese in particular have usually been conspicuous by their absence. Total Japanese investment in western Germany over the period of the 1980s was one-fifth of that in the United Kingdom.

Why have foreign investors shunned Germany? First, Germany is notoriously difficult to penetrate, as Pirelli's abortive bid for Continental showed yet again in 1991 (see also pp. 65–66).

Second, labour costs in Germany are high, overtaking Switzerland's in 1991 as the most expensive in the world and averaging DM 36 per hour. This is not so much due to large increases in hourly rates as to shorter working hours (see pp. 120–121) and to the sustained rise and relative weight of indirect labour costs. In 1991 manufacturers had to pay up an extra DM 83.80 for every DM 100 of salary. (The DM 83.80 broke down into DM 23.70 for the employer's contribution to social security insurance, DM 20.60 for holiday pay, DM 10.00 for the thirteenth month's salary, DM 9.00 for the company's contribution to the employee's pension, DM 5.90 for miscellaneous items, DM 5.40 each for paid **Feiertage** (feast days) and continued wage payments in the event of ill health, DM 2.40 for accident insurance and maternity leave, and DM 1.40 for savings bonuses.)

However, labour costs around the world cannot be compared without taking into account the differences in productivity. During the 1980s productivity growth in western Germany averaged 2.5 per cent per annum, compared with 4 per cent during the 1960s. It came down as the technical progress in the capital equipment lapsed. In the 1980s unit labour costs increased in real terms, and profitability diminished as the rise in real wage costs was not fully matched by productivity improvements. The deceleration in investment growth is clearly linked with the decline in profitability.

Third, the bill faced by manufacturing companies to keep the place clean (DM 21 billion in 1990 alone) is much higher in Germany than elsewhere (see pp. 172–173).

Finally, corporate taxes appear extremely high and profits low. But Germany's flexible accountancy rules allow firms to bury earnings in reserves and accelerated depreciation and the like, which results in lower revealed profits and a lower tax bill (see pp. 183–187).

The debate about Industriestandort Deutschland flared up again in 1992. The issues were, as ever, high wages, shorter working hours, social costs, lower productivity and high taxes. The anxieties reappeared after one of the longest booms in post-war western Germany, which was artificially extended and then suddenly halted by unification and its financial consequences. Companies in the west began to reduce their workforces. Siemens announced several thousand redundancies in Germany in 1992, which were followed by more in 1993, in an effort to reduce the workforce worldwide by 10,000. BMW said it would cut 3000 jobs in Germany between 1993 and 1996, while Mercedes-Benz sprang the biggest surprise of all by stating that it would seek up to 20,000 redundancies inside Germany between 1992 and 1996, and move production units outside the country.

In April 1993 Mercedes-Benz unveiled a $650 million project to build a four-wheel-drive vehicle in America, the first time the company has produced a new car outside Germany. While it was stressed at the inauguration that the project marked a milestone in the company's development from a German manufacturer to a global player, an accompanying announcement shocked the whole of German industry. Jürgen Hubert, head of Mercedes cars, said: 'The time is right to emphasize "Made by Mercedes". Experience has proved that this philosophy can be realized outside Germany without compromising our quality'. The decision to abandon the 'Made in Germany' tag reverberated throughout German manufacturing industry as other goods' producers contemplated the loss of the standard-bearer of the German quality cachet.

A company's choice of business location is not influenced merely by financial considerations, crucial as these are. The innovation potential of an economy, its degree of technological sophistication, and the know-how it produces are all determined to a large extent by the size of its R & D efforts. Here Germany occupies a top position internationally (Table 2.5).

In 1990 Germany spent about 2.9 per cent of GNP on R & D, compared with some 3 per cent in Japan and 2.8 per cent in the United States of America. In western Germany alone 420,000 people have jobs connected with science and research — one-third are scientists, one-third technical staff and one-third support personnel. In 1991 the Federal Ministry for Research and Technology invested some DM 500 million in projects implemented by small companies and targeted at enhancements in their production methods.

Perhaps, however, Germany's most important competitive advantage as a location for industry lies in its system of vocational training and business education, which is regarded as a model by many other industrialized countries (see pp. 144–163).

Table 2.5 *Research spend in western Germany (1971–89) in DM billions*

Research sector	1971	1981	1989
Non-university research institutions	3.01	5.78	8.40
Universities and colleges	4.27	5.87	9.09
Private industry	10.70	26.60	47.30
Research abroad	0.79	1.07	1.88
Total	18.77	39.32	66.67

Source: *Facts about Germany*, 1992

Other factors working in favour of Industriestandort Deutschland are its position in the centre of Europe and its infrastructure (see pp. 35–36). Geographically, Germany lies at the heart of the EC, sharing land borders with Denmark, The Netherlands, Belgium, Luxembourg and France. It enjoys thus ready access to the EC's Single Market of more than 320 million consumers. In addition, it represents a gateway to the east, i.e. to the former CMEA countries, which have become increasingly attractive in commercial terms since the demise of Communism. Moreover, in some countries of central and eastern Europe, an area of erstwhile strong German economic influence, the German language has remained the *lingua franca* of business.

Services

The contribution of the service sector to GNP is considerably lower in Germany than in most other developed countries (less than 60 per cent versus a typical 60–70 per cent). These macroeconomic statistics underestimate, however, the true importance of services, since a large part of the manufacturing sector in Germany actually consists of services.

According to a study in 1991 by the **Institut der Deutschen Wirtschaft** (IDW) (Institute of the German Economy), less than 20 per cent of the German labour force is doing real manufacturing work. This implies that more than half the employees in the manufacturing sector are actually providing services. Such manufacturing-related services encompass office work, training, general services, trading, maintenance, repair work, supervision, planning, R & D, and security. As a result, Germany enjoys an excellent reputation especially in external manufacturing-related services, several of which constitute key critical success factors for many German companies (see pp. 185–186).

This position contrasts starkly with that of the 'pure' services, i.e. those not related to manufacturing. The German business culture has never embraced the notion of work in services constituting 'real work'. Nor has the service sector been favoured by those whose task it is to promote the German economy as a whole. In short, the sector has always led a Cinderella existence compared with manufacturing.

Against this background it is interesting to note that growth in private services increasingly exceeded growth in manufacturing in the 1980s. At two percentage points, the differential over the period from 1979 to 1989 in the west was larger than in most OECD countries. At the same time, however, the rise in service employment was small by international comparison.

The service sector throughout Germany is more highly regulated than manufacturing, and growth in the economy as a whole could be higher if regulations and red tape did not cramp entrepreneurial verve in services. Alfred Herrhausen, the late chairman of the management board of the Deutsche Bank, and regarded by many as the most powerful man in German business until he was killed by a terrorist bomb in November 1989, stated in *The Wall Street Journal* of 6 July 1988: 'Deregulation and open markets are a must: they would promote competition and stimulate demand'.

Indeed growth in service employment has been held back by a whole series of market regulations in western Germany, most of which have also, ironically enough, been imposed on the east. Of these, restrictive practices in insurance and road haulage are just two examples. Insufficient access to seed capital in the early 1980s may also have prevented the creation of small firms, which are particularly important for the provision of services.

Though the postal and telecommunications system in Germany was completely reorganized in 1990, there was little support at the time for privatization of any of its services (see p. 9). Three services formerly controlled by the **Bundesministerium für Post und Fernmeldewesen** (Federal Ministry of Post and Telecommunications) were transferred to three newly-formed public enterprises: Deutsche Bundespost POSTDIENST (postal services), Deutsche Bundespost POSTBANK (banking services), and Deutsche Bundespost TELEKOM (telecommunications). Although the three new companies enjoyed a certain amount of independence and a little more scope for entrepreneurial flair, they still resided under a central administration, and were public, not private, companies. By September 1992 Helmut Ricke, chairman of Deutsche Bundespost TELEKOM, was making no secret of wishing to be released from public ownership: 'As long as Telekom remains in the web of paragraphs of the public service and the public budget laws, it will not achieve the flexibility it needs to secure its long-term survival and make Germany an attractive location for business and industry'.

Typical of the restrictions in this sector of the economy are the regulations affecting the retail trade, western Germany's third-largest 'industry', employing some 2.4 million people in some 380,000 outlets. As the *Financial Times* of 28 October 1987 pointed out, ever since the **Ladenschlußgesetz** (Shop Opening Hours Act) became law in 1956, retail establishments were obliged to follow a strict business routine. Shops could open any time after 7 am, though most actually began business much later, but all had to close by 6.30 pm during the week and by 2 pm on all but one Saturday, usually the first Saturday, in the month – **langer Samstag** (Long Saturday).

However, the Act was full of loopholes. Petrol stations, for example, could remain open later as long as they did not sell goods beyond the motorist's immediate needs — a proviso that was subjected to the most liberal of interpretations by almost every petrol station in the land. Newspaper kiosks were also allowed to remain open at different hours. Yet there were even stranger exceptions, with special rules for retailers in spa towns or shops in rural areas, which could sell certain items on Sundays.

In September 1989 the federal government reformed the Act to let shops stay open until 9 pm on Thursday evening each week, but opposition to even this short extension built up. The trade unions objected on social grounds. They argued that their women members especially would suffer through longer working hours and spend less time with their families. Similarly, the opposition to change included some of the largest retailers. Wulf Ridder, spokesman for Kaufhof, did not believe that there was any pressing need to stay open longer. Other retailers pointed to the large number of shops outside city centres that close early even on the once-per-month Long Saturdays, when they could stay open longer if they wanted.

Progress in the liberalization of the whole services sector looks like being painfully slow. The federal government set up a deregulation commission in the late 1980s, but it did not report until 1991. The commission's findings attracted considerable criticism, not just from the trade unions but also from the CDU, the dominant partner in the ruling coalition. Perhaps the main hope for deregulation rests with the further development of the EC's Single Market, which should enforce liberalization on a grand scale, even in Germany's almost sclerotic services sector.

Agriculture

Two-thirds of Germany's farmers would be forced off the land if American proposals for cutting agricultural subsidies in the Uruguay Round of the General Agreement on Tariffs and Trade (GATT) were implemented. Such was the claim in December 1990 by Baron Constantin Heereman, president of the **Deutscher Bauern-Verband** (German Farmers' Association). He maintained that even the EC's initial GATT offer of a 30 per cent cut in subsidies phased over the 1990s would decimate the agricultural industry's income by up to DM 10 billion a year, and ever more German peasant farmers would find it impossible to survive.

The Association represents the 650,000 small farmers in Germany, and its membership is dwindling by between 15,000 and 20,000 a year. But the power of the German farming lobby is out of all proportion to the fact that this sector accounts for only 1.7 per cent of the western part of the country's wealth and employs only 3.5 per cent of the working population. This is because the farmers produce 80 per cent of western Germany's food, and contribute significantly to preservation of the environment (see pp. 164–181).

Falling incomes and EC quotas are already changing the structure of western German agriculture. At present 95 per cent of farms cover fewer than 60 hectares. In 1989 and 1990 the income of the average 20-hectare farm was a mere DM 40,000 per year, of which one-third was made up of subsidy payments. This is some 20 per cent below the average industrial wage in the country, and means that almost half the farmers had to take a second job to supplement their income.

Agriculture in former East Germany was dominated by state-owned and co-operative farms. In 1989 the total number of people working in agriculture was 820,000, or some 9 per cent of the labour force. This represented a high degree of overmanning, and labour will have to continue to be shed if the sector is to become competitive on international markets. In 1989 more than 80 per cent of all agricultural workers were employed in state-owned or co-operative farms, cultivating 95 per cent of all agriculturally-productive land, growing 75 per cent of the crops, and tending 75 per cent of the livestock. Only about 5 per cent of agriculturally-productive land was cultivated by 3500 private farmers and their families.

It is assumed that a variety of farms will now develop, with different types and sizes of farm. The number of co-operatives will probably decrease sharply as the number of private family farms rises. In 1990 more than 2000 farmers in eastern Germany applied for assistance to establish a family-run farm.

When Communist rule was first imposed there, the farms were amalgamated and most of the barriers between fields were removed. The result is great expanses of land often stretching to several hundred hectares and ideally suited to high horse-power machines. As a consequence of collectivization, eastern Germany with its large fields, and even larger blocks of land run by the co-operatives, offers farmers there the opportunity to cash in on the economies of scale denied them in the west.

Eastern Germany thus holds obvious attractions for farmers in the west. Legal arguments about entitlement to land will obviously continue for some time to come, and there remain the problems of the people who have worked the soil for the past fifty years. In the meantime western German farmers are already making their presence felt in the east. Many are acting as advisers to existing co-operatives, while others are already in place and farming successfully. Where this has happened, yields of cereals, for example, are reported to have been significantly higher. The average improvement is estimated at about 8 per cent. The federal government also lent a helping hand by pumping some DM 12 billion into farming and food products in the east between 1990 and 1992.

Production yields from eastern German farms seem set to climb further over the next few years, as western techniques and management methods are widely introduced, and eastern Germans are given the incentive to till their own soil. All the same, more cuts in EC quotas and the outcome of the GATT negotiations will inevitably combine to render life difficult for Germany's farmers in both west and east.

Transport infrastructure

The transport infrastructure in any country makes its own unique contribution to the smooth operation of manufacturing, services and agriculture. Among other things, the transport infrastructure in Germany consists of a network of trunk roads totalling 221,000 kilometres, including 11,000 kilometres of motorways. In size therefore it is second only to that of the United States of America. The main concern at present is to build new roads and resurface old ones in the eastern states, and to remove bottlenecks and accident black spots in both parts of the country.

Germany's transport infrastructure also implies about 49,900 kilometres of railway track, 16,000 kilometres of which are already electrified. The 13,000 kilometres in the east are to be cut back to about 4,800 kilometres. After the Deutsche Bundesbahn (DB) merged with the Deutsche Reichsbahn (DR) (German Imperial Railways), the total workforce numbered some 500,000. The staff will have to be reduced in numbers, however, in the next few years as a result of rationalization measures.

The showpiece of the western German passenger service for the 1990s is its inter-city express (ICE), linking Hamburg in the north with Munich in the south, and launched in June 1991. The new ICE trains can run at speeds up to 250 kilometres per hour, and fresh routes are planned, e.g. between Mannheim and Stuttgart. The aim is to offer an attractive alternative to air and car travel over distances of up to 500 kilometres. The ICE service is intended to form the hub of a pan-European network twice as fast as cars and half as fast as aircraft.

In February 1993 the federal cabinet agreed to privatize the DB in stages over the next decade, and to write off its debts of DM 70 billion. The new private railway is to be known as Deutsche Bahn.

Part of the transport infrastructure in Germany is provided by the country's efficient inland waterways network. The main international waterway is the Rhine, which accounts for two-thirds of goods transported by inland waterway. Some 3900 vessels ply the country's rivers and canals, which have a total length of 6700 kilometres. **Fossa Carolina** (Charlemagne's Ditch), or to give it its modern name the Rhine–Main–Danube Canal, was completed in September 1992, twelve centuries after it was originally started by the King of the Franks. The 110-kilometre canal connecting the Main and the Danube makes it possible to send bulk goods (2000 tonnes at a time) on barges from Rotterdam to the Ukraine, thus further opening up central and eastern Europe for trade with the west.

Transport infrastructure includes Germany's airports, through which 82 million passengers passed in 1990. In addition, they handled 1.8 million tonnes of air freight. The largest airport is Frankfurt-am-Main, from which 30 million passengers land and take off each year, and through which pass 1 million tonnes of freight. Other German airports are Berlin-Tegel and Berlin-Schönefeld, Hamburg, Bremen, Hanover, Düsseldorf, Cologne/Bonn, Munich, Nuremberg, Stuttgart, Saarbrücken, Leipzig, Dresden and Erfurt. Plans are afoot to enlarge Berlin's airports in particular in the 1990s.

Conclusion

Western Germany has always been most adept at making and selling manufactured items abroad in open competition with other countries. The challenge now is to refurbish and modernize industry in eastern Germany, so that it can emulate its counterpart in the west. If the second of the twin deficits, i.e. that relating to the current account, is to be avoided over the medium and long term, united Germany will have to manufacture and export its way out of its difficulties in the way in which the west of the country did for so many years.

Trade in services hardly ever contributed to the former western German export surplus, partly because western German tourists every year spent some DM 25 billion abroad more than foreign tourists in Germany, and partly because the **Gastarbeiter** (guest workers) (see pp. 100–102) in Germany sent home to their families the approximate monetary equivalent of what German tourists spend abroad.

Exports of agricultural and food products currently make up only 5 per cent of the united country's total exports.

The reconstruction of eastern Germany began with the fundamentals, i.e. with a complete overhaul of the transport and communications infrastructure. This was seen as basic to the future success of manufacturing, services and agriculture there. The more quickly the process is completed, the more easily the five eastern states will be able to contribute in full to the rejuvenation of the economy as a whole, particularly through their manufacturing and exporting capabilities. The much-vaunted zweites Wirtschaftswunder, however, to which so many references were made at the time of unification, appears to have been postponed indefinitely.

3 Business and the law

Introduction

Society in western Germany is ordered and orderly. The platitude **Ordnung muß sein** (order must prevail) is heard from the lips of ordinary citizens with startling regularity. Moreover, the concept of the **Rechtsstaat** (rule of law) is constantly emphasized by politicians, civil servants and business people alike. Indeed it has often been maintained that the Germans in the west assume that anything not specifically permitted by the law is in fact **verboten** (forbidden)!

Society in eastern Germany was also ordered and orderly, kept firmly in its place by the all-pervasive hand of Communism, which was supported by the activities of the infamous **Staatssicherheits-dienst** (Stasi) (state security service). However, the economic and social tensions wrought by unification, in addition to the upheavals in central and eastern Europe, have served to introduce a not-inconsiderable amount of lawlessness into the east of the country. This lack of respect for the law has also had repercussions for the business culture in the east.

Before looking at the area where business and the law come into sharpest focus in both west and east, i.e. the field of commercial law, it is important to place matters within the general framework of the law, the administration of justice, and the legal profession.

The Grundgesetz (GG) (Basic Law)

German law differs in many important respects from Anglo-American jurisprudence. In common with most other mainland European countries, it is based on a code rather than a series of statutes and precedents. Another distinction, at least with reference to the law in the United Kingdom, is that Germany has a written constitution.

On 23 May 1949 the **Grundgesetz** (GG) (Basic Law) was proclaimed in western Germany. The GG was not called a constitution because, according to Article 146, it was to remain valid only until 'a constitution adopted by a free decision of the German people comes into force'.

With the signing of the **Einigungsvertrag** (Unification Treaty) between the two German republics on 31 August 1990, the GG now applies *de facto* in eastern Germany.

By 23 May 1989, when the GG celebrated the fortieth anniversary of its existence to great acclaim in Germany and elsewhere, it had been amended thirty-five times. In essence, however, it has remained unchanged. In fact some parts of the GG cannot be changed at all, not even by the customary two-thirds majority in the Federal Parliament. These parts include the federal structure of the **Bund** (Federation) and the **Länder** (states), and the participation of the latter in legislation wherever their interests are affected.

Article 1 states 'the dignity of man is inviolable', and stipulates that the basic rights of German citizens are binding on all state bodies without further legislation. This article cannot be amended, though the basic rights themselves may be redefined. Indeed, the first nineteen articles guarantee certain 'inviolable and inalienable' human rights to every citizen. These include the right of all to free development of the personality, freedom of faith and creed, equality before the law, freedom of the press and of opinion, the inviolability of the home, the integrity of postal and telecommunications, the right to own property, and the right to asylum. This latter provision in particular was to have enormous ramifications after 1989, with the streams of immigrants and asylum-seekers pouring into the country (see pp. 104−106).

But even basic human rights cannot be unlimited in extent. The GG permits, for example, the prosecution and punishment of criminals though such actions violate the person and restrict the freedom of the individual. Here and in similar cases the federal parliament is especially empowered to legislate as long as the 'essential content' of the basic right is not violated (Article 19/2).

In extreme cases citizens can come personally to the defence of the constitutional order. According to Article 20, 'All Germans have the right to resist any person or persons seeking to abolish that constitutional order, should no other remedy be feasible'. This direct enforcement of the constitution by the citizen is a procedure not usually found in written constitutions, even those containing a Bill of Rights.

The administration of justice

There are two outstanding features concerning the administration of justice in Germany: first, the exercise of judicial authority is shared between the federation and the states; second, judicial power is extensively sub-divided into a constitutional jurisdiction and six other independent jurisdictions (Table 3.1).

Table 3.1   *The court system in western Germany*

Type of jurisdiction	Federal courts	Regional courts
Constitutional jurisdiction	Federal Constitutional Court	Regional Constitutional Courts
Ordinary jurisdiction	Federal Court of Justice	Appeal courts Regional courts Local courts
Labour jurisdiction	Federal Labour Court	Regional Labour Courts Local Labour Courts
Administration jurisdiction	Federal Administrative Court	Regional Administrative Courts Local Administrative Courts
Patents jurisdiction	Federal Patent Court	Local courts
Social jurisdiction	Federal Social Court	Regional Social Courts Local Social Courts
Financial jurisdiction	Federal Finance Court	Regional Finance Courts

Source: Smith, 1981

The **Bundesverfassungsgericht** (Federal Constitutional Court), located in Karlsruhe, is the ultimate arbiter of constitutional issues. It has two main functions: to act as a traditional defender of the constitution and settle differences of opinion between various state bodies, e.g. parliament and government; and to pass judgement on complaints of alleged violations of constitutional rights brought by individuals. The Court's twelve members are all professional lawyers.

In the west of the country, there are 557 **Amtsgerichte** (local courts), ninety-two **Landgerichte** (regional courts) and nineteen **Oberlandesgerichte** (appeal courts). At the apex of this system is the **Bundesgerichtshof** (Federal Court of Justice). The local courts deal with criminal proceedings, civil and commercial disputes, and non-contentious litigation such as probate and land transfers. Forming part of the local courts are the **Familiengerichte** (family courts) dealing with divorce, child custody and maintenance matters. Decisions of the courts of first instance, i.e. the lower courts, may be challenged in a court of second instance, the regional courts, which can review the cases and if necessary call for fresh evidence. The cases can then go all the way to

Table 3.2 *Ordinary courts in western Germany (criminal and civil cases)*

Name of court	Number	Number of judges
Federal Court of Justice	1	100 (in total)
Appeal courts	20	3 for each case
Regional courts	93	3 for each civil case 3 plus 2 lay assessors for some criminal cases
Local courts	638	1 judge sitting alone

Source: Smith, 1981

the top, to the Federal Court of Justice, which considers only legal aspects of the matters affected (Table 3.2).

The Arbeitsgerichte (labour courts) are independent jurisdictions of special interest, the legal basis for which is found in the **Arbeitsgericht-Gesetz** (Labour Courts Act) of 3 September 1954. These courts settle disputes between employers and employees, and questions such as in-house agreements and co-determination rights. Perhaps one of the most salient features of the labour courts is that of a number of honorary judges from the employer and employee sides on an equal footing, always accompanied by a professional judge versed in labour law (Table 3.3).

In the west some 500,000 cases come before the labour courts every year. Approximately 50 per cent of the cases concern issues of remuneration between employers and employees, 25 per cent refer to cases of dismissals brought to the courts by works' councils (see pp. 114–118), and 5 per cent to holiday entitlement and holiday pay; the rest are

Table 3.3 *Labour courts in western Germany*

Name of court	Number of judges
Federal Labour Court	Three judges
Regional Labour Courts	One judge plus two honorary judges (one named by employer and one named by employee)
Local Labour Courts	One judge plus two honorary judges (one named by employer and one named by employee)

Source: Smith, 1981

usually actions by employers against employees and concern damage to plant or products, or leaving the place of work without fulfilling the period of notice.

Verwaltungsgerichte (administrative courts) tackle all disputes under public law which are not of a constitutional nature, e.g. an individual suing a local authority over a refusal to grant planning permission. This is also the forum where **Beamte** (civil servants) can institute proceedings against their employers, and vice-versa.

Patentgerichte (patents courts) settle affairs arising from the registration or the violation of patents and intellectual property rights.

Sozialgerichte (social courts) concern themselves with matters relating to social security, unemployment benefit, war victims' compensation, and sickness insurance.

Finanzgerichte (finance courts) arbitrate on tax disputes between individuals and the state.

In eastern Germany parts of the old court structure have been retained for the time being. Here the county and district courts deal with all matters that in the west are the responsibility of the different types of court. Some of the eastern states have, however, already established labour courts.

The personnel of the law

The law courts in Germany are run by **Richter** (judges), who must have successfully completed legal studies at university for a period averaging five years, in addition to two-and-half years' professional training. Unlike in England and Wales, the judiciary is not appointed from the ranks of experienced lawyers. Judges have a separate career, with a status resembling that of a civil servant. On average, a judge is 29 years old when he or she takes office. After working for about ten years in a court of first instance, a judge may be appointed to an appeal court. Only the very best and brightest have any chance of becoming judges in the Federal Court of Justice or the Federal Constitutional Court.

A judicial career is not usually one for achieving fame, since judicial decisions have only persuasive authority. The name of a judge is hardly ever quoted, except for decisions in the Federal Constitutional Court, where judges are permitted to publish separate and dissenting opinions.

Lay assessors may act in certain types of courts, but only as jurors. This can happen, for example, in the **Schöffengericht** and **Schwurgericht**, which deal with serious crimes at the level of the regional court. Thus almost everyone in the German legal process is professionally trained. All criminal and civil cases are handled by judges who share the same study background as the independent professional lawyers appearing before them as counsel for their clients. This means that the west of the country had, in 1989, some 14,000 judges to deal with criminal proceedings, civil and commercial disputes and non-contentious legislation.

Apart from one or more judges, every German criminal court has a **Staatsanwalt** (public prosecutor). He or she acts on his or her own initiative or, more commonly, on the basis of a complaint received by the police, or by his or her own office. The police investigate on the public prosecutors's behalf and must gather evidence for and against the suspect. The prosecutor alone decides, after scrutinizing the evidence and possibly after a preliminary hearing, whether there are sufficient grounds to proceed and whether it is in the public interest to prosecute. Before the case goes to court, then, the prosecutor acts as an impartial examining magistrate; during the trial, however, he or she presents the case for the state, but only after examination of the accused and the witnesses by the judge. The prosecutor's submission precedes that of the defence lawyer. It asks for a specific sentence. After the defence lawyer's plea, the prosecutor has a further opportunity to speak before the accused is allowed a final say. There were some 3600 public prosecutors in the west of the country in 1989.

The key figure in private legal practice is the **Rechtsanwalt** (professional lawyer), who combines both the function of barrister and solicitor. There is not therefore the traditional division of the profession as found in the England and Wales. The position of the lawyer is particularly strong in Germany, because under the system in general the defendant or the parties concerned is subject to **Rechtsanwaltszwang** (the compulsion to employ a lawyer) in cases that go before most courts. In the regional and appeal courts a party cannot plead without a lawyer. In the criminal division of the local court the judge may appoint a lawyer to assist a defendant if the case is deemed to be complicated. Even parties appearing in the family courts are in general obliged to instruct a lawyer.

The role lawyers play in German courts is different from that of their counterparts in England and Wales, on account of the differences in the procedural systems. Once a German action has been filed, the matter is in the hands of the court, which will direct the proceedings and decide what evidence to take, and the judge will examine the witnesses. There is no place for advocacy in court, and the bulk of the lawyer's litigation work consists in preparing statements on the reasons for or against a case. The lawyer's role is to produce the facts: the judge's to find the law. Of course the lawyer looks up the law to calculate the risks of the case, and the facts he or she presents depend on his or her perception of the legal position. Finally, a lawyer may influence the judge's opinion by legal reasoning. It is a rare event for a judgment to be based on a point of law of which lawyers on both sides were completely unaware.

As a matter of principle, any defendant or party in a civil case who cannot afford to hire a lawyer can turn to the court for assistance. The lawyer is then paid his or her fee from public funds. In contrast to the British system, the legal aid will cover the opposing lawyer's fees even if the case is lost. The German fee-charging system is also different from the one in the United Kingdom. A lawyer must charge fees in accordance with the scale as laid down. The basis of the calculation is the sum in dispute or the value of the object in dispute. In court proceedings the precise amount of the chargeable fees can and must be calculated on the scale. In criminal proceedings, however, only fee guidelines are prescribed for the defence. Where the lawyer's work consists of consultation only, he or she may either charge a fixed part of the fee unit for the sum in dispute or a discretionary proportion of the fee unit, depending on the kind of work the consultation generates.

Lawyers enjoy a fairly modest status on the social ladder, with doctors of medicine, dentists and veterinary surgeons ranking above them. Traditionally, the academic lawyer, the professor, has enjoyed a high reputation, followed by the judge. Following on in third place within the profession are the practising lawyers, whose marks in their final university examinations were perhaps not good enough for them to become judges or civil servants.

Another reason for their social standing may be financial status. There is an enormous gap in earnings between those at the top and bottom of the profession. A rough estimate is that only one in five lawyers makes a decent living out of his or her career, and such problems are becoming more acute as overcrowding increasingly affects the profession. The number of lawyers practising in western Germany rose from 11,818 in 1950 to 18,720 in 1961, 25,851 in 1974, 36,081 in 1980, and in excess of 48,000 in 1989. Some lawyers moved to the east after unification, sensing a greater market opportunity for their skills there.

Nonetheless, German lawyers seem to enjoy a larger share of commercial work than their British counterparts. Some lawyers are company directors. It is also possible to qualify both as an accountant/auditor and a lawyer (see p. 88). Equally, mixed partnerships of accountants and lawyers may specialize as tax lawyers.

Until approximately twenty years ago the one-lawyer practice was the rule. Now, apart from two-lawyer partnerships, partnerships of three, five or up to eight lawyers are quite common in the larger towns, but there are still relatively few partnerships of more than ten to fifteen lawyers, as encountered, for instance, in the City of London.

Within partnerships, lawyers appear to specialize less than is common elsewhere. Even in large partnerships, where there is some degree of specialization, separate departments are quite rare.

The class of lawyer likely to be of most interest to foreigners is that of the **Rechtsbeistand** (law-support officer) because a non-German wanting to practise in Germany would most probably appear in this role. Becoming a fully-fledged lawyer would be a daunting task for a foreigner. Anyone wishing to do so would have to go through the appropriate education at a German university and the training period in the courts. But there is no barrier to a foreigner setting up in practice as a law-support officer, provided that he or she can satisfy the local court as to the character, competence and legal qualifications obtained in the country of origin.

The distinction between the lawyer and the **Notar** (notary) is similar to that in other mainland European countries. While the lawyer is the independent consultant and agent in all legal matters, the notary is a public official, and his or her main function is the documentary authentication of legal acts. This is an activity normally performed by solicitors in England and Wales, but in Germany it has greater importance. The reason for this is that German law prescribes notarial certification and attestation in a very wide range of matters, including every sale or purchase of land or mortgages, every company shareholders' meeting and every sale or purchase in a private company.

In some of the federal states lawyers can combine the functions of both lawyer and notary; in others the professions are completely separate. The **Bundesnotarordnung** (Federal Notary Act) of 1961 acknowledges these historical differences between states. The number of notaries admitted to practice is limited to that held to be necessary in the public interest. This means that lawyers must often wait up to fifteen years or more after qualification before admission as a notary in court jurisdictions where the functions of lawyer and notary are combined.

Forms of business enterprise

The business culture, especially in the west of the country, takes the law very seriously. Business activities are carried out, in general, within the clearly defined framework of the **Handelsgesetzbuch** (HGB) (Commercial Code). In addition, western German companies employ large numbers of law graduates to make sure that neither they nor their business partners break any of the rules. While it is not true that 'business by litigation' is the order of the day, firms in western Germany can be characterized as litigious by persuasion, and legalistic in many of their dealings.

To convey an impression of the legal framework within which companies operate, it will suffice to describe the most important corporate entities encountered in a business context, starting with the most straightforward.

Einzelkaufmann (sole trader)

Such an individual conducts business as a single owner. His or her liability for the settlement of debts is unlimited. The trade name must be registered, and a sole proprietor must use his or her full name but may add to it a description of the business. If the sole trader's business reaches a certain turnover, or if he or she exercises any of the specific forms of trade as laid down in Section 1 of the HGB, the proprietor becomes subject to the provisions of the Code.

Gesellschaft des bürgerlichen Rechts – GbR (civil law partnership)

This partnership is provided for in Section 705 ff of the HGB, and forms the basic model for a partnership under German law. It may be set up for any common legal purpose pursued jointly by the partners, except for commercial undertakings. What constitutes a commercial undertaking is defined in Section 1 ff of the HGB.

A GbR may be initiated *ad hoc* without following any formal incorporation procedure and without the requirement for paying in mandatory capital or other contributions. The partnership has no firm's name. Law firms are a typical example, each partner sharing in office costs but otherwise keeping his or her income as personal earnings. Other examples are building and construction partnerships, and even banks syndicating loans or subscribing to newly-issued shares to be sold to third parties.

The partners are free to decide whether any voting requires unanimity or whether the partners represent the partnership individually or jointly. All partners are jointly and severally liable to third parties when they act jointly. The partners have to indemnify internally those who act on behalf of the partnership. A GbR is terminated upon achievement of the common purpose, upon notice of termination by a partner, bankruptcy, or death of a partner. Finally, it should be noted that partners may be legal persons.

Offene Handelsgesellschaft – OHG (general unlimited partnership)

An OHG is formed, according to Section 105 of the HGB, when at least two partners agree to carry on a commercial undertaking for profit under a common company name, and their liability for the debts of the partnership is not limited. Although the OHG is not a legal person, it does act under a firm's name, may acquire property, and may sue or be sued before the courts. This form of business entity must be registered in the **Handelsregister** (Commercial Register) at a local court.

Any of the partners may represent the firm individually or jointly in transactions within the scope of normal business; extraordinary measures must be taken by the joint action of all partners, e.g. the granting or taking up of substantial loans. However, the powers of the partners may vary greatly, if so agreed and laid down in the partnership agreement.

Regarding the assets of the OHG, title is vested in the partners jointly. All the partners are jointly, severally and personally liable, with no limitations, for the debts and liabilities of the partnership. Thus a creditor may elect to sue in one action the partnership in its company name and in another any or all of the individual partners. Hence a judgment against the partnership may be enforced against its assets as held by the partners in common, and a judgment against any individual partner may be enforced against his or her personal assets.

Unless the OHG provides otherwise, it is dissolved upon expiry of its specific duration, by a decision of the partners, by the bankruptcy of the partnership or an individual partner, by the death of a partner, or by order of the court.

In 1990, there were some 28,000 OHGs in western Germany.

Kommanditgesellschaft − KG (limited partnership)

The KG conducts business under a firm's name, as does the OHG, but with the distinction that while one or more partners are jointly, severally and personally liable for partnership debts, i.e. the **Komplementär** (general partner(s)), the liability of at least one partner, the **Kommanditist** (limited partner(s)), is restricted to his or her liability for the amount of capital contribution. With the exception of specific provisions regarding the limited partner as delineated in Section 161 ff of the HGB, the rules governing OHGs apply.

Thus the KG is not a legal person but may, under its firm's name, acquire property, sue and be sued before the courts. The name of the partnership, the names of the partners, and the amount of each limited partner's contribution must be entered in the Commercial Register.

The limited partner(s) may make contributions of money or in kind, but the management of the limited partnership is the sole right and responsibility of the general partner(s). Although the limited partner(s) are excluded from the conduct of the company's affairs, their consent is required for transactions outside the normal course of the partnership's business.

GmbH & Co KG — (special limited partnership)

The GmbH & Co KG is not a specific form of partnership under German law but a limited partnership whose general partner is a **GmbH** (limited liability (private) company) and whose limited partners may be shareholders in the latter company. Thus the unlimited liability of the general partner is indirectly limited as well. The GmbH may act here at the direction of its shareholders, and its unlimited legal liability is effectively worthless to any unsatisfied creditor because its only asset is its stake in the partnership's capital. This can, however, be as low as zero.

The initial purpose of the GmbH & Co KG was to avoid the double taxation of profits from the company and of the dividends paid to the partners. Yet the business considerations underlying its operations are quite advantageous, too. With a GmbH, the continuity of business operations is more secure, whereas a 'private' partner could pull out at any time. Moreover, the personal assets of the individuals concerned are not liable for partnership debts. Thus the risk is reduced considerably.

The GmbH & Co KG is quite common in western Germany. In 1990 there were some 130,000 such firms.

Stille Gesellschaft — SG (silent partnership)

In an SG a person may participate in a business conducted by another by making a contribution to it in money or in kind, but title to its assets is vested in the other partner. Thus the active partner alone carries out the business in his or her own name, has rights and incurs liabilities *vis-à-vis* third parties. Since no registration requirements exist, the SG is purely an internal one, to which some specific rules are laid down in Section 335 ff of the HGB.

The silent partner has no right to manage the partnership but does enjoy certain control and inspection rights. He or she shares in both profits and losses of the business in proportion to his or her contributions. However, the silent partner's liability to contribute to losses may be excluded by the partnership agreement. A simple loan may be distinguished from a contribution in an SG: a loan is project-bound, whereas a silent contribution is targeted at increasing the business assets in general.

Gesellschaft mit beschränkter Haftung — GmbH (limited liability (private) company)

A GmbH is formed under the **GmbH-Gesetz** (Limited Liability (Private) Companies Act) of 1892 as amended. Basically it allows a business to be conducted with the benefit of limited liability but avoids a complex corporate structure such as the **Aktiengesellschaft (AG)** (stock corporation or limited liability (public) company)

The GmbH is most appropriate for a business requiring comparatively little capital and few shareholders. It is generally selected for family businesses and small companies where the owners wish to exercise close personal control. Moreover, before 1 January 1987 the GmbH was not subject to statutory audits. For all years beginning on or after this data, companies' audit requirements depend on size criteria only, and not on legal form (see pp. 75–77).

The GmbH is a legal person, and must be incorporated by notarial deed. The minimum capital required for formation is DM 50,000, of which 25 per cent, but at least DM 25,000, must be paid in. A one-man or one-woman company is possible.

The **Gesellschaftsvertrag** or **Satzung** (articles of association or statutes) represent the incorporation data and the by-laws in one single document. The GmbH is constituted upon being entered in the Commercial Register. The company name must identify the limited liability by either incorporating the term **Gesellschaft mit beschränkter Haftung** or its abbreviation **GmbH**.

The articles of association may be tailored to the needs and requirements of the shareholders. The latter are free to amend the articles at any time thereafter, provided a three-quarters majority are in agreement. Very few provisions for a GmbH company are mandatory, and these are the ones protecting the interests of creditors. However, a distinct feature of the GmbH is that the registered capital is protected by various provisions against being reduced by either open or hidden payment of dividends and the like. As long as assets do not cover the registered capital, no capital may be repaid or loaned, nor may dividends be paid thereon. Thus this form of company incorporates a basic and strict protection of creditors against misuse of the corporate entity by shareholders or managing directors.

The shares of a GmbH may be traded and transferred freely, provided the articles of association do not prevent such actions. Any transfer would be subject to the formal requirement of a notarial deed. But GmbH shares cannot be traded on a stock exchange, since such shares are not represented by bearer or order certificates.

The GmbH is represented by **Geschäftsführer** (managing director(s)), of which there must be at least one. A managing director usually acts in concert with at least one other managing director, although only one such may be empowered to represent the company individually. He or she may be dismissed at any time by a majority vote of the shareholders.

A shareholders' meeting may be called irrespective of any formalities if all shareholders consent. In addition, shareholders' meetings may be held by proxy. Finally, one individual may be empowered to represent several or all shareholders. In practice a lawyer or notary, who may have to record certain matters in conjunction with the meeting, may represent all shareholders concerned by proxy (Figure 3.1).

Special co-determination rules apply in the steel and mining industries as well as in GmbHs with more than 500 and 2000 employees respectively. The company will then have to establish an **Aufsichtsrat** (supervisory board), which has a variety of control rights (see below).

There were approximately 500,000 GmbHs in existence in western Germany in 1990.

Aktiengesellschaft − AG (stock corporation/ limited liability (public) company)

The AG is the most advanced and complex form of company in Germany. It is a legal person, which comes into existence upon being entered in the Commercial Register. Five founders are necessary to subscribe to the shares in the notarial deed. Thereafter the AG may become a one-man or one-woman company. Such a deed embraces the articles of association, which, as for a GmbH, represent the incorporation data and by-laws in one single document. To a great degree the content of the articles of association is prescribed by the **Aktiengesetz** (AktG) (Stock Corporations Act) of 1965.

The minimum share capital for an AG is DM 100,000, of which at least 25 per cent must be paid in. Share certificates are issued to the nominal value of at least DM 50. Shares without par value are forbidden. In practice almost all shares are bearer shares. The shares are negotiable securities, which may be admitted to a stock exchange listing on one or all German stock exchanges.

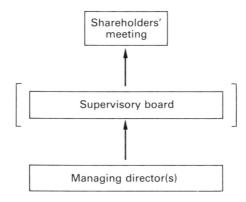

Figure 3.1 *Management bodies of the GmbH − limited liability (private) company*

Owing to cumbersome listing requirements and procedures, a relatively small number of AGs are actually listed on the eight stock exchanges – some 480 in 1990. Shares are mostly bought and sold through banks, with the certificates normally left behind in the bank's custody. Exercise of voting rights by banks or other institutions per proxy is regulated in detail in the AktG.

The transferability of its shares is basic to the concept of an AG. However, some such companies have inserted clauses in their articles of association so that no single shareholder may at any time exercise more than a certain percentage of total voting rights. A typical example is one of the large banks in Germany, whose articles restrict such to 5 per cent. Other companies still have adjusted their articles to ensure that non-voting shares are also issued. Provisions such as these limit the transferability of shares and make it virtually impossible for investors to buy up large quantities of an AG's shares on the stock market. They cannot, in effect, purchase a controlling interest and then take over the management of the company.

A distinct feature of an AG is the two-tier board system. Here the **Aufsichtsrat** (supervisory board) monitors, guides and advises the **Vorstand** (management board). The supervisory board is a body elected by the **Hauptversammlung** (HV) (shareholders' meeting) and by the employees. It represents the shareholders' and the employees' interest, on a permanent basis, in the company. Its main functions are the appointment and removal of **Vorstandsmitglieder** (members of the management board), the approval of the AG's annual financial statements, and certain transactions or measures by the board. The supervisory board can consist of between three and twenty members, depending on share capital and the number of employees in the company. Basically, one-third of the supervisory board members are elected by the employees and two-thirds by the HV. Special co-determination rules apply in the steel and mining industries as well as in large AGs with over 2000 employees. In such companies the supervisory board is composed of equal numbers of shareholder-elected and employee-elected members. The chairman of the supervisory board is always a shareholder representative and has a casting vote (see also pp. 115–117).

The management board is responsible for the daily running of the company. In practice this board consists of several members and a **Vorstandsvorsitzender** (chairman). If the total number of employees in the AG exceeds 2000, one board member must take prime responsibility for personnel matters. This **Arbeitsdirektor** (personnel manager) is required to devote him or herself full time to employee matters. The management board represents the AG in and out of court, mostly by two members jointly. Its members may be appointed for a maximum of five years, and reappointment is possible. Nobody may be a member of both the supervisory and the management boards, since their functions are strictly separate and incompatible (Figure 3.2).

The shareholders of an AG meet once per year for the HV. Their responsibilities are limited in scope. They decide by majority vote on appointment of their representatives on the supervisory board, dismissal of members of the supervisory board, disbursement of profits, appointment of auditors, changes in articles of association, and liquidation of the company.

Amendments to the articles of association require a three-quarters majority of the votes represented in a duly-convened shareholders' meeting. The meetings are recorded by notarial deed. Every shareholder has a right to information.

Thus the AG has a complex corporate structure with various meticulous requirements as to the separation of functions within different corporate bodies and to disclosure (see pp. 79–87). The AG does not have the flexibility of a GmbH. It is mostly chosen as a corporate structure if considerable capital need is anticipated, either on foundation or in the course of its activities, e.g. by issuing new shares or bonds.

There were approximately 2400 AGs in western Germany in 1990.

No contribution on the law and business culture in western Germany would be complete without mention of the **Prokurist**. He or she — it is usually he — is an employee of a GmbH or an AG to whom the power of procuration has been granted by a managing director in a GmbH or a member of the management board in an AG. This means that this person is legally entitled to act for the company in business matters and to bind it *vis-à-vis* third parties. On letters received from GmbHs or AGs two signatures will be found. The one at bottom left belongs to

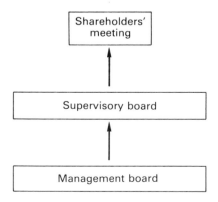

Figure 3.2 *Management bodies of the AG — stock corporation/limited liability (public) company*

the Prokurist. Without this signature, that of a managing director, or that of a member of the management board, the letter would not be legally binding on the company.

The legal incorporation of eastern Germany

In principle the law of the former Federal Republic of Germany now applies in the five eastern states. The comprehensive Unification Treaty of 31 August 1990 laid down the details for the changeover to a social market economy and all that this entails in legal terms, as well as the limited application of special parts of former East German law, and the newly-drafted regulations for transition.

Even during the period after the first free elections and the creation of the first freely-elected East German government in March 1990, comprehensive new ordinances and regulations for the conversion to the social market economy were adopted. In addition, a vast number of laws had to be passed for which there were no precedents, not only for the restitution of land and companies to their former owners but also for the modernization and privatization of former state-owned companies in the east.

The adaptation of the social and legal systems to those in western Germany required their complete reorganization. This could only happen with the establishment of proper institutions, and in several stages, so that no excessive burdens were placed on either part of Germany. Now the new citizens of the united country enjoy the right to equal treatment before the law, e.g. in the field of labour law and in finding employment. A rapid expansion of the **Arbeitsämter** (labour offices) alone would not have sufficed; the number of courts had also to be increased and new ones established. Administrative courts, for example, where the decisions of civil servants are subject to judicial review, were totally alien to the concept of a totalitarian state. Nor could the East German judges working in civil and criminal jurisdiction be expected to administer justice at short notice under an entirely new legal system. For the adaptation of the GG, administrative authorities had to be reorganized as well as many of the legal institutions and the personnel of the law.

Reorganization comprised not only all aspects of economic life but also cultural and public life as well. The aim of the conversion process was the establishment of an economic system based on private owner-ship, which also applied to the means of production, freedom of trade with no regulation of prices by any business person but within a legal framework for the protection of free competition, and social security. As a result of all this, the legal structures of companies had to be changed completely, and real estate reviewed.

The following measures were especially significant for business:

- The **Treuhandgesetz** (Trust Agency Law), to which reference has already been made (see p. 13), was adopted by the transitional government of East Germany. It formed the basis of the complete transfer of all state-owned enterprises into the trust property of the Treuhandanstalt. By act of law, therefore, as of 1 July 1990, all state-owned enterprises were converted into AGs and GmbHs, according to the HGB. The shares in these enterprises were lodged with the Treuhandanstalt.
- Enterprises converted into private companies had to present information required for the Commercial Register at the appropriate court by 16 July 1990.
- The newly-founded AGs and GmbHs were required to present to the Treuhandanstalt by 31 October 1990 draft articles of association in compliance with the Commercial Code, as well as an **Eröffnungsbilanz** (opening balance) retrospective to 1 July 1990. The basic principles for the establishment of the opening balance were laid down in the **DM-Bilanzgesetz** (DM Balance Law), as stipulated in the Unification Treaty (see also p. 89).
- General principles for the return of land and companies to their former owners were established in the **Gesetz zur Regelung offener Vermögensfragen** (Law on the Settlement of Open Questions relating to Assets). These principles allow for **Wertausgleich** (value equalization) and damages in cases where assets no longer represent their former value.
- Any person, their heirs or successors, or company, with property, whether movable or immovable, or other rights or assets, including mortgages, credits and legal claims in eastern Germany, including East Berlin, had until 13 October 1990 to file a claim for restitution. Claims had to be lodged in writing at the central administrative offices of the **Landkreis** (rural district) or **Stadtkreis** (urban district) in which the claimant last lived, or if the claimant had never lived in former East Germany, at the administrative offices in which the property or assets were situated. Where the assets had been expropriated by the state, the application had to demand restitution of the original property rights. No claim could be made for assets expropriated by the Soviet authorities between 8 May 1945, the day the Second World War ended, and 7 October 1949, when the German Democratic Republic was founded. By mid-1991, one and a half million such claims were outstanding.

Conclusion

The passing of laws, the wholesale transfer of judges to administer them, and the eastward migration of western German lawyers to represent clients there have not yet succeeded in establishing a law-abiding business climate in the east of the country. The Business Crimes Office of the Treuhandanstalt registered some 500 cases of bribery, accepting bribes, fraudulent bankruptcy, and offences under the German Official Secrets Act in the course of 1991. Hans Richter, head of the Office, was quoted as saying: 'The control mechanisms are for the most part just not in force in the east'. According to Jutta Limbach, Berlin's justice senator, the German capital city was cheated out of DM 4.5 billion from 1 July 1990 to the end of 1991. Indeed the prevalence of business crime in eastern Germany provoked *Der Spiegel* of 9 September 1991 into commenting: 'The risk of business criminals being caught in the east is scarcely greater than in a Latin American banana republic' (see also pp. 191–192.)

At the time of writing, the culture in the two parts of the country displays an enormous contrast in terms of business and the law. The impression should not be created, however, that it is only eastern Germans who have been breaking the law: many slick operators from the west have also been found guilty of pursuing dubious practices in the less-regulated east. How long it will take for the law-abiding, even law-revering, attitudes prevalent in the west to permeate business in the east remains a matter of conjecture.

4 Business and finance

Introduction

Strength and conservatism, which are such outstanding features of the business culture in western Germany, are nowhere more in evidence than in the major financial institutions. Indeed the performances of the Bundesbank, the Big Three private commercial banks, and to a lesser extent the financial markets, represent some of the critical success factors for post-war western Germany. This should not imply, however, that these financial institutions are without their critics. Nor does it signify, especially in the light of unification, that long-postponed reforms in the financial sector can be delayed. In fact all the country's providers of financial services are currently under scrutiny from one quarter or another, and radical changes can be anticipated.

The Bundesbank

Even by the late 1950s the Germans in the west had come to the conclusion that money was too important a matter to be left to the politicians! Established in Frankfurt-am-Main in 1957 by the **Gesetz über die Deutsche Bundesbank** (Bundesbank Act), the central bank is 'required to support the general economic policy of the Federal government. (But) in exercising the powers conferred on it by this Act it shall be independent of instructions from the federal government'. This high degree of autonomy has been zealously guarded ever since. Moreover, the Bundesbank has seldom shirked from imposing the policies it has deemed to be appropriate, even at the risk of incurring the wrath of the political party or parties forming the federal government at the time.

Indeed Chancellor Konrad Adenauer once complained that the central bank was 'responsible to no one'. Moreover, it is claimed by certain critics that the Bundesbank's policies contributed either directly or indirectly to the breakdown of three western German governments: Ludwig Erhard's in 1966, Kurt Georg Kiesinger's in 1969, and Helmut Schmidt's in 1982.

One of the reasons behind these criticisms is that the Act is quite specific about the central bank's duties: 'The Deutsche Bundesbank shall regulate the volume of money in circulation and of credit supplied to the economy, using the monetary powers conferred on it by this Act, with the aim of safeguarding the currency...' Yet both the independence of the Bundesbank and the stated goal of 'safeguarding the currency' are a reflection of deep-seated German fears of inflation.

Twice in less than half a century, in 1923 and again after the Second World War, the Germans suffered from periods of total inflation when, quite clearly, the currency had not been safeguarded. Memories of these bouts of hyper-inflation are still etched on the popular consciousness. In the first period workers were being paid their wages twice a day, once at lunchtime and again in the evening, taking them home in wheelbarrows, then rushing out to spend their virtually worthless money before the prices in the shops rose even higher. In the second the Reichsmark (RM) had been virtually ousted as the medium of exchange in the west of the country by the cigarette and the nylon stocking! This bout of hyper-inflation was not terminated until the **Währungsreform** (Currency Reform) of 1948, when the Deutsche Mark (DM) replaced the RM.

Given these experiences, it is small wonder that the western Germans should want to leave monetary policy to the technicians, the experts (see also pp. 203–204), in this case the central bankers, and then specifically charge them with the task of 'safeguarding the currency'. Moreover, the Bundesbank's record in controlling inflation has been extremely good (Table 4.1).

Table 4.1 *Western German inflation (1969–93)*

Year	%	Year	%
1969	1.9	1981	6.3
1970	3.4	1982	5.6
1971	5.3	1983	3.7
1972	5.5	1984	2.8
1973	6.9	1985	2.6
1974	7.0	1986	−0.3
1975	6.0	1987	0.3
1976	4.3	1988	1.4
1977	3.7	1989	3.0
1978	2.7	1990	3.4
1979	3.8	1991	4.4
1980	5.1	1992	4.0
		1993	4.2

Source: OECD

Table 4.2 *Inflation in the G7 Countries*

Average consumer price inflation (1957−92)	% pa
Germany	3.4
United States	4.7
Japan	4.9
Canada	5.0
France	6.8
United Kingdom	7.2
Italy	8.5

Source: Deutsche Bundesbank

Over the period 1969 to 1993 the rate of inflation in western Germany exceeded the average rate for all OECD countries in two years only, 1972 and 1973. In other years it has been significantly below the average. If an even longer period is considered, from 1957, the year the Bundesbank was founded, to the end of 1992, average consumer price inflation in western Germany was significantly lower than for any of the other G7 leading industrial countries (Table 4.2).

Since 1974 the Bundesbank has attempted to come to grips with the problem of inflation by means of a medium-term-oriented monetary strategy, with monetary targets announced in advance. Within this framework, since 1988 it has pursued an annual target for the growth of the broadly-defined money stock M3. Before that, central bank money, which is closely associated with M3, served as an intermediate target variable. Now the annual target is derived from a few key variables. These are the price benchmark and the potential growth achievable by the economy on the basis of full utilization of production factors, but without any signs of overheating. In addition, due consideration is given to the fact that the money stock tends to grow faster than the national product. The Bundesbank sees the merits of this procedure, on the one hand, in its emphasis on the medium term, while at the same time establishing an imminently stabilizing policy that acts in an anticyclical manner.

The Bundesbank has enjoyed more success than other central banks in using monetary targets to control inflation. Over the past two decades M3 has been a good indicator of inflation for up to three years ahead. Even the first all-German monetary target, for 1991, was met − but only just. In 1992, however, the target was overshot significantly: in the fourth quarter M3 exceeded the level in the corresponding period of the year before by $9\frac{1}{2}$ per cent, instead of remaining in the envisaged range of $3\frac{1}{2}$ per cent to $5\frac{1}{2}$ per cent. The Bundesbank's critics claim that M3 is now distorted by several special factors, one of which is the increasing use of the DM in eastern Europe.

Nevertheless, the Bundesbank's success in keeping inflation in check has found favour in a whole succession of OECD reports, which constantly praise the central bank's skill and pragmatism. Perhaps the most resounding testimony to its efforts is contained in the *1987—1988 OECD Economic Survey*, which states:

> The sensitivity of the average citizen to inflationary developments and the negative impact of inflation would seem to be much greater in West Germany than in most other OECD countries. Not surprisingly, therefore, price stability objectives have always figured at the top of the policy priorities of German monetary authorities, and the Bundesbank as the 'inflation watchdog' has been constitutionally entrusted with a high degree of independence. Given both the strong commitment to the maintenance of price stability and the wherewithal to fight inflation effectively, the German price record has traditionally been better than generally elsewhere.

Yet even the Bundesbank's independence has limits, and these were cruelly exposed during the acrimonious Gemu debate. Early in February 1990 Karl Otto Pöhl, president of the Bundesbank at the time, described the idea of monetary union between West and East Germany as 'fantastic'. It was, he said, 'an illusion to believe that even one of East Germany's problems could be solved', either by monetary union or by some alternative form of parallel currency arrangement. Yet in the very same week he was obliged to retract this statement and declare his support for Helmut Kohl's policy of monetary unification. The retraction was a demonstration of the limits of the Bundesbank's much-vaunted independence: constitutionally, it is bound to support the federal government's general economic policies.

But the altercations did not stop here. In April 1990 the Bundesbank recommended an exchange rate of one West German DM for two Ostmarks, except for the first 2000 Ostmarks of a person's savings. President Pöhl argued at the time that there was no further room for generosity because higher instant spending power in East Germany would prove to be inflationary, and the Bundesbank was obliged to protect the value of the currency. Again the Bundesbank was rebuffed, its proposals being subsequently amended by Chancellor Kohl, who insisted on an exchange rate of one DM for one Ostmark, for salaries and pensions, as well as for the first 4000 Ostmarks of savings, for all between the ages of 14 and 60. Children were only permitted to exchange 2000 Ostmarks at this rate, while for pensioners the ceiling was 6000 Ostmarks. All other savings were converted at one-to-two, and company debts were also halved at a rate of one DM for two Ostmarks.

Gemu occurred on these terms on 1 July 1990, to the accompaniment of much celebration throughout eastern Germany. The currency switch was overseen by the Bundesbank and handled with brilliant technical precision. But the repercussions for eastern German industry were grave. From Gemu onwards, goods made in eastern Germany were priced in DM, and many of its trading partners in eastern Europe were no longer able to pay at the high, hard-currency exchange rate. The result was a virtual collapse of the export economy. Internally, productivity levels in eastern Germany were approximately 30 per cent of those in western Germany, and product quality was usually inferior. The outcome here was that western German goods were sucked into the east of the country in ever greater volumes. Many parts of the domestic economy in eastern Germany were badly affected (see pp. 26–27). Inflation rates soared (Table 4.3).

Even the cost of dying skyrocketed. The demise of state-run funerals left thousands unable to afford a decent burial. By 1991 coffins were almost twenty-five times dearer than under the old Communist regime, and the total cost of a funeral was often the equivalent of two months' wages. No wonder Herr Pöhl subsequently described the terms of Gemu as 'a disaster'.

In May 1991 he announced his resignation from the presidency of the Bundesbank, emphasizing his desire to devote most of his time to his family. It was, however, an open secret in Germany that he still harboured deep misgivings about the wisdom of grafting a Trabant economy on to a Mercedes business culture. Helmut Schlesinger, Pöhl's deputy, took over as interim president of the Bundesbank on 1 August 1991, after almost forty years' service there. He was succeeded in the autumn of 1993 by Hans Tietmeyer. Both are passionate advocates of the central bank's continuing independence.

Attacks on the Bundesbank's independence have not only arisen from inside the country. Western Germany has been a full member of the European Monetary System (EMS), including the Exchange Rate Mechanism (ERM), ever since its inception in 1979. Indeed the Bundesbank has provided the anchor currency in the EMS, a role into

Table 4.3   *Eastern German inflation (1990–93)*

Year	%
1990	4
1991	10
1992	9.2
1993	8.8

Source: Deutsche Bundesbank

which, it protests, it was pushed and did not seek. In its European policy the central bank has pursued the dictum of 'stability begins at home', maintaining that European developments cannot divert its attention from obligations within Germany, and, furthermore, that a stable DM is very much in the interest of the rest of the EC.

Perhaps the largest external threat to the Bundesbank arose in 1988, when a Joint Finance and Economics Council was set up by the West German and French governments. The Council is composed of the economics and finance ministers and central bank presidents of the two countries. It meets four times a year to co-ordinate policy, and was established under a supplementary protocol to the Franco-German Friendship Treaty. As such, its provisions would have prevailed over those of the 1957 Bundesbank Act, which guarantee the German central bank a degree of autonomy enjoyed by no other. After furious objections from the Bundesbank, and particularly Karl Otto Pöhl, the federal government inserted a memorandum in the treaty to the effect that the Joint Council is consultative and not decision-taking.

Behind this anger lie significant differences between the Bundesbank and the French. The latter complain that the German central bank does little to support their franc in the EMS. The same complaint was heard from the British and the Italians in September 1992, when both the pound sterling and the lira were eventually obliged to withdraw temporarily from the ERM. In fact Bundesbank support operations for the survival of the ERM cost DM 92 billion in September 1992 alone.

Indeed the French have maintained for a long time that the EMS is in reality a DM-dominated zone, in which all other countries have to bow to the Bundesbank's severe monetary policies, which often take the form of high domestic interest rates. Again these complaints were echoed by the British both before and after Black Wednesday, 15 September 1992. Ever since this date, which has also been called White Wednesday and even Golden Wednesday, the Bundesbank has been known in the City of London as 'The Bank that likes to say No'!

Nevertheless, the Bundesbank's statutes are currently being studied closely as a possible model for the European Central Bank, in accordance with the Maastricht Treaty on European Political and Economic Union signed in December 1991. This is consistent with Bundesbank policy ever since 1988. President Pöhl always maintained that he would like to see the establishment of a European Central Bank some time in the future, but only if it had as much freedom from political interference as the Bundesbank itself enjoyed. He contended that inflation in western Germany had been the lowest in the developed world because the central bank had not been obliged to finance large deficits incurred by the federal government or to trim monetary policy to satisfy short-term political expedients, such as impending general election deadlines. The establishment of a politically-dependent European Central Bank would, he felt, promote inflation and jeopardize the limited progress made by the EMS to date. It was thus essential, he concluded, that any European Central Bank must have control of the money supply, which might also necessitate minimum reserve requirements being imposed.

Helmut Schlesinger adopted a similar stance. In 1992 he stated: 'If this European Central Bank has the same tasks as we have of ensuring the stable value of money; if this bank has the necessary instruments to do this; if it is as independent as we are at the Bundesbank, then certainly we could accept it. If these conditions, however, are not met, it will be very difficult for us to explain to the German population why such a bank should be accepted'.

Among the Bundesbank's major preoccupations in the early 1990s was one with its own structure. The seventeen-strong Bundesbank **Zentralbankrat** (ZBR) (Central Council), whose fortnightly pronouncements on German interest rates are anticipated with fear and trepidation by virtually every business person in Europe, had hitherto included a representative from each of western Germany's eleven individual state central banks. In view of unification, the five eastern states might each have sent a representative, thus swelling the council to twenty-two, and since there could be parity between regional representatives and permanent directors, the size of the ZBR might have increased to thirty-two. This, all agreed, would have made it far too unwieldy.

With effect from 1 November 1992, the total number of central bank representatives for the whole country was cut from eleven to eight, with Bavaria, Hesse, Baden-Württemberg and North Rhine-Westphalia boasting one ZBR representative each; Rhineland Palatinate and Saarland, Saxony and Thuringia, and Berlin and Brandenburg sharing one representative per pair of states; Hamburg, Mecklenburg-West Pomerania and Schleswig-Holstein, and Bremen, Lower Saxony and Saxony Anhalt contenting themselves with one representative per trio. In addition, the maximum number of Bundesbank permanent directorate members on the ZBR was cut to eight from the previous ten.

It seems ironic that, whereas eastern Germany united with western Germany in October 1990, it had to wait until November 1992 to join the Bundesbank, and then in much truncated form! Yet perhaps someone of a more cynical frame of mind might find this waiting period not at all ironic – merely a reflection of the relative importance of the central bank!

The Big Three

Standard and Poor's, the US credit-rating agency, regularly awards AAA status to about fourteen banks in the world. The Deutsche Bank, the Dresdner Bank and the Commerzbank, western Germany's Big Three private commercial banks, are prominent members of the exclusive AAA club. Although the west of the country is vastly overbanked, with one branch per every 1370 head of the population, and one bank employee for every 100, the Big Three tend to dominate the banking scene because of their links with big business.

Founded during the late 1800s to provide a complete range of services to industry, the Big Three were broken up at the end of the Second World War but re-formed in the 1950s. Ever since, the ties between the Big Three and large western German manufacturing companies in particular have been the subject of widespread criticism. The links were investigated in the 1970s by the Gessler Commission. It ascertained that the power of the banks lay in the combination of the sheer size of their equity holdings in these companies, the many seats on company supervisory boards to which these shareholdings gave entitlement, the proxy votes cast by banks on behalf of other shareholders at company AGMs, and the **Hausbank-Prinzip** (house-bank principle), which keeps a company firmly linked to one principal lender.

There is lingering concern about the Big Three's influence on non-financial companies. Wolfgang Kartte, president of the **Bundeskartellamt** (Federal Cartel Office), has affirmed much of the criticism of the Gessler Commission. In 1986 the Deutsche Bank had a direct equity holding of 35 per cent in Philip Holzmann (construction), over 25 per cent in Daimler-Benz (vehicles and aerospace), over 25 per cent in Hapag-Lloyd (shipping), over 25 per cent in Karstadt (department store chain), 18 per cent in Horten (another department store chain), and 6 per cent in Allianz (insurance). In the same year the Dresdner Bank held direct stakes of 25 per cent or more in Hapag-Lloyd (shipping), Flender Werft (shipbuilding), Gold-Pfeil (leather), Dortmunder Union (brewing), and Heidelberg Zement (cement). Also in 1986 the Commerzbank owned more than 25 per cent of the equity in Karstadt and further substantial stakes in Sachs (ball-bearings) and Hannoversche Papierfabriken (paper and cardboard).

In addition, the Big Three's investment is sometimes masked by holding companies. The Deutsche Bank had a 75 per cent share of a Frankfurt holding company that owned 25 per cent of Horten; the other 25 per cent of the same holding company belonged to the Commerzbank. Similarly, the Commerzbank held a twice-removed interest in Daimler-Benz through its 25 per cent share in a Munich firm owning 25 per cent of a holding company that in its turn had 25 per cent of Daimler-Benz.

The large equity holdings by the Big Three entitle members of their management boards to sit on the supervisory boards of non-financial companies. In the 1960s Hermann Abs, chairman of the management board of the Deutsche Bank at the time, sat on the supervisory boards of over thirty companies! A law, the so-called 'Lex Abs', has since been introduced to restrict to ten the number of supervisory board seats that can be held simultaneously by any one person. Nevertheless, in the early 1990s, members of the management board of the Deutsche Bank had seats on the supervisory boards of BASF and Bayer (chemicals); Siemens and AEG-Telefunken (electricals); Volkswagen and Daimler-Benz (predominantly vehicles); Thyssen, Klöckner, Rheinmetall and Arbed Saarstahl (steel); Karstadt, Kaufhof and Horten (department store chains); Bertelsmann and Gruner + Jahr (publishing); and many more.

At first glance it would appear that there is a clear case of conflict of interest for a representative of the Deutsche Bank to sit on the board of, say, BASF and Bayer, two companies in the same sector of manufacturing industry. But where is the conflict? The Deutsche Bank has a vested interest in the well-being of both companies: it has put its money into the two companies and wishes to see a return on that investment from both, so it will not be inclined to favour one more than the other. In fact it could be argued that the presence of the manager from the Deutsche Bank actually prevents conflicts of interest.

The supervisory board of a western German company has two sets of clearly defined duties: it hires and fires the management board, and it gives or withholds approval for major financial decisions (see also pp. 51−52). In the example above let us assume that BASF decides, with the assent of its supervisory board, to make a major investment in plant in Country X. Let us further assume that Bayer has been thinking along similar lines. Once the decision has been taken at BASF, the person from the Deutsche Bank might well advise against similar action by Bayer, and since this person is the representative of a major shareholder, he − most unlikely she − would be listened to. Conflict in the sense of 'needless' competition between two domestic companies would thus have been avoided.

The presence on large western German companies' supervisory boards of representatives of the Deutsche Bank, Dresdner Bank and the Commerzbank is also advantageous for companies in terms of consortium formation and consortium management. Each of the Big Three has shareholdings in a vast range of companies, so consortium formation from within that circle of companies is relatively straightforward. Moreover, in the unlikely event that the companies forming the consortium fail to co-operate satisfactorily, the bank could always apply the ultimate sanction.

Approximately 400 large western German companies have banks' representatives on their supervisory boards, and the management boards of these companies welcome their presence. The bankers bring to the manufacturing companies a high degree of financial expertise and, what is more, a high degree of financial security. Their presence means that western German manufacturing companies can look to the long term with confidence. In conditions such as these the management boards can operate, plan, invest and train without worrying too much about the effects of one set of bad figures on the share price of their companies.

Bank representatives on the supervisory boards of manufacturing companies help to ensure that predatory takeover bids, especially by foreign competitors, are virtually out of the question, though attempts at hostile takeovers are becoming more frequent. In 1988 British Steel wished to take over parts of Klöckner, but its efforts came to naught on account of the banks' influence. In 1991 Pirelli, the Italian tyre company, attempted to take over Continental, the largest German tyre manufacturer. This attempt also failed, but the banks saw to it that Horst Urban had to resign from his position as chairman of the Continental management board.

Foreign companies can gain control of western German firms, but usually only when the target company is in deep trouble and when no major German organization objects to the acquisition. Triumph-Adler belongs to Italy's Olivetti, Grundig to the Netherlands' Philips, and Standard Elektrik Lorenz to France's Alcatel. But once it has been decided that a German national asset is at stake, a foreign predator's chances diminish rapidly as the German old boy network swings into action (see also pp. 128–143).

When subjected to criticisms of excessive power, the Big Three defend themselves in the following terms. As for proxy votes, the banks state that shareholders are at liberty to ballot as they see fit, and not to follow the recommendations made by the bank in question. They claim further that many of their large shareholdings in manufacturing companies arose from company rescues, when debt was turned into equity. The bailout of AEG at the beginning of the 1980s, when a banking consortium stepped in to stop the country's second largest electricals group from going to the wall, is a case in point. The banks claim that they lend stability to companies, and take the pressure off the need for short-term profits, being more interested in capital growth. Finally, the banks maintain that, in accordance with the house-bank principle, they remain bankers to their corporate customers through good times and bad, far beyond the point at which financial institutions in other countries might have forced a company into receivership or liquidation.

It could be argued that this degree of support keeps sick companies going, but experience in western Germany has shown that many of the patients make startling recoveries. Again AEG, after its merger with Telefunken, is a case in point. The all-pervasive hand of the banks, which does not hesitate to apply the surgeon's scalpel to management when required, is mainly responsible for administering the cure.

All the same, from the beginning of the 1990s there has been a discernible trend in western Germany for the Big Three to begin to divest themselves of their interests in large companies. They claim that holding equity stakes in other companies ties up their own assets, and their assets are expensive commodities.

Instead, the caring, sharing Big Three have been diversifying. Though each of them was already a so-called universal bank, i.e. heavily engaged in many aspects of banking, from company financing, personal lending and deposit-taking to foreign exchange dealing and stock-broking, they felt it necessary to spread their wings even further. Led by the Deutsche Bank, they entered the fields of mortgage finance, property broking, management consultancy, venture capital, and even insurance, with the aim of offering their clients **Allfinanz** (all-inclusive financial services).

At the end of 1988 the Deutsche Bank decided to establish its own life insurance company. Although this move inevitably resulted in a clash with Allianz, Europe's largest insurance company, in which it had a major shareholding, the leading member of the Big Three felt it had little choice. In 1987 western Germans invested 30 per cent of their savings in insurance policies, up from less than 20 per cent in 1977, with premium income totalling approximately DM 120 billion. Life insurance made up the largest segment of this premium total, which does not include reinsurance. In March 1989 the Dresdner Bank announced that it was also diversifying into the insurance market through a joint venture with Allianz, which had 14 per cent of the life and 16 per cent of the non-life market. In return, Allianz acquired a 22.3 per cent stake in Dresdner, which initially incurred the wrath of the Federal Cartel Office but was eventually sanctioned.

The Cartel Office probably relented in this case on account of the considerable amount of interest being shown in German insurers at the time by large French companies. Among the companies eyeing Germany were Assurances Générales de France (AGF) and Union des Assurances de Paris (UAP). The problem is that German companies are rarely interested in the French, and in the few cases where this is not the case they tend to change their minds. In April 1990 the Aachener und Münchener (AMB), Germany's third largest insurer, made soundings with AGF about a partnership. Before the deal could go through, Helmut Gies, AMB's management board chairman, was smartly replaced, on the insistence of the supervisory board, by Wolf-Dietel Baumgartl, who sent the French company packing.

Another area into which the Big Three are moving is the up-market side of banking. Dresdner Bank has set up an operation managing private clients' portfolios worth DM 5 million or over under the old Hardy banking name. Deutsche Bank has acquired a majority stake in Grunelius, the private bank, and Commerzbank has bought the private financial advisory unit of Matuschka, the western German financial services group.

Diversification at home and expansion abroad were the pre-unification watchwords of the Big Three. As far as foreign operations are concerned, Deutsche Bank bought the Banca d'America e d'Italia, an Italian commercial bank, in 1986, and Morgan Grenfell, the British merchant bank, in 1989; and Commerzbank took a 10 per cent holding in the Banco Hispanoamericano of Spain in 1988.

But these foreign acquisitions were as naught compared with the 'bank grab' in former East Germany. Among the very first acquirers there, one that did not escape the twin accusations of 'gun-jumping' and 'cherry-picking', was the Deutsche Bank, which snatched the major share of the existing commercial banking network in a joint venture with Deutsche Kreditbank, the former East German banking monopoly. Deutsche Bank took 122 branches and 8500 staff in a deal that gave it 49 per cent of Deutsche Kreditbank's DM 600 million capital. Equally quick off the mark was the Dresdner Bank, securing seventy-two Kreditbank branches, which, together with its own new outlets, put its representation in eastern Germany at 107 branches. Likewise, Allianz grasped 51 per cent of the former East German state insurance monopoly with unseemly haste, again much to the consternation of the Federal Cartel Office.

Two years after the bank grab, it seemed the Deutsche Bank in particular had bitten off more than it could chew. When it started its joint venture with Deutsche Kreditbank, Deutsche Bank promised that the 8500 staff it employed would enjoy secure positions. With an average wage of DM 1200 per month, the salary bill for the joint Deutsche Bank Kreditbank (DBK) topped DM 200 million within two years. DBK planned to increase its branch network from the original 122 to 240 by the end of 1992. It refused, however, to repeat its promise to workers but stated that the expansion would absorb staff from overmanned former state branches. Alone among the Big Three, the Deutsche Bank registered a 5 per cent fall in profits for the first ten months of 1992. Analysts blamed at least part of the fall in profits on the group's banking operations in eastern Germany.

Finally, the Big Three often come in for criticism in Germany because it is held that big banks are only interested in big companies. Such criticisms are easily shrugged off because the private commercial banks can point to the public credit institutions, the co-operative banks, and a number of banks that actually specialize in the financing of the **Mittelstand** (small and medium-sized companies) (see pp. 187–189).

Financial markets

In sharp contrast to the private commercial banks, the equity markets in Germany are tiny. Attempts to foster 'equity-mindedness' among businesses and private investors alike have met with only limited success. Nevertheless, changes have been made, and there are more to come. Indeed this is an aspect of the business culture in Germany that could embrace significant developments in the near future. There is certainly plenty of scope for innovation and reform.

The relatively minor role played by share financing, and the consequently heavy dependence on bank finance, have been typical of industry and services in western Germany. Broadly speaking, debt-to-equity ratios have traditionally been about twice as high as in the USA or comparable European countries. Of the two million or so companies in western Germany, approximately 2000 are AGs, or public limited companies, with a joint stock capital structure. At the end of 1987 only 574 domestic companies were actually listed on the markets of the stock exchanges, and companies themselves owned about half the country's equity, often through complicated cross-holdings. Even by mid-1991 the market's capitalization represented only about 20 per cent of GNP, compared to around 80 per cent in the United Kingdom.

The structure of the equity market reflects the dominance of manufacturing industry, with services under-represented. In 1991 chemicals, including the world's three largest companies, Hoechst, Bayer and BASF, were responsible for 25 per cent of the market's capitalization. Banks and insurance accounted for another 16 per cent. The vehicles and engines sector (another 16 per cent) was dominated by Volkswagen, Daimler-Benz and BMW. Utilities (11 per cent), electricals (mainly Siemens, with 9 per cent) and engineering (9 per cent) represented the next largest sectors. Shares in advertising, financial services and consumer goods did not feature significantly.

Apart from a handful of blue chips, most shares are traded so infrequently that share prices are fixed for the day, though trading times were extended from two to three hours per day in 1990. Not surprisingly therefore, the equity market is small relative to the bond market.

The equity market in western Germany is the world's fourth largest, and initial concern about **Finanzplatz Deutschland** (Germany as a financial centre) brought about a number of changes. The year 1983 was declared the Year of the Share, and eleven new companies were launched on to the market. This number rose to twenty-seven, worth some DM 4.9 billion, in 1986. Before the stockmarket crash in October 1987, nineteen maiden share issues and thirty-seven capital stock increases were made. In 1988 there were a mere eight new issues, but this number rose to twenty-two in 1990, and a further twenty-four each in 1991 and 1992. A total of one hundred and sixty-six new issues in ten years may not sound impressive, but this has been accompanied by other significant developments.

One helpful factor was the introduction in May 1987 of a new tier to the market. This might appear strange in a market that already distributes a low turnover over three tiers, but there were good technical reasons. The top tier, **amtlicher Handel** (full listing), is costly for firms. The next, **geregelter Freiverkehr** (regulated free market), has modest reporting requirements but is hardly policed. The bottom tier, **ungeregelter Freiverkehr** (unregulated free market), has no rules governing disclosure or admission and consists entirely of off-the-floor trading between banks. The new **geregelter Markt** (regulated market) comes immediately below the topmost tier. It costs about half the full listing, imposes fewer admission and reporting requirements, and is open to firms with a lower nominal capital. The new market immediately attracted more than fifty existing shares and many of 1987's stockmarket newcomers.

The best news of all came to the financial markets in January 1989, when the federal cabinet approved a bill to revamp the Stock Market Act, which goes back to 1896, and to set up a **Deutsche Termin-Börse** (Options and Futures Exchange). The bill passed through the Federal Parliament in autumn 1989, and the new-look stock exchange and the new futures market started operating in 1990. Although other financial centres have futures exchanges, in western Germany such trading was long regarded as tantamount to gambling. So why the change? The western German experience has been that the absence of an effective hedging instrument was magnifying the swings in their stockmarket, and foreign competition was taking business away from Frankfurt-am-Main. The new Act also implements EC guidelines under which a company accepted for a stockmarket listing in one member state can be recorded in western Germany without further bureaucracy.

The late 1980s and early 1990s have also seen a change in the attitudes of private individuals to investment in equities. Before the start of 1987 the level of equity investment by private persons was low, with only some 5 per cent of households owning shares, and insurance companies holding only 6 per cent of their funds in equities. In addition, relatively few pension funds exist in western Germany, a remnant of the post-war period when companies had little cash to spare for such luxuries. Although private citizens have traditionally been good savers, squirrelling away on average 14 per cent of disposable income, they have been conservative and risk-averse. They usually put their money into local and regional savings banks or hold government bonds. Since the beginning of 1987, however, the number of share-holders in western Germany has jumped by more than 2 million to almost 6 million, or about 10 per cent of the population in the west of the country. Many of the newcomers are in their twenties and early thirties, more cosmopolitan than their parents, and less cynical about shares. Moreover, they belong to a generation that, for the first time this century, will inherit wealth not diminished by war or hyper-inflation.

Neither private equity investors nor efforts to boost the reputation of Finanzplatz Deutschland have been helped by certain puzzling federal government policies over recent years. In 1987 the government announced plans to impose a 10 per cent **Quellensteuer** (withholding tax) on interest income. All investors, large and small, were to be caught in the new tax net. The flight of about DM 45 billion to foreign banks forced the government to withdraw the tax in July 1989, just six months after it had taken effect. The federal government displayed much more reluctance to abolish the notorious **Börsenumsatzsteuer** (stockmarket turnover tax), which was levied at a rate of 0.1−0.25 per cent on all local market secondary trading in western German stocks and bonds. This it promised to do years ago, after it had been called by Karl Otto Pöhl 'A tax with which to subsidize foreign exchanges'. The tax was finally scrapped early in 1991.

Unification has brought pressure on the eight western German stock exchanges to emulate the two former parts of Germany. But rivalry between Frankfurt and the smaller exchanges, and the desire of certain cities in the east such as Leipzig to start up their own exchanges, could lead to fragmentation rather than unification. Although Frankfurt accounts for some 70 per cent of annual turnover of shares and Düsseldorf for 10 per cent, with the remainder split between Munich, Hamburg, Berlin, Stuttgart, Bremen and Hanover, the country's federal structure stands in the way of reform. All eight existing exchanges agree that standardizing their trading systems would bring down costs, but the smaller ones fear that an all-German market could lead to their closure as the bigger ones take the lion's share of the business. Regional stock exchanges are viewed by many as a symbol of the commercial virility of the local economy.

The Frankfurt stock exchange has put forward the idea of a **Deutsche Börse** (German stock exchange), a holding company to incorporate all eight regional exchanges. But ownership of the company and a trading system to link all eight are just two of the problems in such a scheme.

Although Frankfurt has developed IBIS, a screen-based trading system that allows banks and brokers to trade the thirty blue-chip shares composing the **Deutscher Aktienindex** (DAX) (German Share Index), plus some government bonds, its extension to seven other exchanges is proving highly problematical. Resolution of the issue of a pan-German stock exchange is not anticipated in the foreseeable future.

Some new developments have, however, been brought to the huge bond market in Germany by the post-unification surge in public-sector borrowing. Standard government bonds – as opposed to five-year special federal bonds which are issued on tap – had previously been issued by fixed quotas through a consortium of predominantly German banks. Among other things, the system was an irritant for Frankfurt's growing number of foreign banks. Quotas were allocated according to placing power, and rarely altered, leading foreign bankers to complain that they could often sell many more than their allocation. In a radical departure the Bundesbank reduced consortium commissions and began selling a percentage of newly-issued standard bonds by auction as a first step to introducing a calendar auction.

A wider range of debt instruments has also helped to iron out the borrowing process. Since unification, only about two-thirds of net new public-sector borrowing has been funded by the issue of bonds. The balance has been financed by **Schuldscheine** (borrowers' promissory notes). Unlike bonds, these notes can be tailored to investors' needs: maturities can range up to ten years, and even floating rates have been offered. German state governments have long favoured this type of debt, and are responsible for approximately 80 per cent of all such outstanding notes. Since July 1990, most of the borrowing necessitated by the German Unity Fund has been raised in the form of bank loans against borrowers' notes (Table 4.4).

The abolition of the unpopular stock exchange turnover tax in January 1990, together with the withdrawal of the rule requiring Finance Ministry approval for issues of new securities, has opened the way for the first-ever issues of DM commercial paper. The first three financings, for Daimler-Benz, Frankfurt Airport and Südzucker (a sugar refiner), followed within weeks of the lifting of restrictions. All were arranged by the Deutsche Bank. Commercial paper could develop into an alternative form of funding for German companies. It could also undermine the house-bank principle, as banks compete with one another to arrange the most attractive deals, and erode banks' cheap retail funding bases, as competition for investors develops between commercial paper rates and bank deposit rates.

Table 4.4 *German bonds outstanding (1985—90) in DM billions*

	Total (end year)						% increase	
	1985	1986	1987	1988	1989	1990	1989	1990
Public sector								
Federal government	208	252	301	347	375	441	7.9	17.8
Other government	28	34	37	36	37	49*	1.6	33.6
Post & railways	37	43	54	58	57	65	−0.6	13.0
Total	272	330	392	441	469	555	6.2	18.4
Specialized banks	55	65	75	72	81	155**	12.7	91.4
Other banks and industry	602	623	644	638	682	749	6.9	9.7
Total	929	1018	1111	1152	1232	1459	7.0	18.4

* Including German Unity Fund. ** Including East German institutions in the run up to and after unification

Source: Deutsche Bundesbank

Conclusion

Serious efforts are now in train to make Finanzplatz Deutschland more competitive. What is more, unification has given a hefty boost to Frankfurt's chances of overtaking London as the financial capital of Europe. Germany, so the argument runs, is set to use the anchor role of the DM in the EMS and the strength of its economy to carve out an ever-increasing share of western Europe's financial markets. As a bonus, Frankfurt would also be able to play a central role in financing and exploiting the economic revolution in eastern Europe.

However, the 1991 stock exchange enquiry into alleged insider dealing and other irregularities at the Deutsche Bank cast a shadow over such ambitions. The lack of criminal sanctions for insider trading, loose rules about what dealers can and cannot trade for their own account, and inadequate safeguards against trading ahead of orders from clients, had shaken confidence in the system. Indeed one former senior employee at the Deutsche Bank stated in 1991: 'As far as trading ethics go, this is still virtually a third-world country'.

Undeterred by such considerations, however, Theo Waigel, the Finance Minister, increased pressure in 1992 on the EC for Frankfurt, and not London, to be selected as the seat of the future European Central Bank. The implied threat was that Germany could back out of plans for a single European currency if such were not done. Indeed a prominent Bavarian politician had already dismissed the ecu as 'Esperanto money', and the Germans harbour a deep emotional attachment to the DM as a symbol of post-war economic success. The German government clearly saw the choice of Frankfurt as the price for surrendering the DM. The Bundesbank backed the policy, pointing out that Germany, with 80 million inhabitants, is the largest country in the EC and yet still not home to a single major EC institution.

On 30 October 1993 it was decided that the European Monetary Institute (EMI), the forerunner of the European Central Bank, should be located in Frankfurt. Five days later a law was approved by the federal cabinet making insider trading a crime. Theo Waigel hailed the new law as a 'quantum leap' for Germany as a financial centre.

5 Business and accountancy

Introduction

German accountancy principles are tightly specified alongside reporting, disclosure and consolidation requirements in the HGB (Commercial Code). These legal provisions are mandatory and cannot be altered except by statutory instrument. They can only be interpreted with any authority by the appropriate court, although the views of the **Institut der Wirtschaftsprüfer in Deutschland e.V.** (IdW) (Institute of German Accountants), the professional institute, are at least listened to.

Thus legal prescription is the overriding salient feature of German accountancy. Indeed the prime motive of the law has always been to protect the creditor rather than inform the investor. If this consideration is taken in combination with the influence of the tax regulations, then German accounting stands accused of a large degree of conservatism. This aspect of conservatism in the German business culture leads to undervalued assets, silent reserves and understated profits. At the same time, the system incorporates many laudable features.

German accountants, tax advisers, and EC legislation are now beginning to change attitudes to accountancy in Germany. Thus their influence must also be recorded, alongside the system itself, if the position of accountancy within the German business culture is to be illustrated faithfully.

Background

The German accounting tradition was established in the 1920s by Professor Eugen Schmalenbach, whose book *Der Kontenrahmen (The Framework of Accounts)* first appeared in 1927. Ever since, uniform accounting has been a principal feature of the German approach. It was for internal, cost-accounting reasons that uniform formats were first devised in Germany. But uniformity of accounts was also esteemed by political parties, especially the Nazis, because they could be used for inter-firm comparisons within an industry. The publication of the **Reichskontenrahmen** (Imperial Framework of Accounts) in 1937 rendered approximately 200 uniform charts compulsory for the various sectors of German commerce and industry. Indeed uniform accounting was introduced in every country occupied by the Nazis, because it contributed to the prioritization of precious and scarce resources. Only in 1945 did uniform charts cease to be mandatory, and in 1949 several German businesses adopted new uniform charts, the **Gemeinschafts-kontenrahmen** (Communal Framework of Accounts). Thereafter the use of **Industriekontenrahmen** (IKR) (Industrial Framework of Accounts) has been advocated by the **Bundesverband der Deutschen Industrie e.V.** (BDI) (Confederation of German Industry) (see pp. 135–140).

Statutory requirements

All German business entities must keep proper accounting records. These are required to be written up promptly and accurately, with all entries supported by a voucher. The accounts must be designed in such a way that they can be audited by a professionally-qualified person within a reasonable period of time. A complete audit trail must be identifiable from the financial statements to the original vouchers and back again.

The records must be drawn up in DM (with memoranda relating to foreign currency balances), and the financial statements must also be written up in the German currency. Although the financial statements must be in the German language, the books themselves may be kept in any living language. There is no requirement to follow any specific chart of accounts, though many companies in the same sector tend to adopt what has been recommended by the BDI or their particular trade association.

Records and books must be retained for a minimum of ten years after the end of the year in which the last entry was made. The retention period for supporting vouchers and commercial correspondence is six years. In principle the books and records must be kept and retained in Germany unless the tax office responsible for the company gives specific permission for such to be done abroad. The point here is that the tax authorities must be persuaded that the books can be placed at their disposal as and when they require to inspect them.

It can be stated in general that German accounting procedures are of a high standard, yet at the same time they are not deemed to be tiresome by foreign corporate entities, because the latter set at least the same high standards for their own internal financial control mechanisms.

All financial statements must be audited, apart from those of 'small' companies (except those in banking and insurance, where all businesses must be audited, irrespective of size). A company is held to be 'small' if it does not exceed more than two of the following three criteria:

- Balance sheet total.......DM 3.9 million.
- Annual sales revenue.......DM 8.0 million.
- Number of employees.......50.

All other companies' financial statements require statutory audits.

Companies exceeding any two of the three following criteria are held to be 'large' for purposes of financial reporting:

- Balance sheet total.......DM 15.5 million.
- Annual sales revenue.......DM 32.0 million.
- Number of employees....... 250.

It follows, then, that companies not meeting the limits for 'large' but exceeding those for 'small' are held to be 'medium-sized'.

A large company must publish its full financial statements, together with the directors' and auditors' reports, and other specified information in the *Bundesanzeiger (Federal Gazette)*. The same information must be filed in the Handelsregister, where it is open to public inspection. Small and medium-sized companies need only file in the commercial register, but must publish a note to this effect in the *Federal Gazette*. The information these companies are required to file is far less complex than that demanded of large companies. Indeed small companies do not even need to file a profit and loss account or the notes relating to such accounts.

For financial years beginning before 1 January 1990 all German companies controlling one or more domestic subsidiaries were required to prepare, publish and have audited consolidated financial statements if any two of the following three limits were exceeded:

- Consolidated balance sheet total.......DM 125 million.
- Annual sales revenue.......DM 250 million.
- Number of employees.......5000.

As from 1 January 1990, the consolidation requirement was extended to include all foreign, as well as domestic, subsidiaries. The minimum size criteria were also reduced significantly to the following levels:

- Consolidated balance sheet total.......DM 39 million.
- Annual sales revenue.......DM 80 million.
- Number of employees.......500.

The consolidation reporting requirement for German intermediate holding companies can be satisfied by publishing German translations of the consolidated financial statements of the ultimate parent company.

Accounting principles

As in almost every other mainland European country, the impact of taxation on accounting in Germany is highly significant. To a large degree the taxation rules *are* the accounting rules. The Germans firmly believe that the **Handelsbilanz** (commercial accounts) should be the same as the **Steuerbilanz** (tax accounts). There is even a German term for this concept: **das Maßgeblichkeitsprinzip** (principle of bindingness).

Thus taxable profits must be derived from the commercial accounts. In addition, the Germans are convinced that if the result of a particular accounting device is to be claimed for tax purposes, that treatment must be followed in the commercial accounts. For example, the roll-over of capital gains or accelerated depreciation can be claimed only when charged in the accounts. Indeed paragraph 154 (2) of the 1965 AktG states quite specifically that fixed assets may be depreciated at tax rates even if this is excessive in relation to the utilization of the assets. Moreover, the lower valuation can be retained even if the reasons for the accelerated depreciation have ceased to be valid.

Paragraph 149 of the same law insists that the annual financial statement shall conform to **Grundsätzen ordnungsgemäßer Buch-führung** (proper accounting principles). The accounts must be clear, well set out and give 'as true a view of the company's financial position and of its operating results as is possible pursuant to the valuation provisions'.

In addition to these prescribed rules, two unwritten but generally accepted accounting principles form the basis of the German approach: first, the conventions of accounting for an economic entity over a definite period of time, continuity (conformity in the opening and closing balance sheets), and the use of historical costs; second, the concepts of completeness (all business transactions must be accounted for), truthfulness and clarity (financial statements must not be misleading and should truly reflect the financial position), and prudence (the financial position must not be overstated). This latter concept implies that the lowest value must be attributed to assets but liabilities must be accounted for at their nominal values.

Form and content of published accounts

The annual accounts of large German companies must contain the following:

- Agenda for the shareholders' meeting.
- Names of the members of the boards.
- Report of the supervisory board.
- Report of the management board.
- Auditors' report.
- Profit and loss account.
- Balance sheet.
- Consolidated accounts (see pp. 76 and 91).
- Notes to financial statements.
- Resolution on net profit appropriations.

Report of the supervisory board

This report generally conforms to a brief, standard format. It affirms that the supervisory board has kept itself informed of developments in the company, that particular attention has been given to any measures for which the approval of this board is specifically required by the law, and that the chairman of the supervisory board has been in regular contact with the management board regarding the conduct of business.

The report then goes on to state that the supervisory board has examined the financial statements, business report, the proposal for the distribution of profit, and the auditors' report. It usually ends with a declaration of approval of the statements, reports and dividend disbursements.

Report of the management board

This report contains a summary of the year's activities and a commentary on the accounts. The summary includes details of the main company, and its subsidiaries if these exist, as well as listing numbers of employees, together with board remuneration. The commentary on the accounts depicts the principles of valuation. As a minimum it will state that the accounts are in accordance with the law, and that the tax concessions claimed are reflected in the accounts.

Auditors' report

The auditors' report is usually very brief. It normally states that the auditors have duly examined the accounting records, financial statements and business report, and find them in compliance with the law and by-laws. The official form of the German auditors' report reads as follows in the English translation as certified by the IdW: 'The accounting, the annual financial statements and the management report, which I/we have audited in accordance with professional standards, comply with the German law and the company's statutes'. The German auditor may only depart from the above text if he or she wants to draw specific attention to a particular aspect of the financial statements or wishes to qualify his or her opinion.

Profit and loss account

The profit and loss account can be presented in one of two alternative forms: type of cost and cost of sales. Both forms are drawn up in tabular form, showing sales revenue as the first item. The type-of-cost approach then reveals the increase or decrease in finished goods and work-in-progress inventories as an expense or credit item. These are followed by the value of other capitalized 'home-made' fixed assets and sundry recurring business income. Expenses are then deducted under the headings of costs of materials and bought-in parts, employed costs, depreciation and other recurring business expenses. Sundry income and expense items are presented, with a strict distinction being drawn between recurring and non-recurring items. Taxes are then deducted to leave the final net profit for the year from the remaining balance.

Companies opting for the cost-of-sales approach must show the cost of sales as a deduction from the sales revenue, and the gross profit as a sub-total. Then marketing and general expenses are deducted. The rest of the profit and loss account is identical to the type-of-cost approach (Table 5.1).

Table 5.1 *Profit and loss account*

Type of cost presentation	1 January to 31 December	Previous year
	DM	DM
Sales revenue (1)		
Increase/decrease in finished goods and WIP (2)		
Other expenses capitalized (3)		
Other operating income (4)		
Release or writedowns and provisions made for tax purposes only (a)		
Other (b)		
Cost of materials (5)		
Raw materials and goods (a)		
Services (b)		
Cost of employment (6)		
Wages and salaries (a)		
Social security and pension costs, including retirement pensions DM... (b)		

Table 5.1   *(continued)*

Type of cost presentation	*1 January to 31 December*	*Previous year*
Depreciation (7)		
Fixed assets and start-up and expansion costs (a)		
Current assets insofar as unusual or non-recurring (b)		
Other operating expenses (8)		
Release of writedowns and provisions made for tax purposes only (a)		
Other (b)		
Income from profit-pooling agreements (9)		
Income from investments, including associated companies DM... (10)		
Income from other securities and investments, including associated companies DM... (11)		
Other interest and similar income, including associated companies DM... (12)		
Losses assumed under pooling agreements (13)		
Depreciation of investments and securities (14)		
Interest and similar expenses, including to associated companies (15)		
Operating income (16)		
Non-recurring income (17)		
Non-recurring expenditure (18)		
Non-recurring result (19)		
Taxes on income (20)		
Other taxes (21)		
Income from transfer of a loss (22)		
Profit transferred under a pooling agreement (23)		
Profit/loss for year (24)		

Source: Price Waterhouse, 1992

Balance sheet

Capital

Normally shareholders' equity is grouped together as the first item on the credit side of the balance sheet. This position is further divided into the nominal capital, capital reserves, revenue reserves, retained earnings brought forward, and the profit or loss for the year. If the shareholders' equity is negative, it must be displayed as the last item on the asset side of the balance sheet, where it is designated 'deficit not covered by shareholders' capital'.

Any share premiums or comparable amounts received by the company in connection with a capital increase form part of the capital reserve. If a company purchases its own stock, a reserve in the nominal amount of the capital purchased must be created out of profits or silent reserves. This reserve cannot be distributed and is separately shown as a revenue reserve.

Valuation of assets

Accounts in Germany are based primarily on historical costs and the overriding principle of prudence. Apt provision in the form of writedowns or accruals must be made for all anticipated losses, expected liabilities attributable to the year under review or to previous periods, and for impairments in asset values. In contrast, corresponding unrealized profits may not be taken up until realization is assured. The law also demands that accounts as prepared for tax purposes correspond with the statutory financial statements, except for a few minor exceptions. Thus any valuation options taken in the legal financial statements also have their impact on the tax accounts.

As far as assets are concerned, the definition of historical costs is different for fixed and current assets. For fixed assets it is the cost of original acquisition, and an exceptional writedown made in the past can therefore be written back in future periods, provided that it can be proved to be no longer necessary in objective terms. The possibility of writeback is naturally restricted, in the case of depreciable fixed assets, to the book value that would have been shown if 'normal' depreciation had been continued in the usual manner. For current assets, however, the historical cost is deemed to be the opening book value for the year under review. Thus a specific writedown of a current asset item cannot be released until the asset itself is liquidated.

Neither investments nor other securities held as fixed assets may be depreciated on a regular basis. They must be written down below cost whenever it becomes evident that their long-term value to the business has diminished. Subsequent writeups are allowed if the provision originally made is no longer required. In no case, however, may their book value exceed the original cost.

Inventories are valued at whichever is the lower − cost or net realizable value. Cost for raw materials and other purchased items is defined as landed cost. Thus it includes both the purchase price and all freight, customs duties and other costs associated with the acquisition of the goods and their movement to the company's premises. It does not, however, usually include storage, financing and other costs accrued while they are there. As far as manufactured goods are concerned, costs cover not only the direct production costs (fixed and variable) but also administrative and financing costs to whatever degree these can be attributed to the goods affected.

Costs are allocated to specific inventories on hand on either a direct basis or on a moving-average method. Plan or standard costs are also accepted, provided the variances are identified on a regular basis, and appropriate adjustments to the plan or standard costs are made.

In special situations the historical costs of inventories must be adjusted downward if realizable value is lower for manufactured goods and work-in-progress or replacement cost for raw materials and other purchased items. Realizable value is net of any expected selling charges necessarily incurred in connection with their future sale and delivery, but not of any anticipated profit margin.

Real property is required to be valued at its original cost of acquisition, including expenses directly related to such. Land may not be depreciated but buildings must be. The normal depreciation rate for buildings is 2 per cent per annum over fifty years for those on which planning permission was applied for on or before 31 March 1985, and 4 per cent over twenty-five years for those on which this permission was sought after this date.

Plant and machinery, fixtures and fittings, must be depreciated at rates that correspond to the estimated useful lives of the individual assets. The German tax authorities issue a series of detailed tables by type of industry and type of asset, which serve as guidelines. The guidelines are not, however, binding. Usually straight-line rates of 25 per cent for motor vehicles and 10 per cent for other movable assets are accepted by both statutory and tax auditors even if they are applied across the board.

Low-value items costing individually no more than DM 800 may be written off in the year of acquisition.

As an alternative to the straight-line method of depreciation, a company may elect for declining-balance depreciation. This rate may not exceed by three times the corresponding straight-line rate and in no case may it exceed 30 per cent. If a company opts for the declining-balance method, it may change at any time in favour of the straight-line method. The converse option, from straight-line to declining balance, is not allowed.

Investment grants received under incentive programmes are recorded as income in the year of receipt. Investment incentives granted in the form of accelerated depreciation with tax effects must also be taken up in the legal accounts as an expense, thus reducing the potentially distributable dividend.

Legal reserve

Large companies are required to establish a considerable reserve by means of annual transfers of 5 per cent of the annual profit, decreased by losses from previous years, until the reserve is equal to 10 per cent of the share capital or even a higher amount if the company's articles so specify. Premiums on the issue of shares or convertible bonds must also be transferred to the legal reserve. This legal reserve may be actually used only under the following circumstances:

- When it does not exceed 10 per cent of the capital or a higher ratio in accordance with the articles, in order to compensate a loss for the year insofar as it is not covered by a profit carried forward from the previous year and cannot be compensated by a release of silent reserves.
- Or to compensate a loss carried forward from a previous year, with the same provisos.

Liabilities

Liabilities are stated at the amount due on maturity apart from those of four years or more, i.e. of a long-term nature, such as pensions provisions. Disclosure occurs by way of note of all pension payments disbursed during the year as well as the anticipated payments in percentages of that amount for each of the following five years.

Some contingencies should be disclosed even when there are equivalent claims of recourse. These are liabilities from warranty contracts, liabilities from the granting of collateral security for another's liabilities, liabilities from the negotiations and transfer of promissory notes and drafts, liabilities from sureties, and guarantees of promissory notes, cheques and drafts (Table 5.2).

Notes to financial statements

Accounts disclosure in the form of footnotes is required on a series of items. The twelve items figuring most prominently are given below:

1   Accounting principles and valuation methods used.

Table 5.2   *Balance sheet at 31 December 19..*

	Disclosure requirements for large companies
Assets	DM

Unpaid capital (A)
Start-up and expansion costs (B)
Fixed assets (C)
  Intangibles (I)
      Concessions, trademarks and similar
        rights and licences (1)
      Goodwill (2)
      Payments on account (3)
  Tangible assets (II)
      Land and buildings (1)
      Machinery (2)
      Equipment and fixtures (3)
      Payments on account and construction in
        progress (4)
  Investments (III)
      Holdings in associated businesses (1)
      Loans to associated businesses (2)
      Holdings in other businesses (3)
      Loans to other businesses in which a
        holding is held (4)
      Other loan term securities (5)
      Other loans (6)
      (Loans 2, 4 and 6 include DM ... secured
        by mortgage on real estate)
Current assets (D)
  Inventories (I)
      Raw materials (1)
      WIP (2)
      Finished goods (3)
      Payments on account (4)
  Receivables and other assets (II)
      Receivables from customers (of which not
        due within one year, DM ...) (1)
      Receivables from associated businesses (of
        which not due within one year, DM ...)
        (2)
      Receivables from businesses in which a
        holding is held (of which not due within
        year, DM ...) (3)
      Receivables from GmbH shareholders (4)

Table 5.2 *(continued)*

	Disclosure requirements for large companies
Other assets (of which not due within one year, DM . . .) (5)	
Securities (III)	
In associated companies (1)	
Own shares (2)	
Other securities (3)	
Cash (IV)	
Prepaid taxes (E)	
Prepayments (F)	
Loan discount (1)	
Other (2)	
Accumulated deficit uncovered by shareholders' equity (G)	

Source: Price Waterhouse, 1992

2   Any changes to such principles and methods, together with their repercussions insofar as these are quantifiable.

3   Lack of comparability of any items on the financial statements with previous years' figures.

4   The degree to which the year's results have been affected by claiming tax benefits.

5   Accelerated depreciation or non-recurring writedowns.

6   Pension expense not provided for.

7   Commitments and contingencies.

8   Analysis of sales by sectors of activity and by geographically-defined markets, though this information need not be given if it would result in a 'serious disadvantage' for the business or indeed any other businesses.

9   Average number of employees by group of companies.

10   Management board remuneration and supervisory board fees for each group of companies.

11   Information on any loans granted to members of management or supervisory boards.

12   Summary of information on equity or subsidiary holdings unless this might harm the businesses concerned.

The necessity for providing either notes or disclosure is overridden by

Table 5.2   *(continued)*

	Disclosure requirements for large companies
Capital and liabilities	DM

Shareholders' equity (A)
  Issued share capital (I)
  Capital reserve (II)
  Revenue reserves (III)
      Legal reserve (1)
      Reserve for own shares (2)
      Reserves required by the company's
        statutes (3)
      Other reserves (4)
  Profits/losses brought forward (IV)
  Profits/losses for the year (V)
Writedowns and provisions made for tax
  purposes only (B)
Accruals (C)
  Pensions (1)
  Taxes (2)
  Deferred taxes (3)
  Other (4)
Payables (D)
  Loans (of which convertible DM...) (of which
    not due within one year, DM...) (1)
  Banks (of which not due within one year,
    DM...) (2)
  Payments on account received (3)
  Trade payables (of which not due within one
    year, DM...) (4)
  Notes payable (of which not due within one
    year, DM...) (5)
  Associated businesses (of which not due
    within one year, DM...) (6)
  Business in which a holding is held (of which
    not due within one year, DM...) (7)
  Other liabilities (of which taxes DM... and
    social security DM...) (of which not due
    within one year, DM...) (8)
Deferred income (E)

Source: Price Waterhouse, 1992

the consideration of 'the well-being of the Federal Republic of Germany or of one of its states'.

Resolution on net profit appropriations

Once the management board has received the auditors' report, it must present its proposals for the appropriation of profit to the supervisory board. These proposals must encompass disbursement to shareholders, transfer to disclosed reserves, profit carried forward, any additional expenses incurred if the resolution is passed in accordance with the management board's proposals, and retained earnings.

The two boards acting together may determine the accounts or they may leave this to the shareholders' annual general meeting. If the shareholders' meeting determines the annual financial accounts, a maximum of 50 per cent of the annual profits may be transferred to the silent reserves, but only after the legal reserve requirements and any losses carried forward have been met.

The shareholders enjoy full rights to the retained earnings, provided this is not disallowed by the law or the articles, and they may make appropriations from retained earnings to the reserves. Otherwise the two boards may also transfer a similar amount to the silent reserves. These may not, however, exceed by more than 50 per cent the total share capital.

Interim dividends are not permitted but the management board may make an interim payment on the basis of the preliminary annual accounts. Such disbursements are not normally encountered.

The resolution on net profit appropriations must be included in the published accounts.

Accounting profession

Audits of financial statements must be performed by professionally-qualified accountants or accounting firms with German professional qualifications. Audits by persons or firms holding foreign qualifications or by other persons, such as the internal auditors of the parent company, are not recognized. Statutory auditors must be independent of the body whose records are under examination, though they may act for it in other professional capacities, such as tax consultancy.

German auditing standards are absolutely comparable with those of other countries in Europe. The auditing standards are laid down by the IdW. A basic principle is that the German auditor exercises due professional competence and is guided by his or her own independent judgement.

In the course of their professional duties, performing full-scope audits, German auditors accumulate a detailed information base on the subject of the companies and their accounting systems. They are thus well placed to provide other professional services, such as tax consultancy or management consultancy. Moreover, their pre-accountancy education has also contributed to this facility.

Any candidate training for the profession of **Wirtschaftsprüfer** (WP) (accountant/auditor) must have a first degree in economics, business economics, law, engineering or agriculture. In theory all these first degrees have equal validity as far as WP training is concerned, but since economics, taxation and the law are the subjects in Germany with most relevance for professional practices, it is normal to find that approximately 75 per cent of all candidates have read either economics or business economics at university. It is relatively rare for candidates to have studied engineering or agriculture. (If a person has practised for at least five years as a **Steuerberater** (tax adviser) and if, as part of this activity he or she has carried out independent audits, he or she will be recognized as possessing the appropriate first degree.)

There is no minimum age qualification, but the requirement for a university degree or its equivalent, in addition to the further requirement of five years' practical experience, mean that any candidate is unlikely to qualify as a WP before the age of 29. In practice the normal qualifying age is between 30 and 35.

The practical training precedes the theoretical examinations. Before admission to the IdW's examinations, the candidate must have had at least five years' experience in the business, four of them concerned with auditing. This requirement is met if the candidate has carried out major audits in 'outside' companies. A company is considered to be outside if the candidate is not associated with it as a director or employee. Experience as an accountant with an 'inside' company, or as a tax adviser, can be deemed to be the equivalent of two years' experience. Approximately 85 per cent of all candidates for the WP examination have already passed the tax-adviser examination.

As far as the theory is concerned, no specific programme is required, nor is any formal guidance provided as to the manner in which the candidate should develop his or her theoretical knowledge. Private organizations offer training programmes, as does the IdW.

The examination consists of seven written papers (two each on auditing, economics, and tax law, and one on commercial law) in addition to an oral examination, which may not exceed two hours. This final hurdle usually takes the form of a grilling before an eight-person panel of the accounting great and good — mainly drawn from professional ranks.

There are some 9000 WPs practising in Germany, compared with about 120,000 accountants in the United Kingdom. In 1990 approximately one-third of Germany's WPs were active in former East Germany, preparing the opening DM balance sheets of the 8000 original state companies due for privatization. All 8000 companies were expected to present their balance sheets by 31 October 1990 (see also p. 54). Full audits of these companies were scheduled for 30 April 1991 at the latest. Many failed to meet either deadline.

Under the Gemu terms, Ostmarks were translated into DM at a rate of two-to-one, but this could only be applied to debtors and creditors. For other items the issues were much more complex. All assets and liabilities had to be revalued on a prudent but going-concern basis. Land and buildings had to be revalued at market value, whatever that was, and, in cases of difficulty, estimates could be made based on western German values, or, for buildings, replacement costs could be used.

Plant and machinery were to be stated at replacement costs, less an allowance for depreciation and obsolescence. In practice this often meant a value of nil. Any raw materials not valued at scrap had to be stated at replacement cost, while finished goods were to be valued at net realizable value.

Share capital was often only a temporary estimate of what would be appropriate for the business, and reserves were sometimes bolstered by an amount receivable from the Treuhandanstalt, especially representing the balancing figure on the balance sheet.

Since July 1990, normal western German rules have applied.

EC influence

The two major EC initiatives to date towards accounting harmonization are the Fourth and Seventh Company Law Directives. The Fourth Directive was adopted in 1978, and came into force by 1984 in all member states with the exception of Italy, Portugal, Spain, Greece and Ireland. But it had been implemented even in these countries by the end of 1992.

The Seventh Directive was adopted in 1983. Again, Ireland, Portugal, Italy, Denmark and Belgium were somewhat tardy in enacting it. The Directive had, however, been implemented in all EC countries by the end of 1992.

The Fourth Company Directive

The Fourth Directive applies to individual company accounts. Its major objectives are:

- Common presentation formats for balance sheets and profit and loss accounts.
- Comparable valuation principles.
- The presentation of standard minimum footnote disclosure in order to achieve a 'true and fair view' of a company's financial standing.

The Fourth Directive is still the subject of intense debate, and not all of its provisions have been observed even by those countries that have enacted it. Nevertheless, it has brought about two new aspects of European business culture. First, there is now a common European concern for company accounts. From the very birth of the Fourth Directive company financial experts, accountants and auditors began to speak to one another in a more-or-less common language. Second, the effect of the Directive was to spread the use of company accounts, and of their disclosure to the public, much more widely.

Germany is a good case in point. Before the Fourth Directive was enacted, some 500,000 Mittelstand companies forming the backbone of German industry had never had to disclose accounts. Now they must do so, though it must be said that to date very few have disclosed fully. It was calculated in 1993 that only 10 per cent had conformed with the Directive, but the figure is slightly misleading in that all the medium-sized companies towards the 'large' end of the medium-sized scale have complied. What is important is that wide disclosure is now required and is happening, though falteringly.

Yet the Directive still meets with resistance inside Germany because of the tradition of conservatism in the business culture. Witness, for example, the pained expressions on the faces of the managing directors of medium-sized or small companies when they have to show just their management accounts to their bankers! And, literally, these management accounts are 'shown': even bankers are rarely allowed to make photocopies of them.

The enactment of the Fourth Directive also gave rise to a high-class 'demarcation dispute' in Germany. One of the stipulations, on enactment, was that the accounts of all companies affected by the Directive should be audited independently by WPs. This naturally included some of the GmbHs. Yet the tax advisers, of whom there are some 40,000 in Germany, had traditionally done the 'voluntary audits' of these companies, audits that had, over recent years, become more and more in demand by banks and other creditors.

The tax advisers, under the president of their Association, Heinz Bachmann, set up a furious lobbying campaign. They argued that the Directive prevented them from working for their largest block of clients, the GmbHs. Moreover, they claimed that if they lost their roles as 'voluntary auditors' to the GmbHs, then their real function — that of advising on tax matters — would also be taken over by the WPs.

The dispute was eventually resolved, after much public acrimony between Herr Bachmann and Dieter Thümmel, head of the **Wirtschafts-prüferkammer** (Chamber of Accountants/Auditors — the profession's self-governing body responsible to the Federal Ministry of Economics), by allowing easier access for tax advisers to the WP qualification. In addition, a second-tier auditing qualification, that of the **vereidigter Buchprüfer** (sworn accountant), was resuscitated in the later 1980s for the auditing of GmbHs.

The Seventh Company Directive

The Seventh Company Directive sets similar objectives to the Fourth, but this time for consolidated accounts. In addition, it establishes common definitions and methods of preparation.

The Seventh Directive complements the Fourth in that it prescribes the way in which company accounts for subsidiaries must be incorporated into the consolidated accounts. Above all, it defines what subsidiary companies actually are, i.e. companies where the parent exercises a controlling influence, either through possession of a sufficient number of shares, through the capability of appointing the management, or through its ability to control company policy. Where such circumstances apply, companies are obliged to provide consolidated accounts.

The Seventh Directive relies heavily on the Fourth for both the layout and the selection of items in the accounts. It then proceeds to define how the subsidiary's assets and liabilities must be taken into the consolidated accounts.

The prime advantage of the Seventh Directive, in the view of the accounting profession, is that consolidated accounts are ignored by the tax authorities. This means that various tax-driven departures from the 'true and fair', such as occur in Germany, are no longer required. Moreover, there is a considerably improved comparability of result. However, this applies obviously only to groups of companies, not to individual companies.

Conclusion

The United Kingdom and German approaches to accountancy represent in many ways the two ends of the spectrum. While the former has established that company accounts must faithfully reflect the company's financial performance — the 'true and fair' maxim — German accounts, very much in line with the German business culture in general, are very conservative and prudent, and tend to understate profits.

The reason for this is, broadly speaking, that the United Kingdom approach is shareholder-driven and the German tax-driven. United

Kingdom companies in general rely on the financial markets for the provision of their capital. As a result, they must demonstrate to these markets, in their accounts, that they have been successful. If they played down their financial performance, the markets might write down their shares or even dismiss their managements.

In contrast, the equity market in particular in Germany is less developed, as we have observed (see pp. 68–69). Thus German companies look to their banks for the provision of capital. In addition, the German tax authorities use published company accounts as a yardstick for company taxation. Hence the binding principles of German accounting are prudence in the valuation of assets and the disclosure of the lowest profit possible as allowed under the tax laws.

Touche Ross, the UK-based firm of accountants, has devised a model to demonstrate the varying results that can be derived from the same company performance under the different accounting procedures prevalent in the EC. Taking the United Kingdom and Germany, the model illustrates that the minimum achievable profit varies from 171 monetary units in the United Kingdom to 27 in Germany. The maximum possible profit is 194 units in the United Kingdom but only 140 in Germany.

The remaining differences in the two systems, despite European harmonization, are highlighted when a German company takes over a United Kingdom one or vice-versa. Though the technical differences in the structures of the balance sheets can be overcome with relative ease, even if this entails double reporting, in both German and British mode, the variations in the underlying philosophies do still present problems. Bitter experience in the United Kingdom in the early 1990s has shown that the profit in the bottom line sometimes owes as much to the skills of accountants as to the good stewardship of management. This inevitably clashes with the German convention of conservatism. Yet at least with the German approach nobody receives any unpleasant surprises. A company that looks, from previous years' accounts, apparently healthy does not appear to get into difficulties virtually overnight.

With further harmonization of EC accounting standards in the fullness of time, perhaps a dose of conservatism in the British approach and a dash of bravado in the German will become institutionalized.

6 Business and the labour market

Introduction

Business activities in western Germany in the 1980s were conducted against the background of a declining and ageing indigenous population. In contrast, the working population increased, thus contributing to higher unemployment over the decade than might have been expected from such an inherently strong economy. Special groups within the working population were disproportionately affected by the scourge of unemployment. By the end of the decade they had been joined on the labour market by large numbers of **Aussiedler** (returnees of ethnic German origin from eastern Europe), **Übersiedler** (refugees from former East Germany) and **Asylanten** (asylum-seekers).

Officially, as in all the former Communist states, there was no unemployment in East Germany. Post-unification, however, citizens of eastern Germany had to bear the full brunt of Gemu as factories were closed and workforces reduced. Unemployment, especially among women, and short-time working soared. At the end of 1993 prospects for the labour market in the east looked even bleaker, since Germany as a whole was in recession.

Demographic trends

Before unification, politicians and political parties in western Germany were concerned that their fellow citizens might gradually be dying out. In 1970, 23 per cent of the population were under fifteen years old; by 1987 the proportion had sunk to only 14.6 per cent, western Germany having the second-lowest fecundity rate in Europe (1.3 children per woman). In addition, from 1970 to 1987, those aged over sixty-five increased from 13.2 to 15.3 per cent of the population. In 1989 the **Rentnerquotient** (dependency ratio) — the number of old-age pensioners in relation to the number of people paying in contributions — had reached 50 per cent. In other words, two persons in employment were making contributions for every retired person receiving a pension.

After unification, such problems have been postponed but not resolved. In 1990 the united country had a population of some 79,790,000 persons (including 5.6 million foreigners); 22 per cent of total population were under twenty, 58 per cent between twenty and sixty, and 20 per cent over sixty. The population is forecast to rise to just over 81,000,000 by the year 2000, but then begin to tail off. In addition, the former problems of fewer young people and more pensioners will begin to reassert themselves. By the year 2010 the population is forecast to decline to 78,858,000, with 19 per cent under the age of twenty, 55 per cent between the ages of twenty and sixty, and 26 per cent over sixty. Matters will look even worse by the year 2030, with only 17 per cent of the population below twenty, 48 per cent between twenty and sixty, and 35 per cent over sixty.

Unemployment in the west

The declining population figures in the west in the 1980s were not reflected in low unemployment rates partly because the working population actually increased from 26.3 million in 1970 to 28.2 million in 1987 (Table 6.1).

No single factor can be blamed for the high percentages of the dependent labour force out of work in the 1980s in western Germany. At the beginning of the decade the effects of the second oil crisis of 1979 and the world-wide recession were clearly reflected in the steep rises in the unemployment statistics. In the mid-1980s factors common to most OECD countries, such as rapid technological change and fierce Japanese competition, combined with particular western German circumstances to produce in 1985 the worst annual set of unemployment

Table 6.1 *Western German unemployment rates (1979–93)*

Year	%	Year	%
1979	3.8	1986	9.0
1980	3.8	1987	8.9
1981	5.5	1988	8.7
1982	7.5	1989	7.9
1983	9.1	1990	7.2
1984	9.1	1991	6.3
1985	9.3	1992	5.9
		1993	8.2

Source: OECD

figures since the proclamation of the 'old' Federal Republic in 1949.

Low growth rates in the western German economy throughout most of the 1980s have already been noted (see p. 8), and these were no doubt partly responsible for the high unemployment figures. So why was no attempt made to reflate the economy and thus reduce the number of jobless? The test of reflation is whether greater domestic demand would improve output rather than increase prices. In addition, between 1965 and 1985, the west of the country witnessed a rise in the rate of unemployment relative to capacity utilization. This indicates, as *The Economist* observed on 26 October 1985, 'that even if capacity were fully used, unemployment might remain high. The reason is familiar: too much capacity deepening (men replaced by machines) and too little capital widening (expansion of capacity) because of what the OECD calls western Germany's "real wage rigidity"'. In effect western German wages are less flexible than those in most EC countries, and inter-industry wage differentials are virtually negligible.

Towards the end of the 1980s higher growth rates did contribute to a decline in the unemployment rates, and between 1983 and 1988 1 million new jobs were created. The increase in employment originated in the gradual expansion of the services sector, which has been slower to grow than in most comparable countries on account of the over-regulation already noted (see pp. 31–32).

The higher growth rates were sustained into the 1990s by unification, with unemployment actually dipping below 6 per cent in July 1991, the lowest monthly figure for over a decade. Indeed, in the year from 1 July 1990 to the first anniversary of Gemu, 600,000 jobs were created in the west. It was not until early 1993 that the recession throughout the country began to increase unemployment in the west.

Unemployment in the east

The contrasting fortunes of the dependent labour forces in western and eastern Germany were mainly responsible for repeated references to Schumpeter's dictum of 'creative destruction': during the immediate post-unification period western Germany enjoyed the creation, eastern Germany the destruction (see also p. 27). After unification, many former East German state-owned companies were closed down completely, among them the Trabant plant and the Pentacon works. Even the 600-person, 100-animal East German State Circus had to fold its tents. The People's Army ballet, orchestra, cabaret and ensemble suffered a similar fate, but the army choir was allowed to remain.

From 1 July 1990 the number of registered unemployed in the east rose from 270,000 (approximately 2.8 per cent of the unsus-

Table 6.2   *Eastern German unemployment rates (1990−93)*

Year	%
1990	5
1991	12
1992	14.5
1993	15.8

Source: Statistisches Bundesamt

tainably large labour force) to 1,060,000 (12 per cent) by October 1991 (Table 6.2). Over the same period the number on short-time working rose from 660,000 (6.7 per cent) of the labour force to 1,450,000 (13.5 per cent). In the first fifteen months after Gemu therefore the real 'underemployment rate' (the percentage of unemployed plus the percentage on short time) was in excess of 25 per cent. Moreover, these figures did not include a large, but undisclosed, number of redundant employees of the former East German state whose employment relationship was 'suspended' pending a decision about their future deployment (see p. 162). In addition, some 450,000 easterners were commuting daily to the west over this same period. At the end of 1989 approximately 9,750,000 million were employed in eastern Germany, at the end of 1990 the figure was 8,855,000, at the end of 1991 7,166,000, at the end of 1992 6,125,000, and at the end of 1993 5,834,652.

The reaction of the German government to such alarming falls in employment in the east was to galvanize the **Bundesanstalt für Arbeit** (Federal Labour Office) into action, and 2000 of its officials were dispatched to the east to assess needs and set up appropriate programmes. Not only were the labour market and unemployment benefit programmes it administers in the west extended to former East German territory, but a number of special transitional regulations and measures were introduced:

- **Arbeitsbeschaffungsmaßnahmen** (job-creation measures) were financed under particularly favourable conditions for programme sponsors. The Federal Labour Office authorized up to 100 per cent financing of the wages and social security contributions of participants. By October 1991 there were 280,000 eastern participants on job-creation programmes.
- **Aus- und Umbildungsmaßnahmen** (training and retraining measures) were expanded considerably, company-based training schemes in former East German **Betriebsakademien** (company academies) having been discontinued as a result of the economic crisis (see also p. 162). By October 1991 the number of workers in the east on training and retraining schemes was 320,000.
- **Frühpensionierungsmaßnahmen** (early-retirement measures) were

introduced for unemployed East German workers as part of the Unification Treaty. Unemployed persons who had reached the age of 57 were eligible for **Altersübergangsgeld** (old-age transition payments). They received 65 per cent of their average net pay for a maximum of three years until they became eligible for normal early retirement in the pension system (usually at the age of 60). Employees whose claims began before 1 April 1991 were entitled to 70 per cent during the first year. Until the beginning of 1991 women were eligible under especially attractive terms (at the age of 55 and for a maximum of five years). By October 1991 early retirement schemes accounted for 566,000 persons.

Perhaps the most controversial of these schemes were the job-creation programmes. Here some 400,000 workers were being employed by the end of 1992. Under these programmes the government pays participants between 90 and 100 per cent of their previous wages or salaries. This makes job-creation programmes more attractive than the training or retraining programmes, where wage and salary levels of only 70 per cent are on offer. In addition, all salary and social contribution costs are paid for by the government. The general fear is that job-creation programmes will do little to foster a training ethos in the east and could crowd out private investment there. Both effects would only serve to prolong the agony of the unemployed.

The first signs of an upswing, and with it possible slight relief for the labour market, became visible in 1992. By then the western German Mittelstand had begun to invest in the east. Vofa, a specialist company employing approximately 1000 people making cables for the automobile industry, was building a new plant at Gehren in Thuringia. Henkel, the chemicals, cosmetics and detergent manufacturer, another family concern but at the top end of the medium-sized scale, had also started investing in the east.

If real jobs are to be created in sufficient numbers, many more small and medium-sized companies, the backbone of western Germany's economy, will have to follow Vofa's and Henkel's examples. Investment cannot be left to the government and to the large companies alone. In addition, greater numbers of eastern German citizens will have to make their own individual contributions by founding their own businesses (see p. 189). Equalization of unemployment rates between the west and the east of the country, which is essential to ease the social tensions between Wessis and Ossis, will take a considerable time to achieve. There is no chance that such will be done before December 1994, the date of the second pan-German elections.

It is against this background of recession in the west and faltering investment in the east that Helmut Kohl first mooted his plan for a Solidarity Pact. Only one of the problems is how to fulfil his pledge that the 'cores' of eastern German heavy industry — chemicals, textiles, etc. – will be retained even though they have lost their markets, because they are still the largest employers in the east. Western employers have promised to make even more investments, and buy more goods of eastern German origin, but this is still not enough to solve the problem. Kurt Biedenkopf, Saxony's minister president, insists that annual transfers of DM 120 billion are essential until at least the year 2008.

Disadvantaged groups

Female workers in the east

Of the special segments of the eastern German labour force, women have probably been affected the hardest of all by unemployment. In former East Germany women represented a high proportion (some 47 per cent) of the workforce and enjoyed very favourable rights, designed to foster the compatibility of parenting and work. Many of these rights have been severely curtailed since unification:

- Paid maternity leave after birth now amounts to only eight instead of twenty weeks.
- The maximum duration of maternity leave with reinstatement rights is down to eighteen months from thirty-six.
- The right of working mothers to an additional day of paid leave per month, **Hausarbeitstag** (housework day), was abolished on 31 December 1991.
- The right to paid leave for the care of sick children is now limited to five working days per year and applicable only to children under eight years old, in contrast to the previous generous system of unpaid leave for the care of children under fourteen and paid leave for single parents and married women with two or more children.
- The special dismissal protection for parents of infants has been curtailed.

In 1992 women in eastern Germany were even being sterilized to escape the dole queue. With almost twice as many women (63 per cent) as men out of work in the east at the time, employers were able to pick and choose. Potential employers began asking how long women would be available for work. Unmarried mothers, desperate to earn money, were particularly vulnerable. Some had been told that they would be offered work only on condition that they could guarantee they would never have another pregnancy. In Saxony-Anhalt, there were even cases of women as young as nineteen being sterilized.

Young people and graduates in the west

Special groups within the western German labour market have also experienced contrasting fortunes over the last decade. Young people under the age of twenty-five and graduates point up the contrast.

Western Germany has the best record of any country in the EC for providing employment for its young people under the age of twenty-five. In April 1992 the jobless rate among young men was 4 per cent, while among young women it was even better, at just 3.5 per cent. These figures compare starkly with Spain's (27 per cent and 38 per cent), Italy's (26 per cent and 36 per cent), France's (17 per cent and 23 per cent); and the United Kingdom's (20 per cent and 15 per cent). The average EC figures were 17 per cent and 19 per cent respectively.

There are a number of reasons behind the low rate of youth unemployment in western Germany. These include compulsory schooling until the age of eighteen and the widespread apprenticeship system (see pp. 147–149); national service, which keeps young men out of the labour market for at least fifteen months and usually more; and the exceptionally low birthrates during the 1970s.

One group of relatively young people, but usually over the age of twenty-five, for whom prospects look bleak are the graduates of western German **Fachhochschulen** (polytechnics) and universities. The total number of unemployed graduates passed the 100,000 mark in 1984 and increased fivefold from 1980 to 1985. Among the graduates registered as unemployed in 1985 were:

- 29,546 teachers.
- 22,010 engineers of all types.
- 13,168 economic and social scientists.
- 6722 natural scientists.
- 3728 doctors of medicine.
- 3348 lawyers.

Unemployment rates among graduates in western Germany have continued to rise throughout the 1980s, and early 1990s and, unification notwithstanding, there is little hope of significant improvement in the situation. In fact matters could get worse. According to the **Institut für Arbeitsmarkt- und Berufsforschung** (Institute of Labour Market and Vocational Research), there were in the west in 1980 a total of 1,501,000 graduates, 874,000 of whom will still be employed by the year 2000. There will also be a demand for an additional 627,000 graduates on account of retirements in the interim. But by the year 2000 total graduate supply will have reached 2,983,000, leaving 1,482,000 graduates unemployed!

Patterns of graduate employment are also forecast to change. Hitherto

60–70 per cent of graduates have found employment in the public sector. But in view of federal and state government determination to cut public spending, especially in the west, it is doubtful whether such take-up rates will ever be achieved again. Economic growth rates up to the end of the millenium would have to be truly phenomenal to absorb such large increases in graduate supply.

Though there are some openings for western German graduates in the east of the country, many are deterred from taking up permanent residence there by the prevailing social conditions. Accommodation is difficult to obtain, levels of crime are high, air pollution soon puts a stop to life-style activities such as jogging or brisk walking, badly surfaced roads take their toll on cars, and public transport is unreliable and uncomfortable. What is more, the presence of western graduates is often resented by Ossis, who perceive jobs in the east as their prerogative.

Perhaps the best prospects for unemployed western German graduates lie outside the country. Their chances of taking up employment in another EC state are enhanced by the Single European Market (SEM), one of the provisions of which is the free movement of labour between member states.

Gastarbeiter (guest workers) in the west

Another segment of the labour market in western Germany that has been disproportionately affected by unemployment during the 1980s and up to the mid-1990s is that formed by the guest workers (Table 6.3).

The percentage of unemployed guest workers was lower than the national average until 1974, the year after the first oil crisis. Thereafter it has been significantly higher. This is because most of the guest workers are unskilled and thus regarded as more dispensable in a harsher economic climate.

The first agreement on the recruitment and placement of foreign workers in western Germany was signed with Italy in 1955. Further agreements followed with Spain (1960), Greece (1961), Turkey (1964), Portugal (1967) and former Yugoslavia (1968). Although the signing of an agreement with a particular country inevitably confirmed the *status quo*, it did not mark the date of arrival of the first immigrant worker from that country.

The guest workers originally came to western Germany on account of the push factors in their countries of origin (high unemployment, low wages) and the pull factors in the Land of the Economic Miracle. Here they mostly perform tasks indigenous workers are increasingly unwilling to undertake: they work in tedious jobs (on assembly lines),

Table 6.3   *Gastarbeiter (June 1993)*

	Employed	Unemployed
Turks	652,097	86,121
Former Yugoslavs	375,082	30,157
Italians	165,050	24,658
Greeks	102,831	13,800
Spaniards	42,363	4,791
Portuguese	44,521	2,862
Others	654,210	80,379
Total	2,036,154	242,768
Total Gastarbeiter population	2,278,922	

Source: Bundesanstalt für Arbeit

in dirty jobs (street-cleaning), in dangerous jobs (coalmining), and weather-sensitive jobs (construction and allied trades).

The guest workers in Germany are unpopular with the native population, but not so unpopular as certain of the asylum-seekers (see p. 104). A poll back in 1981 revealed that two-thirds of western Germans believed that the guest workers should return to their countries of origin. They stand accused of defiling western cities by living in untidy ghettos, bleeding the country dry by sending home a high proportion of their wages, failing to integrate into society, and, above all, taking jobs that rightfully belong to western Germans.

One of the fundamental reasons for the unpopularity of the guest workers is the mismatch between original expectations and reality. When they first arrived, the guest workers were perceived by western Germans as a simple solution to a simple problem. The country needed workers, and the guest workers needed jobs. In addition, the guest worker was regarded as ideal economic man. He − but hardly ever she − would be a healthy individual in the prime of life, come to western Germany without a family, stay for a few years, and then return home. Young and fit, he would require no medical support services, though he would naturally pay health insurance charges; without a family he would exert no pressure on social and educational facilities, though the normal deductions for such would be taken from his pay packet. He would naturally pay income tax and pension contributions but would be long gone before any benefits fell due.

The reality has been quite different: although some guest workers did return home, especially in the early years, most have stayed. What is more, they have been joined by their wives and children in the interim, and they have had further children 'Made in Germany'. In fact, they have become a permanent feature of the western German labour market, and are over-represented in the unemployment statistics through little fault of their own.

In 1990 66 per cent of all Turks, 72 per cent of Italians, 76 per cent of the people from former Yugoslavia, and 87 per cent of the Spaniards had lived in Germany for ten years or more. In addition, 12 per cent of all the children born in western Germany in 1990 had foreign parents.

On 23 November 1992 Yeliz Arslan, a ten-year-old, German-born Turkish girl was burned to death in her bed as a result of her home being firebombed by neo-Nazis. Her aunt and her grandmother died with her in Mölln, a town near Hamburg. The arsonists responsible telephoned a warning to the police ending with the words, 'Heil Hitler!' Opel, the car company, offered a reward of DM 100,000 for help in finding the culprits.

Gastarbeiter in former East Germany were relatively few, consisting of a mere 100,000 Vietnamese in the early 1980s. Their number had dwindled to below 20,000 by the time of unification. Attempts have been made in the interim to repatriate them, but Vietnam has stubbornly refused to co-operate. As a result, they eke out a miserable existence in Germany, some of them living off their wits by smuggling contraband cigarettes.

Aussiedler (returnees)

Since 1987 the situation on the labour market in western Germany has become even tighter on account of a strong rise in immigration. Many of these immigrants are accounted for by returnees of ethnic German origin from eastern Europe. The total number of returnees between 1987 and the end of 1991 was 1,273,541, with 1991 recording the peak numbers. The vast majority come from the former Soviet Union, Poland and Romania, where some 3.5 million ethnic Germans continue to live.

The age composition of the returnees was relatively youthful. Some 80 per cent were below the age of forty-five, while 32.4 per cent were under the age of eighteen. Only 7 per cent were sixty or over. In addition, the overwhelming majority possessed formal vocational qualifications.

Particularly keen interest was aroused by a study published in 1992, showing how ethnic German immigrants from Poland and the former Soviet Union had settled down in western Germany's most densely-populated state, North Rhine-Westphalia, over the period from 1988 to 1991. In all cases the researchers found that unrealistic initial expectations had to be abandoned. Opinions on standards of living depended to a great extent on whether acceptable accommodation and regular work had been found. By the third year such had been attained by the majority of respondents. Many immigrants had had to abandon hopes of pursuing their chosen careers and accept positions that they held to be inferior. Nevertheless, matters had generally improved by the third year. Economic integration, it would appear, presents fewer problems than social and cultural integration.

Many ethnic Germans, especially those from Poland, came with social expectations similar to those of western Germans. They prefer, for example, to live in nuclear families in an urban environment. Further assimilation is, however, impeded for a long time by language barriers. Even after three years in the country, the ethnic Germans from Poland had scant command of the language. Within the family Polish continued to be spoken to help the children become bilingual.

As a rule the ethnic Germans from the former Soviet Union speak better German. They also tend to live in extended families and settle mainly in rural areas, where they prefer to buy a dwelling – even a humble one – than settle for rented accommodation. Many of them believe they have left the land of 'persecution' and arrived in the country of 'temptation'. Such is their perception of the consumer society.

German–Polish relations have improved to a great degree since, after unseemly shilly-shallying, Chancellor Kohl finally acknowledged the Oder-Neisse line as marking the eastern border of the new Federal Republic of Germany. Equally, German–Russian relations are on a much friendlier footing than at virtually any time during the Soviet era. The German government wishes to use these improved diplomatic relations to dissuade further ethnic Germans from returning to Germany. The problem lies not so much with Poland as with Russia, where, according to Mikhail Gorbachev, there were 5 million ethnic Germans still resident in 1989. The federal government sees the possible creation of a Volga Republic for German communities in Russia as an alternative to emigration to Germany. It has even toyed with the idea of paying these ethnic Germans to stay where they are.

Übersiedler (refugees)

The returnees were joined in western Germany, from 1989, by large numbers of refugees from East Germany. In the first half of 1989 alone some 45,000 refugees entered western Germany (compared to 40,000 for the whole of 1984, the year of the last large wave of arrivals from East Germany). This stream turned into a flood from the summer of 1989 onwards, when the Hungarian border with Austria was opened, and there followed mass occupations of West German embassies in

Budapest, Warsaw and Prague. The tide was stemmed for a while when the East German authorities banned visa-free travel to former Czechoslovakia, but this restriction was lifted on 4 November 1989. Disaffected East German citizens then crossed over to West Germany via the Czech border at a rate of some 9000 per day, or 375 per hour. On 9 November 1989 the East German government made its historic decision to open the border with West Germany.

A survey conducted at the reception camps at Rasatt and Giessen established that 56 per cent of the new arrivals were under the age of thirty and only 17 per cent over forty; 86 per cent had gone through an apprenticeship or some other form of vocational training; 8 per cent held graduate-level qualifications; and 87 per cent had previous work experience. However, a large proportion of the returnees (36 per cent) had worked in the service, administration and education sectors. But it is precisely in these sectors that there is already an over-supply of labour in western Germany. Moreover, the skills of these refugees are to a large extent not transferable. Teachers and academics, for example, have been trained in accordance with the requirements and values of a totally different social system (see pp. 157–159), while former engineers lack familiarization with the latest technology and the organization of work in western companies (see p. 206). The greatest problem facing former shopfloor workers may well be adjustment to the faster tempo of work in the west.

Asylanten (asylum-seekers)

In 1987 57,379 asylum-seekers arrived in western Germany, but one year later the figure almost doubled to 103,076. From 1984 to 1990 the total number was 853,382. In 1991 asylum-seekers coming to Germany numbered 225,492, and in 1992 the total went up to about 450,000. Some 50 per cent of the asylum-seekers come from eastern Europe (Poland, Romania, Russia, Albania and Bulgaria), 30 per cent from Asia (India, Sri Lanka, Pakistan and China) and 20 per cent from Africa (Morocco, Algeria, Uganda, and Ghana).

Many of them enter Germany across the Oder or Neisse rivers, which form Germany's eastern border with Poland. These 'wetbacks' cross in makeshift boats or on airbeds; they wade or swim across particularly sluggish stretches of the rivers, even on bitter winter nights, with their children. In just four weeks in March 1993, 3110 were arrested crossing the rivers along the 910-kilometre border. Others enter via the Czech Republic with the aid of motorized, highly-paid **Schlepper** (sherpas), cross the wooded border on foot at night, then rejoin their helpers for the rest of the trip inside Germany. In 1992 a total of 18,454 potential asylum-seekers were caught entering Germany illegally. Many of those who were arrested and deported returned to try a second or even third time. Illegal immigration exceeds 100,000 people per year.

The problem is that Germany has one of the most liberal asylum laws of any country in the world. Article 16 (2) of the GG states simply: 'Persons persecuted on political grounds shall enjoy the right of asylum'. Thus Germany is open to anyone who believes that he or she has been politically discriminated against. The law also insists that applications for asylum must be processed legally and thoroughly, which also means slowly. While their cases are assessed, the asylum-seekers can remain in Germany with government support (which was reduced to a quarter in 1992). In the same year Germany had a backlog of over 500,000 cases awaiting assessment, and the bill to the German taxpayer had risen to DM 15 billion per annum. Of the 107,000 applicants refused permission to stay in 1992, 65,000 used other legal means of staying, while a further 21,500 defied the law and stayed in hiding.

The federal government maintains that only a fraction of the asylum-seekers are victims of political persecution with a legitimate claim to asylum: they are for the most part 'economic refugees', fleeing from hunger and poverty and seeking to establish a life in the 'golden west'. Applications for asylum are often submitted, it is claimed, because they ensure that the individual concerned can stay at least for the duration of the recognition process and any ensuing appeal.

The government and opposition have been wrangling over a solution to the problem ever since 1988. In March 1993 an 'asylum compromise' was reached between the political parties, one that still retains the individual right to asylum, but 'manifestly unfounded cases' will be deported more quickly − back to Poland, the Czech Republic, Austria and Switzerland. Border guards will be able to decide, often on the spot, whether to prevent individuals from entering, even if they invoke Article 16. Germany urgently wants common European rules on asylum, and European sharing of the burden of refugees from former Yugoslavia, of whom Germany had taken 220,000 by the end of 1992.

But even if common European legislation is successfully enacted, as long as wages in eastern Europe are one-tenth of those in Germany, the asylum-seekers will keep on coming. The most that they can aspire to on the official labour market in Germany is sorting rubbish. Because of Germany's draconian packaging laws (see pp. 176−179), town halls are having to employ a whole new category of **Müllologen** (rubbishologists). Here Bosnians, Sri Lankans and Ghanaians are only too happy to oblige by raking through other people's dustbins for the princely sum of DM 16.32 per hour!

In 1991, 1992 and 1993 there were a series of savage attacks by skinheads and neo-Nazis on hostels for asylum-seekers in some twenty towns, mainly in eastern Germany, from Rostock in the north to Hoyerswerda in the south. Eleven people were killed. The miscreants were partly aided and abetted by municipal leaders insisting that the local populations would simply not accept any more asylum-seekers. Egged on by headlines in the tabloid press such as 'Gypsy asylum-seeker roasted my cat', Germans are more hostile to Romanians than to any other group. But their case is complicated: most Romanian asylum-seekers are gypsies, and they do face genuine persecution in their home country. Moreover, Germans have a bad conscience about them, because some 500,000 of their people were murdered in concentration camps by the Nazis.

Unfortunately the Romanians do not help their own cause. In 1990, among the larger ethnic groups, they recorded an alarming crime-to-population ratio of 54 per cent. The next closest were the Bulgarians with 28 per cent. Moreover, hordes of Romanian gypsies loitering in railway stations and shopping malls have helped turn the question of **Ausländerkriminalität** (crime by foreigners) into political dynamite. Extreme right-wing agitators have been making great play with the rising crime figures, claiming **Überfremdung von Volk and Heimat** (over-foreignization of people and homeland). In its turn this has led to a charge of **Ausländerfeindlichkeit** (hatred of foreigners) directed at the native population at large.

Helmut Schmidt, the former Federal Chancellor, has blamed Helmut Kohl for lack of leadership in his handling of the asylum-seeker issue, though Kohl did go on television in August 1992 in the aftermath of the Rostock riots and say that 'hatred of foreigners is a disgrace to our country'. A nation-wide campaign against racism and enmity towards foreigners was launched in Berlin's Deutschlandhalle in October 1991, with a nine-hour pop concert supported by leading sports people and entertainers. In November 1992 the Federal President, Richard von Weizsäcker, led a rally in Berlin against racist violence. In addition, there has been a national advertising campaign by the *Hessischer Rundfunk (Radio Hesse)* to combat racism. Here the four largest Frankfurt-based advertising agencies put together a campaign of television commercials and posters aimed at showing the irrationality of xenophobia.

In March 1993 all the parties in the Federal Parliament finally grasped the nettle by proposing changes in the law to allow more immigrants to become German citizens. The rules for granting immigrants citizenship were among the most restrictive in Europe, and based on a 1913 law embracing the notion of **ius sanguinis** (the German people being united by blood rather than territory). This anachronistic law was the real obstacle to creating a multicultural society in Germany and did little to discourage the xenophobia of fringe nationalists.

Conclusion

In 1993 there were 6.5 million foreigners resident in Germany, making up about 8 per cent of the population. Many have made, and are continuing to make, a significant contribution on the German labour market. In the same year one in twelve jobs in western Germany was held down by a guest worker, and in the same year foreign citizens were responsible for one-tenth of GNP in the west. Many have moved out of the heavy industry into which they were recruited and into the service sector, opening garages and restaurants, and creating 140,000 new jobs.

Despite the enterprise of foreigners and native Germans alike (see pp. 182–194), Heinrich Franke, who retired as president of the Federal Labour Office in 1993, was pessimistic about medium-term developments on the German labour market. He went on record as stating that unemployment will remain at high levels until the second half of the 1990s. According to Franke, the EC's Single Market, with its provision for the free movement of labour, only serves to exaggerate movements on all of Europe's labour markets.

In 1993 there were 17 million unemployed persons in EC states, and the figure was expected to rise by a further 3 million in 1994.

7 Business and trade unions

Introduction

Germany has been a united country since 3 October 1990. Full convergence of the industrial relations systems in the country's western and eastern regions had not, however, been attained by the end of 1993. The progress achieved in the interim has been based on a gradual adaptation of the eastern model to the western. It is therefore appropriate to devote most attention to systems and attitudes in the west while at the same time not neglecting their incorporation in the east.

The trade unions in western Germany can look back on the 1980s and early 1990s with a certain satisfaction. Despite the existence for much of the time of a CDU-led centre-right coalition ostensibly committed to free markets and deregulation, the strength of the unions remains virtually unaffected. In 1991 approximately 34 per cent of the dependent labour force in the west was still organized in unions, with membership density having declined by just three percentage points since the start of the 1980s. Although the unions' reputation as entrepreneurs in their own right has latterly suffered severe setbacks, they have achieved notable gains in collective bargaining, and successfully contributed to the system of **Mitbestimmung** (worker co-determination). In addition, some of them have pulled off major recruitment coups in the east.

Umbrella organizations

After the Second World War the tradition of a multiplicity of relatively small, craft-based unions was abandoned in western Germany, and blue-collar workers especially were organized in fifteen large unions, one for each major industry. Thus a chauffeur and a typesetter working in a printing plant would if they so desired — no one can be forced to join a trade union — be members of the same union. Every one of these industrial unions joined the **Deutscher Gewerkschaftsbund** (DGB) (Confederation of German Trade Unions), as subsequently did the **Gewerkschaft der Polizei** (GdP) (Police Trade Union).

The DGB was formed in Munich in 1949 and is now located in Düsseldorf. As the umbrella organization for the sixteen trade unions, its role is to co-ordinate the activities of the member unions, provide advice on legal and social security matters, contribute to education and training programmes, and to speak for the unions in national affairs. It is not affiliated to any of the political parties, nor is it associated with any of the churches.

The DGB is run by its Federal Board, which consists of twenty-seven members: the president of the DGB, two vice-presidents, the sixteen presidents of the member unions, and eight full-time DGB officials, who are the heads of the special committees. Two of these officials have usually been card-carrying members of the CDU or CSU. The DGB meets every three years for its Federal Congress.

At the end of 1990 the unions affiliated to the DGB represented between them over 7,937,000 workers. The largest and most powerful affiliate was the **IG Metall** (Metal-Workers' Union). Indeed, with over 2.7 million workers in western Germany (and an estimated 3.6 million in Germany as a whole), it is the largest single union in the world (Table 7.1).

Apart from the DGB, three other notable organizations are based in the west of the country. The largest of these is the **Deutsche Angestellten-Gewerkschaft** (DAG) (German Union of Salaried Employees), with approximately 575,000 members. It is not an industrial union in the sense outlined above but groups together white-collar workers, on a horizontal basis, from the most varied branches of industry. In so doing, the DAG competes with DGB affiliates for members, particularly in the public sector, banking, insurance, and retail trades. The DAG's general policies and programmes show a marked similarity to the DGB's, though relations between the two have often been characterized by a degree of friction.

The **Deutscher Beamtenbund** (DBB) (German Civil Servants' Federation), with about 1 million members, is the main organization for permanent civil servants. The DBB is not a union in the real sense, since Beamte do not under German law enjoy either the right to collective bargaining or the right to strike. The DBB mainly exercises a lobbying function, but terms and conditions for its members are determined by the state.

The DBB competes with the DGB for members, with numbers divided almost equally between the two organizations, the DGB recording some 800,000 civil servants among its members at the end of 1990. The two organizations hold diametrically-opposed views on the structure

Table 7.1   *The member unions of the DGB (German Trade Union Confederation),*
1990

Industrial unions/trade unions (western Germany)	Members (in thousands)	Share in DGB %
Non-metallic minerals	462.7	5.8
Mining and energy	322.8	4.1
Chemicals – paper – ceramics	675.9	8.5
Railway	312.3	3.9
Education and science	189.1	2.4
Gardening, agriculture and forestry	44.1	0.6
Trade, banks and insurance	404.7	5.1
Wood and plastics	152.7	1.9
Leather	42.6	0.5
Media	184.7	2.3
Metal workers	2,726.7	34.4
Food, drink and tobacco – gastronomy	275.2	3.5
Police	162.7	2.1
Post	478.9	6.0
Textiles – clothing	249.8	3.1
Public sector, transportation and traffic	1,252.6	15.8
	7,937.9	100.0

Source: DGB

of the public service. The DGB, which counts among its members
three different groups of employees – civil servants, **Angestellte** (white-
collar workers) and **Arbeiter** (blue-collar workers) – advocates a single
legal status for the three, as well as collective bargaining rights and the
extension of the right to strike to all employees. In contrast, the DBB
emphasizes the special status of civil servants and maintains that more
advantages can be gained for its members from legislation, which
it believes it can influence significantly, than from the vagaries of
negotiations.

The **Christlicher Gewerkschaftsbund Deutschlands** (CGB) (Christian
Trade Union Federation), founded in 1955, numbers some 310,000
members among its affiliated unions. Christian trade unionism has
lost its former significance, and the CGB has not succeeded latterly in
exerting either major political influence or establishing itself as a force
in collective bargaining.

The **Freier Deutscher Gewerkschaftsbund** (FDGB) (Free German
Trade Union Federation), the central association of trade unions in
former East Germany, organized approximately 90 per cent of the
workforce. In addition, it administered the country's social insurance
funds and played a key role in furnishing workers with subsidized

housing and holidays. But it also operated a Stalinist 'transmission belt' for disseminating the ideology and policies of the SED (Socialist Unity Party) to the workplace. Like the former education system in the east, it was regarded as one of the 'Schools of Communism' (see pp. 157–160).

The FDGB did not represent a federation of independent trade unions but was in effect one of the mainstays of the party and the Communist regime. Discredited by its association with the SED and by allegations of corruption among its leadership, the FDGB was faced with a collapse of confidence among its membership, and the organization formally dissolved itself on 30 September 1990. Its affiliated member unions also dissolved themselves during 1990 and 1991, either recommending individual members to join the corresponding DGB trade union or bringing them in collectively. The figure for union density in the east is put by the DGB at about 50 per cent of the workforce.

Entrepreneurial activities

One of the features that distinguishes some of the trade unions in western Germany from those in other countries is, or rather was, the extent of their activities as entrepreneurs. Although union subscriptions, at 2 per cent of gross wages or salaries, and unions' individual contributions to their umbrella organization, at 12 per cent of revenue, are in themselves modest enough, the DGB and its affiliated unions had succeeded, by the early 1980s, in building up considerable business interests. Through a holding company, they controlled, *inter alia*, the Volksfürsorge life-insurance company, the third largest of its type in western Europe; Neue Heimat, the biggest construction company in Europe; the Bank für Gemeinwirtschaft, the fifth most powerful non-state bank in western Germany; and the Co-op, based in Frankfurt-am-Main.

The trade unions justified these large company interests by referring to them as an attempt at an alternative form of business activity based on the co-operative principle – **Gemeinwirtschaft**. They pointed out that their experiments at capitalism with a human and acceptable face dated back to the early part of the century, with the establishment of the Volksfürsorge in 1912 to combat the high premiums being demanded by other insurance companies at the time. Neue Heimat was founded in 1950 in order to alleviate the catastrophic conditions existing on the post-war housing market.

In the mid-1980s, however, the whole concept of Gemeinwirtschaft received a series of blows from which it never recovered. Neue Heimat was shattered by allegedly corrupt management practices to such an extent that this massive company was sold in September 1986 to an obscure Berlin bakery-owner, Horst Schiesser, for a token DM 1. The banks, however, to whom some DM 12 billion was owed, out of total liabilities of DM 17 billion, forced the trade unions to take it back. Because of the financial repercussions of the Neue Heimat affair, the unions were obliged to sell 51 per cent of the Bank für Gemeinwirtschaft to the Aachener und Münchener insurance group.

Mismanagement on a massive scale, including alleged presentation of falsified balance sheets, credit fraud, and tax evasion shook another union-owned company, the Frankfurt-based Co-op, in 1988. Total debts were estimated at some DM 600 million, and a consortium of foreign banks bought up 72 per cent of the shares. The evident inability of the trade unions to manage their companies adequately has thus forced the DGB and its affiliates to rethink their strategy on Gemeinwirtschaft. In 1989 plans included the sale of 25 per cent of the unions' holding in the Allgemeine Hypothekenbank and even the disposal of 75 per cent of their stake in the Volksfürsorge. The fourteenth DGB Federal Congress, held in Hamburg in May 1990, took an historic decision to abandon Gemeinwirtschaft, in view of the damage caused to the unions by the series of corruption scandals.

Collective bargaining

Historically, German employers' associations (see pp. 128–135) were never keen to enter into wage negotiations with the trade unions. It was not until 1918, with the signing of the Stinnes–Legien Accord, that they formally recognized the trade unions as their negotiating counterparts. Although a collective bargaining system of sorts did eventually emerge – over 14 million employees were covered by collective agreements as early as 1922 – its effectiveness was hindered by lingering distrust on the part of many employers. As a consequence, wage negotiations were frequently deadlocked during the period of the Weimar Republic, 1917–33, and the state had to intervene, not always happily, in an effort to arbitrate. In view of the unfortunate legacy of state arbitration, the concept of **Tarifautonomie** (bargaining autonomy), which is characterized by an absence of government intervention, was established after the Second World War.

The **Tarifvertragsgesetz** (Collective Agreements Act) of 1949, amended in 1969, forms the legal basis for collective agreements. These are of basically two types: the **Lohn- und Gehaltstarifvertrag** (wages and salary agreement), which affects solely pay; and the **Manteltarifvertrag** or **Rahmentarifvertrag** (framework agreement), which regulates, in addition, such matters as hours of work, holidays, benefits, dismissal and redundancy provisions. The former has traditionally been concluded for twelve months at a time, and the latter for perhaps several years.

Collective bargaining for industry- or sector-level agreements takes place between the trade union and the corresponding employers' association. Once signed, these agreements are legally binding on employees and companies alike. An agreement can, however, be extended to cover all employees in the relevant sector by being declared **allgemeinverbindlich** (generally binding). This can be done by the **Bundesminister für Arbeit und Sozialordnung** (Federal Minister of Labour and Social Affairs), or by a state Minister of Labour, if companies employing at least half of all the employees in the sector have signed it, and if such an extension would 'serve the general interest'. At the end of December 1990 the total number of agreements in force was about 35,500, consisting of some 24,700 sectoral agreements and 8800 company agreements.

Collective bargaining in Germany normally takes place at the sectoral level, with negotiations being conducted either nationally or regionally. Either sectoral or regional bargaining is common for such industries as engineering and chemicals, and the retail trade. **Firmentarifverträge** (company wage agreements) are relatively unimportant, and apply principally to small companies that are not members of employers' associations. Exceptions include, however, Volkswagen and certain companies in the energy sector.

After the 1991 pay negotiations had been completed, the trade unions in western Germany were accused of attempting to punish Chancellor Kohl for his pre-unification 'tax-lie' (see p. 9). They were responsible, it was claimed, for launching a wage-price spiral in the west and contributing to mass unemployment in the east through insisting on wage equalization there. As for the first accusation, in 1990 real net wages per worker in western Germany rose by 4.8 per cent, which, on account of tax cuts, was the largest annual increase since 1970. In 1991, due in part to the tax increase to pay for German unification, real net wages declined slightly, the seventh year of negative real pay since 1981. Between 1980 and 1990 workers' purchasing power rose by only 7 per cent. Wage claims averaging 9 per cent for 1992 were a reflection of unions' determination to achieve improved standards of living for their members despite the incipient recession.

Indeed, the eleven-day strike by the union of **Öffentliche Dienste, Transport und Verkehr** (ÖTV) (Public Service and Transport Workers) in April and May 1992, western Germany's biggest since the end of the Second World War, provided further evidence, if such were needed, that ordinary workers' patience with the high price of unification was running thin. The strike was eventually resolved by the union leadership accepting a wage increase of between 5 and 6 per cent, thus setting a benchmark for the rest of the 1992 wage-bargaining round.

The settlement was felt to be inadequate by rank and file members. In contrast, negotiations in September of the same year between Lufthansa's hard-pressed management, the ÖTV blue-collar and DAG white-collar trade unions resulted in a pay freeze. Thus allegations that western Germans had at last contracted the dreaded 'British Disease' were revealed as being much exaggerated.

In the negotiations for the 1993 wage round the trade unions were asking for only 5 per cent rises, roughly half the 1992 claims. The recession had put them on the defensive, but certain other adverse trends might continue even after the economy picks up. These are: fiercer foreign competition, which could depress wages in the future; services growing at the expense of manufacturing, which usually dilutes union membership; and eastern German companies negotiating lower wages and in some cases actually breaking wage agreements. In addition, continued union consent will be crucial for the success of Chancellor Kohl's **Solidarpakt** (solidarity pact), the government's scheme for refinancing the modernization of eastern Germany's industry.

Industrial relations at the workplace

It is often maintained that industrial relations at the workplace in Germany have a 'dual' structure, though this assertion is open to question. At industry level interest representation is conducted voluntarily through the mechanism of collective bargaining between unions and employers' associations. At company level negotiations are conducted on a statutory basis between the **Betriebsrat** (works' council) and the individual employer.

The statutory framework for industrial relations at the workplace is furnished by the **Betriebsverfassungsgesetz** (Works Constitution Act) of 1972. Under this legislation works' councils may be elected in all companies or plants with over five employees, and are thus given the responsibility of protecting employees' interests at the workplace. To this end, the legislation confers upon them significant participation rights in management decision-making processes (see p. 117).

In addition to rights, however, works' councils also have certain duties imposed upon them. Under Article 2 of the Act works' councils and employers have to work together 'in a spirit of mutual trust, having regard to the applicable collective agreements and in co-operation with the trade union and employers' associations for the good of the employees and the establishment'. Works' councils are also enjoined to respect the 'peace of the establishment'; and resorting to industrial action as a means of settling disputes is prohibited.

Works' councils are formally independent of the trade unions, and are elected by the whole workforce, both union and non-union. Legislation prohibits them from bargaining over such issues as wages, which are already regulated in a collective agreement. Thus, where payments are made above and beyond collectively agreed rates, these are inevitably of an informal nature, consisting of unilateral pay rises on the part of the employer, which can in theory be withdrawn at any time.

Besides the works' councils, the unions maintain a network of **Vertrauensleute** (stewards) at the workplace. Unlike the works' council, the **Vertrauenskörper** (body of stewards) in a plant is an integral part of union organization and not subject to the Works Constitution Act. The stewards play an important role at the workplace, recruiting members, collecting union subscriptions, distributing information, and mobilizing members in industrial disputes. These functions, it is claimed, cannot be performed by works' councillors because of their small numbers and because of their obligations under the Act.

Nevertheless, the vast majority of seats on works' councils have always been won by union candidates, and in practice the works' council and the leadership of the union stewards usually consist of the same persons. As a result, the statutory rights of works' councils have *de facto* become union rights. Whatever the legal distinctions, the outcome of practical experience is that the statutory institutions and trade-union organizations at the workplace have to all intents and purposes merged with one another.

Industrial democracy

The business culture and the business climate in western Germany have both been favourably affected by the degree of integration of trade unions and works' councils into corporate structures. Although this integration was not always welcomed by employers, at least not initially, they have come to accept it as a fact of business life. Moreover, possibly as a result of close trade-union involvement in decision-making processes, employers and trade unions refer to themselves collectively as the **Sozialpartner** (social partners), thus at least avoiding the adversarial rhetoric encountered in other countries, and pointing to a higher degree of consensus than is found elsewhere.

Industrial democracry in Germany looks back over a long history:

1920: Works' councils recognized as bargaining counterparts of employers in companies with more than twenty employees.
1951: Parity co-determination introduced for the coalmining, iron and steel industries. Capital and labour representatives have equal voting strength on supervisory boards. Voting deadlock is prevented by an

additional 'neutral man', appointed by the state, if the board is split.
1952: Companies with over 500 employees forced to allocate one-third of the seats on their supervisory boards to labour representatives.
1972: Companies with over five employees permitted to have a works' council. In addition, works' councils are given full co-determination rights on issues of working hours and the introduction of new technology, unless these matters are already covered by wage negotiations between unions and employers' associations.
1976: **Mitbestimmungsgesetz** (Co-determination Act) passed through Federal Parliament. It embraces AGs and GmbHs normally employing over 2000 persons, which must have a supervisory board composed of half shareholders' and half workers' representatives. Companies with between 500 and 2000 employees have supervisory boards with one-third worker representation (Table 7.2).

The trade unions are not entirely happy with the 1976 Act for several reasons. First, it affects only relatively few large companies, and not the vast majority of small and medium-sized firms in the country. Second, the unions claim, the Act does not deliver true parity co-determination. It ensures that, in the event of voting deadlock, the capital owners will prevail because the chairman of the supervisory board is always a shareholders' representative with a casting vote. Moreover, one of the worker representatives must be a **Leitender Angestellte** (senior manager), who, it is alleged, is likely to side with the shareholders.

The employers were not happy with the 1976 Act either. In June 1977, just as the Act was due to come into force, nine companies and twenty-nine employers' organizations submitted a complaint to the

Table 7.2 *Forms of co-determination and their scope*

	No. of employees	Company size and/or type
No co-determination	3.4 million	Small firms (less than five employees)
Internal co-determination	3.6 million	Public sector
Internal co-determination	9.3 million	Remaining industry
One-third participation	0.6 million	Medium-sized companies
Co-determination in coal, iron and steel industries	0.5 million	Coal, iron and steel sector
Co-determination under the Act of 1976	4.0 million	Large companies

Source: *Facts about Germany*, 1992

Bundesverfassungsgericht in Karlsruhe to the effect that it contravened the GG. In March 1977 the Constitutional Court rejected the employers' injunction.

Since 1979 companies in western Germany have come to terms with the provisions of the Co-determination Act, which has been subject of minor amendments in the interim. Most will concede that worker representatives on the supervisory board make a positive contribution to the smooth operation of companies. This has been achieved both through their direct inputs into the decision-making process and through the dissemination of information on decisions taken at high levels in the company, although the works' councils in western German companies were already privy to large amounts of company information. Indeed, for ordinary workers in the average company, the focus of industrial democracy lies neither with their representatives on the company supervisory board, nor with their trade union, but with the works' council.

Industrial conflict

The right to strike is implied, though not expressly stated, in Article 9, Section 3, of the GG. This right is, however, subject to a series of restrictions and qualifications, the most significant of which are:

- The parties to a collective agreement are bound by a **Friedenspflicht** (peace obligation), according to which neither party is allowed to take industrial action over issues that are regulated in the agreement.
- The Federal Labour Court has stipulated that industrial action must conform to the **Verhältnismäßigkeitsprinzip** (principle of proportionality). According to this principle, industrial action should be necessary and commensurate with the realization of its objectives; may be initiated only after all other methods of resolving a dispute have been exhausted; should be conducted according to the principle of fairness; and should not aim at the destruction of the opposite side.
- Essential services may not be endangered by industrial action.
- Secondary strikes and 'political' strikes are illegal.
- Civil servants, as already indicated, are not allowed to go on strike.

Settlement procedures

The procedures for resolving industrial disputes in Germany differ according to whether the dispute is one of right or one of interest.

Disputes of right, i.e. those stemming from the interpretation of a collective agreement, may not be resolved, at least initially, by resorting to industrial conflict, on account of the peace obligation that obtains during the whole life of an agreement. Instead, such disputes are handled by the labour courts (see pp. 41–42).

In cases where a trade union and an employers' association have failed to resolve a dispute of interest, this dispute is normally submitted to a **Schlichtungsverfahren** (voluntary mediation procedure). Though such procedures are relatively common in the private sector, the actual form of mediation varies from industry to industry. Nevertheless, conciliation clauses in collective agreements usually provide for a mediation panel composed of an equal number of employee and employer representatives and an independent chairperson. If the panel concludes that it is unable to resolve the dispute, the mediation process comes to an end, the peace obligation ceases to be valid, and industrial action may begin.

It is vital to distinguish such industry or sector-level dispute procedures from those obtaining at plant level. Here negotiations between works' councils and local management may lead to the conclusion of a **Betriebsvereinbarung** (works' agreement). Should any disputes arise over the interpretation of these agreements, they would, again, be referred to the labour courts. But if local management and works' council cannot conclude a works' agreement, e.g. in the case of a dispute of interest, it must be submitted to an **Einigungsstelle** (arbitration committee). This body would consist of an equal number of members appointed by management and works' council and a neutral chairperson acceptable to both sides.

In post-war western Germany there has never been a national arbitration and conciliation service on account of the unhappy experience of state intervention in industrial relations during the period of the Weimar Republic.

Industrial relations in general

Workers and employers are not only adversaries: they also co-operate in many ways. First, there is the day-to-day co-operation on the shopfloor. Yet above and beyond this, representatives of both sides' organizations also meet in many forums. For example, there are representatives of labour and management on the committees that oversee the final examinations for apprentices (see p. 148). In the labour courts that rule on certain employment disputes there are lay assessors at all levels from both sides (see p. 41). In addition, the leaders of various organizations frequently attend meetings with the politicians responsible for their areas of interest (see p. 131).

The social consensus between trade unions and employers in post-war western Germany, as graphically illustrated by the relatively few working days lost through industrial disputes, has continued, for the most part, throughout the 1980s and early 1990s (Table 7.3). Compared to most other EC countries, the incidence of industrial action has been low. Thus in the 1970–90 period the average number of working days lost per 1000 workers in all industries and services amounted in western Germany to 40. This is above the level for the Netherlands (28), but below that for Portugal (133), France (145), Denmark (211), the United Kingdom (435), Ireland (579), Spain (708), Greece (867) and Italy (1042). The whole post-war pattern of relative industrial harmony is in marked contrast with Germany's experience before 1914 and during the period of the Weimar Republic, when the level of industrial conflict was high.

Moreover, it is highly significant that the issues that have divided trade unions and employers most in recent years are those concerned with working hours. This is undoubtedly a reflection of the sea-change taking place in western Germany today, away from the erstwhile **Leistungsgesellschaft** (high-performance society) and towards the **Freizeitgesellschaft** (leisure society).

The older generation rarely tires of recalling how Germans in the west used to work: women in headscarves passing bricks from hand to hand as they toiled in the rubble to rebuild a country devastated by war; men who laboured long hours in the factories and fashioned an economic miracle; unions that used to sit down with employers, not to argue over a shorter working week but to hatch out strategies for

Table 7.3 *Working days in western Germany lost through disputes (1980–93)*

Year	Working days lost
1980	128,386
1981	58,398
1982	15,106
1983	40,842
1984	2,921,263
1985	34,505
1986	27,964
1987	33,325
1988	41,880
1989	100,409
1990	363,547
1991	153,587
1992	1,545,320

Source: Bundesministerium für Arbeit; Bundesanstalt für Arbeit

greater efficiency and higher output. But as the country has prospered and achieved the **Wohlstandsgesellschaft** (affluent society), attitudes have changed. People have adopted a more relaxed attitude to life and are taking things more easily. They want more time to enjoy the money they are earning, and are more interested in holidays abroad than in overtime in factories at home. (In 1991 Germans again retained the title of Travel Champions of the World, which they have held since 1981, with citizens from both parts of the country spending DM 51 billion on trips abroad in that year.) But what has happened to the good old western German work ethic?

Opinion polls provide an answer of sorts. Young people are more interested in being with their families. They do not believe that they should produce ever more and work ever harder; and they are increasingly unwilling to trade off leisure for more pay. Such findings have led some commentators to deduce that the Germans in the west are becoming idle, a notion abhorrent to the older generation. But this is not even part of the real answer. The circumstances of the post-war reconstruction period were very special. Not only were enormous efforts necessary to make the country habitable again, but hard work was a form of guilt expiation for the atrocities of the war, a way in which western Germans could regain their dignity in their own eyes, and the respect of the rest of the world. The nature of work in the 1980s, however, changed radically. The introduction of a vast amount of new technology, such as computer-numerically-controlled (CNC) machine-tools, industrial robots, just-in-time (JIT) and flexible manufacturing systems, into plants alienated many employees and left them feeling ill at ease at the workstation.

One manifestation of this is the number of days per year that German workers report sick. Despite their long holidays and frequent visits to health spas, Germans appear to be among the world's sickliest workers. They take more time off for health reasons than their counterparts in any of the six G7 industrialized countries. In 1992 the average German engineering-worker reported 'ill' on eighteen days, compared with eleven in the United Kingdom and the United States of America. The sickness rate jumps sharply on Fridays and Mondays.

It is against this background that the disputes between trade unions and employers over shorter working hours should be viewed. The Working Hours Act of 1938 still regulates the length and distribution of working hours, breaks and overtime. However, its provisions are based on the 48-hour week, and it is now of limited relevance for the last decade of the millennium.

In 1984 the Metal-Workers' Union went on a strike lasting eight weeks for the 35-hour week. They successfully broke the 40-hour week barrier and settled with **Gesamtmetall** (Metal Trades Employers' Federation) for 38.5 hours. In May 1990 they achieved a further major agreement for the introduction of the 35-hour week, to be phased in over a period of five years. The working week was to be cut to 36 hours in April 1993 and finally to 35 hours by April 1995. Also in May 1990 a similar agreement was concluded between **IG Medien** (Print-Workers' Union) and the **Bundesverband Druck** (Printing Employers' Federation) to introduce the 35-hour week over a similar period of time.

While the working week has been shortened in western Germany, holiday entitlement has risen. Again the legislation lags far behind reality. The Federal Holidays Act of 1953 provides for an annual minimum holiday of 18 working days. In 1989 holiday entitlement averaged 27.3 working days; in 1990, average length of holidays was 27.5 working days. By 1992 collective agreements provided for almost 70 per cent of workers' entitlement to 30 days' holiday. Where age is used as a criterion, thirty, thirty-five or forty is the age at which employees usually attain their maximum holiday periods, while maximum service-related entitlements are between five and fifteen years' service.

In 1992 94 per cent of employees received additional holiday pay in one of three forms: 44 per cent of all employees averaged 47 per cent of basic pay; 31 per cent of employees were given a flat-rate cash payment to cover the entire holiday period, amounting to DM 677 on average; 19 per cent of employees received a flat-rate cash payment for each day's holiday, which averaged DM 25 per day. Moreover, some 92 per cent of employees received an annual bonus, usually expressed as a percentage of a month's salary (the so-called thirteen month's salary), and in 1992 this percentage averaged 69 per cent of gross monthly pay. Taken together, additional holiday pay and the thirteen month's salary averaged 92 per cent of a month's normal salary, while about two-thirds of all employees received a total bonus equivalent to at least one month's salary.

Given fringe benefits such as these, it is hardly surprising that an area of growing conflict is that of weekend working. Working on Saturday or Sunday separates not only trade unions and employers but has also sown divisions among the unions themselves, and between unions and works' councils. In the 1950s and 1960s the unions succeeded in gaining acceptance of the five-day working week, but recently there has been renewed pressure by employers to reintroduce weekend working, particularly Saturday working.

In 1988 both Opel in its Kaiserslautern plant and BMW in the new Regensburg works brought back Saturday working. Similarly, Siemens and IBM introduced weekend working to permit continuous production of megabit chips at their factories in Regensburg and Sindelfingen respectively. Goodyear insisted that a DM 100 million investment at

Fulda be made dependent on the acceptance of Saturday working by the works' council. In the autumn of 1990 Mercedez-Benz inserted Saturday shifts at its plants in Sindelfingen, Untertürkheim and Bremen.

Article 139 of the GG states: 'Sunday and the public holidays recognized by the state shall remain under legal protection as days of rest from work and of spiritual edification'. Exceptions included in the **Gewerbeordnung** (Trading Regulations) cover mainly the utilities, transport and health services, as well as the leisure sector. In contrast, there are no legal restrictions on Saturday working. Wage agreements expressly stipulating a Monday-to-Friday working week apply to some 265,000 employees only.

Employers maintain that weekend working is necessary because working hours have become shorter, thus leaving expensive equipment idle for long periods (see also p. 132). The inclusion of Saturday as part of the normal working week would thus allow employers to incorporate more effective equipment working times. Dr Werner Stumpfe, President of the Metal Trades Employers' Federation, has stated that, whereas the incorporation of Saturday as a normal working day was a necessity Sunday working was required for technical, i.e. maintenance, reasons and not on economic grounds.

The Metal and Print-Workers' unions are opposed to either Saturday or Sunday working. They claim that weekend working isolates employees from friends, sport and culture, disrupts family life, and places further strain on the environment. The **IG Chemie** (Chemical-Workers' Union), traditionally a more moderate union than the engineers or printers, maintains that although works' councils initially rejected the introduction of weekend working, in many cases ensuing arbitration found in favour of employers. The union consequently decided that where Saturday working seemed likely, it would trade this off against shorter working hours and reductions in overtime. In 1992 17 per cent of blue-collar employees regularly worked on Saturdays and 7 per cent on Sundays.

In view of the large differences between the various parties, it appears unlikely that this conflict will be resolved in the short term. At present the employers appear to be winning, partly because they can drive a wedge between official union policy and works' councils. They also point to increased competition from Japan and the Pacific Rim countries, where employees put in an average of 42 hours per week, including weekends, and to some countries in the EC with similar working practices. Thus, the employers conclude, current German trends place the country at a competitive disadvantage.

Trade-union activities in the east

It is perhaps a matter of some regret that the DGB has not given a stronger lead in helping to refashion the business culture in eastern Germany. Instead, it has been embroiled in an unseemly wrangle over the ownership of the assets that belonged to the former **Allgemeiner Deutscher Gewerkschaftsbund** (ADGB) — the main trade union confederation before 1933. A commission ruled at the end of 1991 that the DGB is not the legal successor to the **Freier Deutscher Gewerkschaftsbund** (FDGB) — the union confederation of former East Germany — and therefore is not entitled to take over its assets. The DGB's view is that property belonging to the ADGB before 1933 should be transferred automatically to the DGB, and that property acquired by the FDGB after 1945 should be sold to the DGB 'at a fair price'.

In general, the Unification Treaty between the two Germanies provides for the extension of western German collective bargaining structures, industrial relations law, social security institutions and labour law to eastern Germany. In many instances, however, special transitional regulations were introduced until full harmonization is achieved. The areas affected include notice periods, employment security and unfair dismissal legislation. It should also be noted that in some areas former East German labour law was more beneficial to employees than the new regulations of West German origin, particularly in relation to working women with children (see p. 98).

The main contribution to the business culture in eastern Germany the individual unions affiliated to the DGB have made to date appears to be in the area of high wage claims. These have met with varying degrees of resistance from employers' associations, but wage awards have risen considerably since Gemu, partly, though not entirely, as a result of high inflation in the east (see p. 60). **Tarifunion** (the harmonization of pay and conditions with workers in the west of the country) has also been one of the major driving forces.

In fact it could be argued that it is in the area of wages that the economies of the two parts of the country have grown closest together. The ratio of wages per employee in the east to that in the west rose from 32 per cent in the second half of 1989 to about 50 per cent in the first half of 1991. On account of declining output, labour costs per-hour-worked in eastern Germany increased by 73 per cent between the second and fourth quarters of 1990.

The first signs of industrial unrest appeared in the east in November 1990, when 250,000 Deutsche Reichsbahn workers walked out for two days, bringing all rail traffic in the eastern states, including 550,000 goods trains, to a grinding halt. The railway workers, whose numbers were expected to be halved, secured a forty-hour week as from April 1991, and a phased harmonization of pay with workers in western Germany.

In December 1990 insurance employees marched through Leipzig and Berlin, protesting at the low levels of their salaries. The DAG promised to back their cause. Eastern German insurance employees were earning approximately 40 per cent of the rate of their western counterparts.

It was, however, the settlement achieved by the Metal-Workers' Union that set the pace for wage deals in the new states. In their 1991 negotiations for the east the union secured wage rates, from April 1991, of 62.5 per cent of their western equivalent, an outcome much nearer the 65 per cent claim than the 50 per cent offered by the employers. Moreover, the negotiations provided for an increase to 71 per cent of western German pay as from April 1992, a further increase to 82 per cent of rates in the west from April 1993, and finally an increase to 100 per cent of western German pay by April 1994. Whether the 2800 engineering companies in eastern Germany can actually afford such wage increases is a different question, especially in the light of the recession. According to calculations in 1993, implementation of these agreements would destroy some 70,000 of the 400,000 jobs in the engineering sector in the east. Yet many there were insisting that **Versprochen ist versprochen** (a promise is a promise).

Metal-workers in eastern Germany went on a twelve-day strike in April 1993 after employers tore up the above agreement, the first legal stoppage in the region since Hitler banned trade unions in 1933. The employers claimed that the ravaged condition of much of eastern German industry meant that the money did not exist to pay for the 1993 increases. A compromise was reached whereby eastern rates were raised to 80 per cent of western wages by December 1993, eight months later than in the original agreement. Parity is envisaged by July 1996.

The race to catch up with wages in the west is proving a boon for some unions eager to boost their membership. By January 1991 the Metal-Workers' Union had thirty-five offices in eastern Germany through a merger with **IGM-Ost**, its counterpart in the east, and was targeting over 1 million new members, or 12.5 per cent of the total workforce in the eastern states, as early as March 1991. Other trade unions based in the west have not been so successful in persuading the citizens of eastern Germany that subscriptions of 2 per cent of their hard-earned salaries represent a good investment. The pressure is on these unions to produce results in the form of handsome wage settlements. Greater membership will then be their reward.

Medium-term concerns

Apart from their concerns about eastern Germany, the trade unions are anxious with regard to developments in two major areas over the medium term: protection of the environment and future trends in the EC.

Environmental protection is one of the issues to which German unions are devoting increasing amounts of energy. While many of their initiatives are still at the formative stage, some plants are already covered by works' agreements on the subject, and there appears to be little doubt that environmental questions will increasingly form part of the collective bargaining agenda in the mid-to-late 1990s (see p. 178).

Western German unions have rejected the view of those who perceive environmental problems as providing justification for the abandonment of industrial society. While acknowledging that there might be short-term conflicts between unions' economic rationale and the interests of the environment, they are gradually coming to the conclusion that in the long term the pursuit of environmental protection cannot be separated from the social interests of workers. In a policy document entitled *Umweltschutz und qualitatives Wachstum (Environmental protection and qualitative growth)*, the DGB outlines its main reasons for this:

- Environmental protection is needed to enhance the social aspects and quality of workers' lives.
- Environmental protection is inevitable if the economy is to survive in the long term.
- Environmental protection can lead to the creation of more jobs.

Trade unions have as yet concluded relatively few agreements which deal expressly with environmental protection matters. But outstanding among them is a communiqué issued on 20 August 1987 by the Chemical-Workers' Union and the Chemical-Employers' Federation. It recommends, *inter alia*, that a company's **Wirtschaftsausschuß** (economics committee), which has to be established in all companies with over 100 employees, should regularly deal with environmental matters; that works' councils should be informed of measures taken in accordance with safety and environmental protection requirements; and that works' councils should discuss environmental protection concepts in relation to the introduction of new product lines and questions relating to the storage and transport of dangerous goods. In addition, some thirty works' agreements on environmental protection issues have been concluded. They embrace the plants of most major chemicals manufacturers, including Bayer, Henkel, Hoechst and Beiersdorf.

As far as the EC is concerned, with the highest pay and best fringe benefits in Europe, the German trade unions believe they have the most to lose from the greater mobility of labour and companies anticipated in the Single European Market. The unions are confident that they can retain most of the skilled-labour and high-value-added jobs, especially in the west, on account of the outstanding system of education, training and development there (see pp. 147–151). But they have worried that some lower-skilled manufacturing jobs could be exported to relatively low-cost countries.

Many of their fears could be groundless. Some of the very large companies, particularly in the car industry, have already moved to Spain and Portugal. Moreover, the swift modernization of these two countries in the Iberian peninsula has also entailed an equally swift increase in labour costs there. Nevertheless, the Single Market has inspired a few smaller companies, particularly the car-component makers, to emigrate south after the multinationals.

But the south of Europe is not the only focus of trade-union worries. They are painfully aware that the United Kingdom is the main target for outward German investment in Europe, and the United Kingdom has opted out of the Social Chapter of the Maastricht Treaty on European Political Union. The trade unions fear that German employers could indulge in 'social dumping' in the United Kingdom.

This is the nub of German trade union objections to EC developments. They claim that 1993 merely marked the advent of a 'Europe of Capital' and focus on the opposition of such countries as the United Kingdom to the Community Charter of Fundamental Social Rights as tabled by Jacques Delors. They point to the rejection of the Vredeling Initiative in the early 1980s, which incorporated much of the western German system of worker co-determination, and fear that, yet again, what might be adopted as the European standard is the lowest common denominator.

Conclusion

Notwithstanding German trade-union fears about protection of the environment and the 'Social dismantling of Europe' in the medium term, the unions do not have their troubles to seek in the short term. Recession, unification problems, and de-industrialization in the east are all perceived as a threat to their many accomplishments. Although they have won for their members some of the world's highest rates of pay and some of the shortest working hours, and offer in return skills and productivity that many countries envy, they are distinctly anxious about their future prospects.

The Chemical-Workers' and Coal-Miners' Unions plan to merge in the hope that larger unions are stronger unions. Experience would suggest otherwise. In 1992 the DAG endeavoured to conclude a collective agreement covering some 400 different professions but caved in after a protracted strike. As a consequence, the DGB is planning a thorough structural overhaul by May 1996, the date of its sixteenth Federal Congress.

8 Business and employers' organizations

Introduction

Compared to the trade unions, German employers' organizations receive scant coverage in the media in general, or in the specialist business press, outside Germany. These organizations do not usually attract the attention even of correspondents on industrial relations abroad, except perhaps when certain of them figure as the trade unions' wage-negotiating counterparts. This contrasts starkly with the situation inside Germany, where the presidents of these associations, or their spokes-persons, are constantly quoted in the newspapers, on radio and television.

The employers' organizations provide invaluable forums where employer can meet employer, discuss matters of mutual interest, hatch out compatible strategies, and indulge in a frenzy of networking, the like of which is not witnessed anywhere else in Europe. A deeper understanding of employers' organizations, their structures and current concerns can thus lead not only to a better insight into industrial relations in Germany but also to an enhanced appreciation of the unique contribution they make to the business culture.

Background

The first employers' organizations were formed in Germany in response to the emerging trade-union movement. They grew rapidly, and in 1913 the **Vereinigung der Deutschen Arbeitgeberverbände** (VDA) (Confederation of German Employers' Associations) was established. Like the trade unions, employers' organizations disappeared under the Nazi regime. Their resurgence after the Second World War was in conformity with the principle of unity displayed by the trade unions.

Employers' organizations receive formal recognition in the GG or in alternative legislation. They are commonly referred to in Germany as **Die Verbände** (the Associations), and there are in excess of 1200 of them in the country at large. Since unification, their numbers have continued to swell as newly-founded organizations become established in the east of the country.

One must be careful to distinguish in Germany between **Arbeitge-berverbände** (employers' associations) and **Wirtschaftsverbände** (business associations). Employers' associations represent their members on social policy issues and industrial relations. Their most important field of interest is wages policy. Business associations concern themselves with economic, monetary, business and technological policies on behalf of their member companies. This distinction is rarely made in other EC countries, where employers' organizations normally lobby on behalf of their members on both sets of issues.

A further distinction must be drawn between employers' and business associations on the one hand and the **Industrie- und Handelskammern** (IHKs) (chambers of industry and commerce) on the other. The latter are self-regulating bodies under public law, which supply a platform for their members to participate directly in public policies affecting the broader interests of the local business community. They also differ from employers' and business associations in that membership of the local chamber is compulsory for any German business entity paying **Gewerbesteuer** (trade tax), no matter what its size or sector. Membership is on an individual, or a company, basis, not on an association basis, as in employers' and other business organizations.

Umbrella organizations

The central organization of the employers' associations is the **Bundes-vereinigung der Deutschen Arbeitgeberverbände** (BDA) (Confederation of German Employers' Associations), located in Cologne. The top organization of the business associations is the **Bundesverband der Deutschen Industrie e.V.** (BDI) (Confederation of German Industry), also located in Cologne. The IHKs are organized at national level in the **Deutscher Industrie- und Handelstag** (DIHT) (Association of German Chambers of Industry and Commerce), which has its seat in Bonn.

Together with the leading organizations of other branches of business, e.g. the banks', the BDA, BDI and DIHT have formed the **Gemein-schaftsausschuß der Deutschen Gewerblichen Wirtschaft** (Joint Committee of German Trade and Industry) (Figure 8.1). The Joint Committee is not, however, a representative body for the whole of German business: it is merely a forum where its member umbrella organizations can meet to discuss matters of common interest.

The BDA, BDI and other associations have established the **Institut der Deutschen Wirtschaft (IDW)** (Institute of the German Economy).

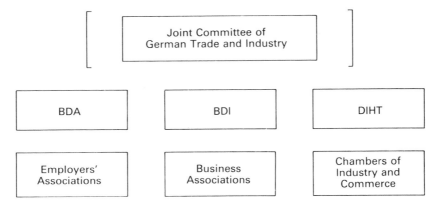

Figure 8.1   *Employers' organizations in Germany. Source: BDI*

This research institute carries out studies on economic and social policy issues, and should be viewed as the employers' counterpart to the DGB's research foundation, the **Wirtschafts- und Sozialwissenschaftliches Institut** (WSI) (Institute of Economics and Social Science).

In former East Germany the employers were represented by the **Vereinigungen Volkseigener Betriebe der DDR** (Associations of Nationally-Owned Enterprises of the German Democratic Republic), though there is no evidence that the associations ever developed a collective bargaining role. Independent employers' organizations were established in the wake of unification. Their structures have been closely modelled along western German lines, and in some sectors, e.g. engineering, east–west mergers have taken place.

The BDA

The BDA consists of forty-six **Fachspitzenverbände** (branch associations) and fifteen **Landesverbände** (state associations), Berlin and Brandenburg sharing one state association. A further 720 employers' associations, either regional interprofessional or regional branch associations, gain indirect membership of the BDA through the direct member associations. Estimates of the organization's membership density would suggest that it represents, through its constituent associations, approximately 70 per cent of all eligible firms. These companies employ almost 80 per cent of all persons working in the private sector.

In contrast to other employers' associations in Europe, e.g. the CBI in the United Kingdom, the BDA does not count public-sector employers among its members. These employers are catered for in the **Vereinigung der Kommunalen Arbeitgeberverbände** (Confederation of Communal

Employers' Associations) and the **Tarifgemeinschaft Deutscher Länder** (Collective Bargaining Association of German States). Nor does the BDA embrace a handful of employers in the private sector, such as Volkswagen, and firms in the oil-refining and energy sectors, because these companies prefer to negotiate separately with the trade unions.

One major employers' association specifically excluded from membership of the BDA is the **Arbeitgeberverband Eisen- und Stahlindustrie** (Employers' Association of the Iron and Steel Industry). Under the 1951 **Montanmitbestimmungsgesetz** (Co-determination Act for the Iron, Steel and Coal Industries), employee and trade union representatives enjoy the right to elect an **Arbeitsdirektor** (personnel director) to the company's management board. As a member of this board, the personnel director would be authorized to represent management in the employers' bargaining committees. The BDA, however, refuses to countenance the notion that the presence of a union-linked representative can be compatible with the operations of employers' organizations, especially in such a sensitive area as wage bargaining.

The BDA's main tasks are:

- To represent its member associations' interests on social policy questions, to government at both the federal and state levels, to European and other international organizations, to the media, the public at large, and to the trade unions. In fulfilling its task as a political lobby, the BDA attaches great significance to the process of drafting legislation in the field of social welfare. The roles of both the BDA and the DGB are formally recognized by the federal government, which sanctions their participation on various standing committees of the **Bundesministerium für Arbeit und Sozialordnung** (Ministry of Labour and Social Affairs).

  Within this framework the BDA's activities in eastern Germany have been concentrated since unification on education, information and counselling services for its new regional associations there. Particular attention has been focused on establishing links between schools and business in the east of the country. In addition, the BDA has pledged that its members will make extra investments in the east, guarantee more jobs for apprentices there, and buy more goods of eastern German origin.

- To co-ordinate the collective bargaining policies of its constituent employers' associations. It should be noted that, unlike employers' confederations in some other European countries such as France and Sweden, the BDA itself does not take part in collective negotiations. It does, however, co-ordinate, to a limited degree, the various bargaining stances of its member associations by publishing general recommendations on matters of policy at large. Though such recommendations are in no way binding on member associations, they are broadly followed. The recommendations themselves generally arise from the deliberations of the BDA's main committee, the highly-influential **Lohn- und Tarifpolitischer Ausschuß** (Wages and Collective Bargaining Policy Committee).

All this has not prevented Klaus Murmann, who became president of the BDA in 1986, from airing his views on collective bargaining issues in public. On 5 August 1992 he started an uproar with an interview given to *Bild*, in which he inveighed against Germany's drift towards the shorter working week. He said that workers should be able to put in up to 42.5 hours per week for higher pay. (In 1992 German industrial employees worked an average of 37.5 hours per week.) 'Germany must be made more attractive as a production site', Murmann told the country's daily newspaper with the largest circulation. 'If we cannot lower costs, we must at least be able to let the machines run longer.' He repeated the popular assertions that German workers are the highest paid in the world, with the shortest working hours, that powerful industrial unions often prevent workers from doing overtime, and government regulations prohibit night-time and weekend working in many industries. 'Rigid and short work shifts must be extended as needed in small and medium-sized firms', Murmann said. 'Why not work on Saturday if it benefits both worker and employer?'

- To uphold solidarity among member employers, especially during industrial disputes. Here the BDA has published a code of conduct under which companies are urged not to seek a competitive advantage over other firms entangled in industrial conflict. One of the guidelines states, for example, that no company should accept an order which has previously been placed with a firm engaged in an industrial dispute. Another guideline urges that no company should employ either strikers or locked-out workers from other firms.

Employers' associations and wage negotiations

The **Gesamtverband der metallindustriellen Arbeitgeberverbände** (Gesamtmetall) (Metal Trades Employers' Federation) is the largest employers' association or, strictly speaking, federation of employers' associations, affiliated to the BDA. It encompasses thirteen autonomous regional employers' associations, with membership from some 10,000 companies employing approximately 2.9 million workers. Although Gesamtmetall is untypical of the national associations affiliated to the BDA in terms of its sheer size and diversity of membership, it has developed a sophisticated decision-making process that has served as a model for other employers' associations in their pay negotiations.

Moreover, its settlements have tended to act as yardsticks for other industries.

As was noted in the previous chapter (see pp. 112–113), **Lohntarif-verträge** (wage agreements) in Germany are usually settled on a regional basis between the particular trade union and its negotiating counterpart, the employers' association. These agreements concentrate on a **Tarif-gebiet** (bargaining area), which is frequently identical to the geograph-ical boundaries of an individual state. Here collective bargaining competence lies with the regional employers' associations. In contrast, the national employers' federation negotiates **Manteltarifverträge** (framework agreements). These settlements normally concentrate on non-wage matters such as holidays, working hours, definitions of overtime, arbitration procedures, etc.

Gesamtmetall's primary objective is to co-ordinate a common bargaining policy. This is formulated by its **Tarifpolitischer Ausschuß** (Collective Bargaining Policy Committee). On the committee sit the Gesamtmetall's president and vice-president, the chairmen of the regional negotiating committees, and chief executives of the member associations in an advisory capacity. From this large policy-making committee is formed a core commission making up one-third of the committee but possessing a right of veto. The outcome is a structure capable of furnishing a unified collective-bargaining stance on the employers' side. This particular structure, and similar ones in other industries, may also help to explain German employers' willingness to resort to the lockout.

The BDA maintains that, in principle, the lockout was declared legal by the Federal Labour Court in judgments of 28 January 1955 and 21 April 1977. The Federal government (SPD/FDP at the time) also held the right of lockout to be legal in a parliamentary answer of 18 April 1978.

Over the past fifteen years German employers' associations, and especially those in the engineering industries, have been distinguished from their counterparts in other European countries, *inter alia*, by the greater use of the lockout. This anti-strike weapon has been employed, the associations claim, as a response to the tactic of **Schwerpunktstreiks** (selective strikes), latterly favoured by the trade unions over all-out strikes. In selective strikes key companies in one or two bargaining areas are targeted by the trade unions under a strategic master plan, with a view to causing maximum industrial disruption to the companies but at minimum cost to the trade unions in terms of strike pay.

The employers see the lockout as a particularly effective weapon against selective strikes. They maintain that such strikes could ruin the companies targeted by the trade unions. But the drain on the particular trade union's strike fund would not be too great because only the employees in a limited number of companies would have to receive strike pay. Yet if all the employers in a particular industry in a particular bargaining area countered the selective strike with a lockout, the risk of bankruptcy or grievous financial harm would be spread more evenly. Moreover, the trade unions would not be able to afford strike pay for all their employees affected out of current income, which would force them to liquidize some of their not-inconsiderable assets to raise the necessary strike pay. This is only fair and just, the employers argue, because their own fixed costs continue, as does interest on borrowings, during a strike.

The trade unions are, quite naturally, unhappy about this state of affairs, and have even gone so far as to state that it is the employers' intention to bring about their financial ruin! The trade unions also attack the lockout on legal grounds, maintaining that it is a denial of one of man's basic rights, i.e. the right to work as laid down in the GG. Moreover, they claim that the lockout is expressly forbidden in certain state constitutions, e.g. Hesse's which actually predates the GG.

The employers hit back with the contention that outlawing the lockout would be against the general interest. In the absence of the lockout they would be exposed to a wage diktat by the unions, and this could entail unforeseeable repercussions for the economy as a whole. If too much were given away in wage settlements, there could be large numbers of company failures, with losses of jobs on a massive scale. Finally, the employers contend, the lockout is a means to force the other side to the negotiating table in an industrial conflict, and has been used 'since time immemorial.'

In 1984 negotiations between Gesamtmetall and the Metal-Workers' Union broke down, leading to a strike over the issue of the shorter working week. Selective strikes were organized in two bargaining areas — Hesse and North Württemberg/North Baden. These strikes were countered by the use of the lockout by the employers' associations. The escalation of industrial conflict was intended to make the strike more expensive for the trade union, which was obliged to issue strike pay to all its members who were locked out, and not merely to those on strike. Companies included in the selective lockout were not necessarily those affected by the strike. In this dispute over 1.5 million more working days were lost as a result of lockouts rather than strike action.

Latterly, the Federal Labour Court has ruled that lockouts are not the main source of employers' bargaining strength and can therefore only be used with justification where the balance of power is held to have shifted towards the unions. The court indicated that such a situation might occur where unions do resort to selective strikes within a bargaining region. In such circumstances employers may resort to a defensive lockout, provided the scale of such remains within defined bounds. For example, employers may not lock out more than 50 per cent of employees within a bargaining region, and if at least 50 per cent of workers are on strike within a region, lockouts are not admissible.

Yet the very fact that companies do obey their employers' associations' occasional call to lock out their workers is proof of the high degree of solidarity among German employers. There are various reasons for this solidarity. They lie partly in the employers' perception of a need for central cohesion and discipline in order to confront large and well-organized trade unions such as the Metal-Workers' Union. They are also partly of a financial nature. Solidarity is fostered by the maintenance of funds from which financial support is furnished to companies incurring costs as a result of industrial disputes. The engineering employers originally set up their own mutual support funds at the level of their regional associations. Subsequently, however, the separate regional funds were amalgamated in a central **Gefahrengemeinschaft** (mutual aid fund), administered by Gesamtmetall, with the aim of increasing solidarity.

Like several large German companies, such as Volkswagen and Robert Bosch, the BDA has set up a number of foundations. Among them figure the **Walter-Raymond-Stiftung** (Walter Raymond Foundation), inaugurated in 1959, which makes possible a forum for the exchange of opinions between representatives of the worlds of industry, politics and science, in the form of colloquia. In 1974 the **Otto A. Friedrich-Kuratorium** (Otto A. Friedrich Curatorium) was established; this organization concerns itself with research into the ownership of property in a social market economy.

The BDA publishes its own journal, *Der Arbeitgeber (The Employer)*, which appears fortnightly and serves as the voice of the employers' associations.

The BDI

The BDI is the major organization representing the interests and pro-mulgating the policies of German industry. It is a confederation of thirty-four **Zentralverbände** (business associations), ranging from the automobile business association to the sugar-producers' association, organized at national level. In their turn these thirty-four associations are organized into some 500 trade and state associations. Finally, the latter associations together represent, in a united Germany, about 95,000 private companies, large, medium-sized and small, employing over 10 million persons.

The BDI itself is organized as follows:

- The members' assembly consists of the thirty-four business associations. It elects the president and eight vice-presidents, and approves the budget and the level of subscriptions. Like the heads of other employers' organizations, the president of the BDI is a powerful figure whose voice is often heard in the media. In August 1992, at the height of the debate on Germany as an industrial site, Heinrich Weiss warned in the *Berliner Zeitung* of an erosion of German competitiveness. 'We are apparently forgetting that we have to create wealth again and again. Unfortunately, people will only wake up when they realize that their wealth is no longer growing the way it does in other countries', he said.

- The board is composed of the president, the vice-president and the chairmen of the individual business associations. The board sketches out the basic thrust of the BDI's work.

- The president's committee is formed by the president, the vice-presidents, and up to thirty-four other members. The chairmen of the BDI's regional association and its small and medium-sized business committee, and the president of the IDW are permanent members. Moreover, one member of the BDA's president's office and the BDI's chief managing director can be co-opted to this committee for the duration of their periods in office. The presidents of the BDA and the DIHT are also permanent guests on the president's committee, which furnishes the directives for the BDI's work.

- Committees and working parties are formed by the BDI's board, on which representatives of companies and managing directors of the associations work hand in hand. These bodies represent the vital link between the BDI's work and everyday industrial practice.

- There are four managing directors at the BDI, headed by one chief managing director, who are responsible for executing the workload at any one time. This work is organized in four departments (Figure 8.2).

Department I is concerned for the most part with economic, competition, social and European policy. It conducts a constant dialogue with the German political parties, ministries, and European institutions. On behalf of the BDI, it supports the process of European integration, has permanent representatives in Brussels, and maintains a database on the current state of the Single European Market.

Department II takes care of research, infrastructure and education. The BDI is only too aware of the extent to which applied research and technology affect businesses of all types. Thus it attempts, through this department, to act as an interface between the latest state of the art and its possible application in member business associations. It also tries to lobby the appropriate German ministries to accept its notions of desirable developments in the area of transport, logistics, and in

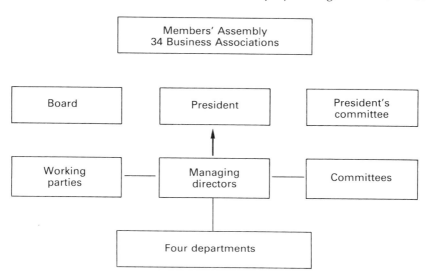

Figure 8.2   *The organization of the BDI. Source: BDI*

particular vocational education. This department is also especially active in attempting to influence German environmental policy (see pp. 164–181).

Department III concentrates on taxation and legal matters, public procurement and policies towards small and medium-sized companies. Its work in the latter area is particularly important, since such firms represent 98 per cent of all companies, employ 57 per cent of all persons in private industry, and are responsible for 61 per cent of output (see pp. 183–185).

Department IV looks after export policies and those concerned with the promotion of private companies in developing countries of the Third World. In its former role it contributes to Germany's relations with international organizations such as the General Agreement on Tariffs and Trade (GATT), as well as in bilateral arrangements with trading partners. It is an extremely important department, since Germany exports more than any other country in the world, not only on a per capita basis but also overall (see also p. 25).

BDI branch activity

The BDI's national-level business associations are organized according to branches of activity. A notable example is the **Zentralverband Elektrotechnik- und Elektronikindustrie e.V.** (ZVEI) (German Electrical and Electronic Manufacturers' Association), which in 1993 celebrated the seventy-fifth anniversary of its existence. Founded in the last months of the First World War, the ZVEI has since represented the business interests of electrical manufacturers. Even by the end of 1919 its 200 member companies had some 200,000 people working for them.

In 1993 the ZVEI was organized differently, with its direct membership deriving from thirty **Fachverbände** (trade associations) in ten **Landesstellen** (state bodies), located in both parts of Germany and covering over 1 million workers. Its headquarters are in Frankfurt-am-Main, and it is run by three full-time managing directors, headed by one chief managing director. It has eight business departments, covering such areas as industrial policy, statistics, sales promotion, law and taxation, public procurement, etc.; and five technical departments, concentrating on general electrical technology, information technology, energy technology, research and manufacturing technology, and vocational education. It has maintained an office in Brussels since 1990 and established another office in Dresden in 1991.

One of the ZVEI's member trade associations is the **Fachverband Kommunikationstechnik** (Association of Communications Technology), which represents the business and technological interests of German manufacturers of communication systems and equipment. A comprehensive range of services enables its approximately 150 member companies, primarily small and medium-sized firms, to remain informed about the markets for their products and to stay abreast of rapid technological change. Over 100,000 employees are represented in the 100 member companies. The Association co-operates with network operators and providers of telecommunication services within both Germany and Europe. Moreover, it is represented on national and European committees for the development of new technical standards and testing and certification procedures. Its influence at European level is guaranteed through its co-operation with both the Association of European Telecommunications and Professional Electronics Industries (ECTEL) and the European Association of Manufacturers of Security technology (EURALARM).

The BDI in the east

The BDI was not slow to establish itself, post-unification, in eastern Germany. Its work in Saxony, the most heavily industrialized of the eastern states, and Thuringia, one of the least industrialized, will serve as typical illustrations of its efforts there.

Saxony

The **Landesverband der Sächsischen Industrie** (LSI) (State Association of Saxon Industry) was founded as early as 5 October 1990, and was the first of the BDI's representations in eastern Germany. The LSI regards it as its task to make an active contribution to the restructuring of industry in Saxony, and to create the general prerequisites for successful industrial activities there.

As far as questions of privatization and reprivatization are concerned, the LSI works closely together with the Treuhandanstalt, the appropriate federal and state ministries, and the BDI. It develops models of privatization in its committees, on which sit representatives of the former state institutions affected by the changeover to the social market economy. Similarly, expert seminars and lectures are held for members on selected topics, such as public procurement, Hermes export guarantee insurance, and industrial support schemes, again in an effort to ease the transition to the social market economy.

The position of Saxony's industry is reviewed in half-yearly reports. These are then distributed both among the other German states and abroad, in an effort to attract domestic as well as foreign investors to one of the traditional homes of German industry. In this respect Saxony was probably the most successful of the states in eastern Germany in the first three years after unification.

Thuringia

The **Verband der Wirtschaft Thüringens** (VWT) (Association of Thuringian Industry) assumed the status of a BDI state association in November 1991. The timing is significant because the VWT was established in a period of political upheaval in the state that led to both administrative restructuring and industrial chaos, particularly among Thuringia's relatively few large companies.

Thus the VWT has focused its aims on founding a viable economic structure based on medium-sized and small companies, even at the risk of creating certain de-industrialized areas where the large companies formerly existed. Although the core of Thuringian industry, microelectronics, has been secured, for the present at least, the VWT is paying special attention to the establishment of innovative industries such as waste-recycling and environmental protection. These industries have been identified as being compatible with Thuringia's position as a tourist area.

Nonetheless, the state is still plagued by problems of infrastructure. Any economic upturn would have to take place along the east–west motorway axis from Eisenach to Hermsdorf. A new north–south link is held by the VWT to be a top priority for sustained economic prosperity.

The BDI maintains a very active press and information office in Cologne. Its periodicals *Information und Meinungen (I + M) (Information and Opinions)* and *Mittelstandsinformationen (Information for Small and Medium-sized Companies)* appear monthly; *Industrie-Konjunktur (Industry and the Economy)* and *Grafiken zur nationalen und internationalen Wirtschaftslage (Diagrams on the National and International Economic Situation)* are issued quarterly; *EG-Konjunktur (EC Economy)* comes out every six months. In addition, the office publishes numerous brochures and pamphlets, some of which appear in English versions. It has even produced a 16 mm film video, *Innovation − Die Zukunft unserer Wirtschaft (Innovation − the Future of our Economy)*, which is available in German, English, French and Spanish.

The DIHT

The DIHT was founded in Heidelberg in 1861. Today it is located in Bonn. Before unification, the DIHT had sixty-nine individual IHKs affiliated to it in western Germany; in addition, it had established thirty-eight chambers of commerce in various locations abroad (Figure 8.3). Since unification, the DIHT had founded a liaison office in East Berlin, together with fifteen IHKs in eastern Germany, from Chemnitz to Zwickau, by the end of 1991, with more being added all the time.

The DIHT's main tasks are:

- To co-ordinate the views of its member chambers and to make representations on their behalf at the federal level before any legislation is passed.
- To analyse and evaluate the effects of new Acts, Laws and Ordinances on its members.
- To act as expert witness in labour, finance, tax and social courts.
- To organize the publicity work of the associated chambers.
- To co-ordinate the work of the IHKs that have been established abroad.
- To manage the response of German companies to the completion of the EC's Single Market.

The IHKs

The IHKs represent the interests of all businesses, but especially small businesses, on a regional as well as sector basis. Collectively they are

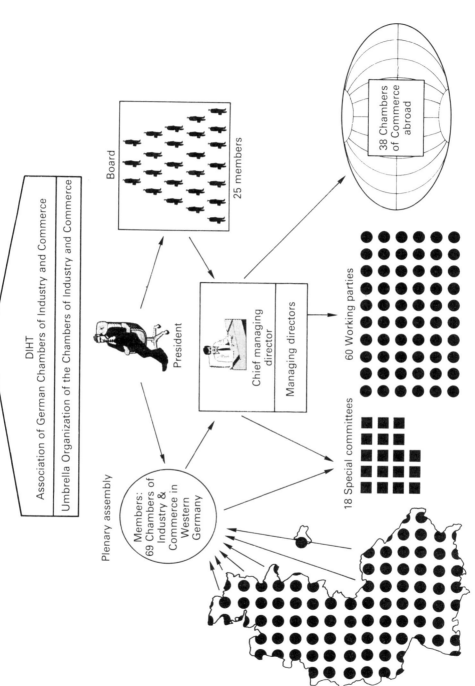

Figure 8.3 *The organization of the German chambers of industry and commerce (pre-unification). Source: DIHT*

DIHT
Association of German Chambers of Industry and Commerce

Umbrella Organization of the Chambers of Industry and Commerce

Board

25 members

Plenary assembly

President

Members:
69 Chambers of
Industry &
Commerce in
Western Germany

Chief managing
director

Managing directors

38 Chambers
of Commerce
abroad

60 Working parties

18 Special committees

frequently misunderstood abroad, especially in countries that either do not possess chambers of commerce or where their roles are of lesser significance. The IHKs are not government agencies, not lobbies in favour of particular customs regulations or DIN standards in any one industry, nor employers' associations concerned with pay bargaining.

All IHKs must act in accordance with the **Gesetz zur vorläufigen Regelung des Rechtes der Industrie- und Handelskammern** (IHKG) (Act for the Provisional Regulation of the Law on the Chambers of Industry and Commerce) of 18 December 1956. Thus an individual IHK is obliged to concern itself with the general economic interests of its particular region. The IHK is, however, committed by law to objectivity and neutrality in its assessment of economic developments in its region. It is therefore forbidden by statute to adopt a 'beggar-my-neighbour' approach to adjacent regions.

The primary task of an IHK is to perform an analysis of the economic conditions and climate in its region. This report is then submitted to the appropriate state and to any affected **Gemeinden** (communes) in its catchment area. Indeed a Prussian Ordinance of 11 February 1848 expressly stipulated that an IHK's main duty was to keep its local authorities informed of all economic developments!

Second, under the IHKG, all IHKs must promote the **gewerbliche Wirtschaft** (trading economy) in their region. This they do by advising member companies. Their advisory activities extend, however, far beyond their own members and take in such public bodies as the Deutsche Bundespost TELEKOM and the Deutsche Bundesbahn (DB). In addition, they act as honest brokers in disputes between members in their own region and/or in neighbouring regions.

In their efforts to promote the trading economy, IHKs are also empowered to buy, run and maintain plant, equipment and buildings. In the past they have operated ice-breakers, ports, warehouses, and stock exchanges. Moreover, they are permitted under the IHKG to form associations leading, say, to the construction of a motorway or canal.

Third, every IHK is called upon, when requested, to act as an expert witness in matters such as trademarks, and the eligibility of non-EC foreigners to act as traders in its region. More than one IHK has in the past also been called upon by the appropriate court to act as expert witness in the postponement of national service for male German nationals.

Fourth, as will be detailed in the following chapter (see pp. 147–148), the IHKs oversee the training of apprentices in technical and commercial professions. They also play a major role in the award of higher vocational qualifications. Latterly they have even entered the area of management development.

Finally, the appropriate IHK furnishes certificates of origin for goods 'Made in Germany' — documentation that is still required for the export of certain products to certain countries.

Conclusion

The employers' associations, the business associations and the chambers of commerce in Germany wield immense influence on account of their role in organizing and representing German business. The federal government consults them before articulating any policy or drafting any laws that might affect either the economy as a whole or certain sections of business. All state governments act similarly.

The degree of cohesion and solidarity with which German employers normally act is due in no small measure to the breadth and depth of employers' associations, business associations and chambers of commerce, and their all-pervasive influence. Maverick employers going their own way or bucking the trend are a distinct rarity in the German business culture.

What is more, these institutions provide an important forum where employers meet on a regular basis. The networking possibilities for employers are almost endless. Neither the Old School Tie network in the United Kingdom nor the network formed by graduates of the **grandes écoles** (schools of business and administration) in France are as powerful. German employers know one another; German employers know one another's staff; German employers know one another's businesses; and German employers know one another's products and services. Should anyone be surprised that German companies prefer to buy from other German companies?

9 Business, education, training and development

Introduction

The influence exerted on business culture by education, training and development is perhaps stronger than any of culture's other determinants for any country, or part of a country. Since the education systems of the former West and East Germanies present such contrasts, it is appropriate to consider them separately before speculating on how they might grow together and eventually make their own contribution to forming a more homogeneous society, with all that such would imply for the business culture.

Ever since the establishment of the 'old' Federal Republic of Germany, all citizens have had the right freely to develop their personality and to choose their profession or occupation. This is a fundamental human right, guaranteed in the GG. As a result, the government must provide all its citizens with the greatest possible opportunities to receive the type of education best fitting their interests and abilities. Moreover, such educational opportunities should be available throughout life, and not merely restricted to the normal educational period.

As an industrialized country blessed with relatively modest raw materials, western Germany relies heavily on its highly-educated managers and skilled workers, and is therefore required to invest substantially in the formation of this 'human capital'. In 1989 federal and state governments, together with local authorities, industry and commerce, spent DM 156 billion on education, in its broadest sense, in the west. This spend represents approximately 7 per cent of GNP.

The business culture in western Germany has been constantly enriched by the existence of a well-educated and highly trained workforce. Education at school, vocational training in the **Duales System** (Dual System), job-related courses at polytechnics and universities, and management development in companies, all make their own unique contributions. Currently an attempt is being made to have the widespread training ethos underpinned yet further by the concept of lifelong learning through extra paid holidays for self-improvement. The concept itself is welcomed by the employers, but they are putting up stiff resistance to the notion of even more holidays!

School education in the west

Education in Germany is for the most part the responsibility of the individual states. School attendance is compulsory from the ages of six to eighteen, i.e. for twelve years. During this period full-time attendance is required for nine years, and at least part-time attendance at vocational school thereafter. In some of the states ten years of full-time schooling are required. As a rule, boys and girls are educated in mixed classes. Attendance at all state schools is free, and certain private schools receive state grants.

The GG demands that religious instruction is a regularly-taught subject in schools, but from the age of fourteen pupils may drop it. Confessional schools have lost their former importance in recent decades. Most states have 'interdenominational schools oriented to Christian principles', i.e. schools based on the Christian ethos in which only religious instruction is given in confessionally-separate classes.

For most young Germans, education of a sort begins in a **Kindergarten**. This German institution, which has been adopted in many other countries, is intended to develop the personality and the ability of the children to express themselves cogently, and generally encourages them to become useful members of society.

The Kindergärten do not form part of the official school system. Attendance is purely voluntary, and usually parents have to contribute to the cost. In the west of the country there are over 24,000, which are run by local authorities, churches, associations, companies or private individuals. Above 80 per cent of all three to six-year-olds attend.

Children enter the **Grundschule** (primary school) at the age of six. In most states attendance lasts for four years, in Berlin six. Children are first assessed, then graded at primary school. After four years there, they attend the next level of school that is deemed to be commensurate with their abilities. Here the fifth and sixth school years are termed the 'orientation phase', when children and parents can revise their choice of school (Figure 9.1).

Approximately one-third of children move from the primary school to the **Hauptschule** (general school). The range of subjects taught at this type of school has been substantially improved over recent years. It is now possible, for example, to receive instruction in a foreign language, mainly English. Most pupils also receive vocational orientation to facilitate the transition from school to working life. The

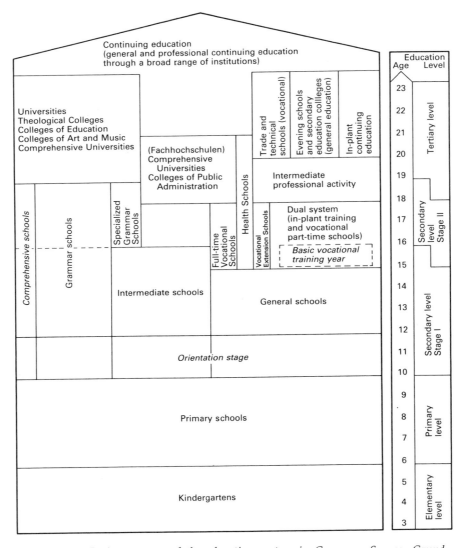

Figure 9.1 *Basic structure of the education system in Germany. Source: Grund- und Strukturdaten 1992/93*

award of the **Hauptschulabschluß** (general school leaving certificate) concludes attendance at this type of school.

Schooling at the **Realschule** (intermediate school) lasts as a rule for six years, from years five to ten inclusive. Successful completion of education at this type of school leads to the award of the **Realschul-abschluß** or **Mittlerer Abschluß** (intermediate school leaving certificate). Possession of this certificate qualifies young people for attendance at a

Fachschule (technical school) or **Fachoberschule** (higher technical school) offering vocational training at upper secondary level. Approximately one-third of all pupils obtain the intermediate certificate.

The nine-year **Gymnasium** (grammar school) takes pupils from the fifth to the thirteenth school years. The former split into ancient-language, modern-language and natural-science grammar schools is not nowadays frequently encountered. It has been replaced by the 'reformed upper phase' in the eleventh to thirteenth years, where elective courses have in many cases replaced traditional classes. Some grammar schools specialize in business or technical studies. The final leaving certificate is the **Abitur** or **Reifezeugnis**, possession of which affords legal right of entry to universities or polytechnics.

Despite considerable expansion of the tertiary system, the number of young people obtaining this certificate has increased to such an extent over recent years that not all those who wish to study can be given university places, and admission restrictions have been imposed on a number of subjects in the form of a *numerus clausus*. The available places are distributed by the **Zentralstelle für die Vergabe von Studienplätzen** (Central Authority for the Allocation of Study Places) in Dortmund. For particularly popular subjects such as medicine, dentistry and veterinary science, there is a selection procedure, which takes account of the applicant's average Abitur mark and the time spent waiting for admission. There are also tests and interviews, and special consideration is given to cases of hardship. In such courses as **Volkswirtschaftslehre** (VWL) (economics), **Betriebswirtschaftslehre** (BWL) (business economics), law and computer science, the available places are also subject to central allocation. Every applicant is assigned to a particular institution of higher education, where possible according to choice.

Vocational training in the west

The vocational training system in western Germany is the envy of many of its competitors and a cornerstone of business success. Although it has not entirely escaped criticism, it has helped to keep youth unemployment in the west down to approximately 5 per cent during the 1980s and early 1990s (see p. 99).

In 1991 almost 550,000 young people embarked on vocational training courses, which mostly last for three years, giving a total of some 1,650,000 **Lehrlinge** (apprentices) in the west of the country. In that year 39 per cent of the apprentices had come from general schools and 46 per cent from intermediate schools. The remaining 15 per cent had attended grammar schools. Partly for demographic reasons, there were approximately 100,000 more training places than apprentices in the west (see pp. 93–94), but this was also the result of some young people from the grammar schools preferring the direct route to university.

Vocational training takes place for the most part in the dual system. This comprises on-the-job learning in companies and theoretical instruction in **Berufsschulen** (vocational schools). Thus industry and commerce, on the one hand, and state governments, on the other, are jointly responsible for vocational training.

Practical training takes place in some 500,000 companies in all branches of the economy, including the public service and the so-called 'free professions', among which figure doctors' and dentists' practices. Some large companies have their own training workshops, but much of the training takes place at the workstation. Large companies tend to overtrain and then offer jobs only to the best. This helps cover for smaller companies but is less altruistic than it seems: trainees' work sometimes contributes substantially to the (tax-deductible) cost of training.

More than half the **Auszubildende** (Azubis) (trainees) are catered for by small and medium-sized companies, some of which are too specialized to impart all the necessary knowledge. Thus some 600 inter-company training centres, where trainees can broaden their vocational skills, have been set up. The IHKs and the **Handwerkerkammern** (Craft Chambers) are responsible for inspecting the 500,000 approved training firms on a regular basis, as well as for monitoring the training content of the 380 recognized training occupations. Apprentices are also registered, supervised and examined by the Chambers.

In addition to on-the-job learning, the apprentices must attend vocational school on one or two days per week for three years. These schools, of which there are some 1500, teach both general subjects and the theory underpinning the profession being learnt. Vocational schools are not attended only by apprentices, they are also compulsory for the approximately 5 per cent of under-18s not attending any other type of school. The vocational schools cost DM 9 billion per year to run.

In 1991 most school-leavers in western Germany plumped for apprenticeships in the services sector. First choice for school-leavers from the intermediate and grammar schools were commercial apprenticeships, with banking being the most popular of all. Some young people possessing the Abitur regard such apprenticeships as a rite of passage on the way to a university. After the commercial apprenticeships, the favourite occupations for young men were motor mechanic, electrician, fitter, painter and carpenter; and for young women, hairstylist, sales assistant and doctor's or dentist's assistant.

At the end of their apprenticeship courses 90 per cent of candidates pass the final examination at the first attempt. The drop-out rate over the average three-year course is less than 5 per cent.

Apprentices are paid an **Ausbildungsvergütung** (training remuneration). The average monthly rates in 1991 for the various apprenticeships were:

Bricklayer	– DM 1322
Bank clerk	– DM 1011
Cook	– DM 905
Doctor's assistant	– DM 763
Painter/decorator	– DM 740
Baker	– DM 702
Motor mechanic	– DM 683
Hairstylist	– DM 506

Training remuneration in 1991 was on average DM 838 for all professions and all years of apprenticeships. This is between 20 and 40 per cent of the starting salary of a **Facharbeiter** (qualified skilled worker).

The cost of **Ausbildung** (initial vocational training) to the company is very often not cheap. Training just one apprentice costs AEG, the electrical company, approximately DM 25,000 per year; Deutsche Lufthansa, the national carrier, DM 27,500 per year; and Deutsche Genossenschaftsbank DM 50,000 per year. If costs of this magnitude are measured throughout the economy, the annual spend by industry alone for its 1.65 million trainees is approximately DM 41 billion, though the net figure is likely to be around DM 30 billion after allowing for trainees' contribution to products and services.

Not only the cost of the system but also its rigidities occasion adverse comment by German industry from time to time. Questions are raised, for example, as to whether training a car sales person should take three years, or whether 380 different trades and professions are realistic towards the end of the twentieth century. Updating the training content of certain courses also takes an inordinate amount of time, as companies, chambers of commerce and vocational schools argue among themselves. On balance, however, most in industry, commerce and the public services agree that the system works very well and that they should stick with it.

Higher vocational training in the west

On successful completion of the apprenticeship, the erstwhile trainees become qualified skilled workers. Now they have gained social status, and possess a qualification they can show to their present, or possibly future, employer. Qualified skilled workers also earn more than the unskilled, even when working in trades or crafts other than their own. But most important of all, the possession of this qualification gives access to a range of higher vocational qualifications, and, with them, opportunities for career progression into supervisory and possibly management positions.

In theory any qualified skilled worker with two years' experience of his or her trade could go on to **Fortbildung** (higher vocational training) and attempt one of the higher qualifications. In practice the average age of those sitting the **Industriemeister**, **Fachwirte** or **Fachkaufleute** examinations is approximately thirty years. In 1991 7245 qualified skilled workers passed the Industriemeister, 5565 the Fachwirte and 4189 the Fachkaufleute examinations.

Part-time preparatory courses for these higher vocational qualifications are held at almost all the IHKs in the west of the country. Full-time courses are also available at some locations, but 75 per cent of all candidates prefer the part-time alternative. Although attendance at a preparatory course is not compulsory, chances of success without such in the final examination would be minimal. Usually some 600 to 900 hours of instruction are required to complete the courses. The cost of the longest was approximately DM 6500 in 1991, half of which was refundable by the German Federal Labour Office.

Those who have gained their initial vocational qualification as a skilled worker in one of the so-called 'technical' trades can proceed to one of the Industriemeister courses, of which there are some fifty different versions. Qualified skilled workers who have completed a so-called 'commercial' apprenticeship can opt for the higher vocational qualifications of Fachwirte and Fachkaufleute. The difference between these two awards is that Fachwirte are related to a particular branch of services or industry, e.g. **Bankfachwirt** or **Leasingfachwirtin**; and Fachkaufleute are associated with a particular functional area of business, e.g. **Fachkaufmann für Marketing** or **Personalfachkauffrau**.

Whereas the Industriemeister awards at certain IHKs date back over fifty years, the Fachwirte and Fachkaufleute qualifications are of relatively recent origin. Before 1971 there had been no higher vocational awards for ex-commercial apprentices to aim for. Consequently promotion of experienced, commercially-qualified skilled workers into supervisory or management ranks without paper qualifications was fraught with difficulty in a business culture that sets such store by titles and awards.

Moreover, the initiative for these higher vocational qualifications came *inter alia* from the employers in small and medium-sized companies. They feared that, on account of the explosive growth of university and **Fachhochschule** (polytechnic) attendance in the late 1960s and 1970s, the lower and middle ranks of management in their companies might quickly become filled with graduate theorists. They suspected that these graduates might lack the relevant experience and insights of those who had been with the company since leaving school and had taken the commercial apprenticeship under the combined aegis of company, vocational school and IHK.

While the possession of a higher vocational award is, without doubt, a necessary prerequisite for entry into management for non-graduates, it is by no means a guarantee of success. So many other factors of a personal, organizational, or even fortuitous, nature come into play. Nevertheless, we do witness in western Germany practice-oriented Industriemeister, Fachwirte and Fachkaufleute working alongside more theory-oriented graduates from universities and polytechnics in lower and, less frequently, even middle, management positions. There is often healthy competition between such non-graduates and graduates for lower management posts, and the German penchant for the **Praktiker** occasionally outweighs the widespread obsession for more academic awards.

Higher education in the west

Most managers come, however, from the polytechnics and universities. The vast majority of today's 120 polytechnics in western Germany were set up in the early 1960s. At this time the individual federal states were keen to promote the expansion of non-university higher education because:

- Polytechnic courses were intended to be considerably shorter than their university equivalents, i.e. a maximum of three to four years.
- Polytechnic courses, particularly in business economics, were to be more practice-oriented and pragmatic than their theory-encumbered counterparts in universities.
- Polytechnic courses were to address more directly the regional demand for study places and to provide a supply of graduates commensurate with the needs of industry, commerce and the public service in their particular states.

In 1991 every third new student was enrolling at a polytechnic, with 1 per cent per annum more young people with the Abitur qualification electing to study at a polytechnic in preference to a university. The main subjects, in order of popularity, studied at polytechnics are mechanical and production engineering, economics and business economics, social studies, electrical engineering, public administration, architecture, and civil engineering.

Most polytechnic courses are divided into a **Grundstudium** (foundation course), which lasts for two years, and after which an examination must be taken; and a **Hauptstudium** (main studies section) lasting one year or more.

Polytechnic studies conclude with a degree examination, the **Diplomprüfung** (diploma examination). To distinguish polytechnic qualifications from university qualifications in similar fields, some states insist that their polytechnics confer awards such as **Diplom-Ingenieur (FH)** or **Diplom-Betriebswirt (FH)**, the abbreviation in brackets referring to Fachhochschule.

The average age on graduation from a polytechnic is 26 years.

Universities in Germany differ from polytechnics in several ways. Most universities are ancient seats of learning, e.g. the University of Heidelberg was founded in 1386. From approximately 1810 to 1960 many universities attempted to pursue the ideal established by Wilhelm von Humboldt at the University of Berlin. According to the Humboldt model, learning and research were to be pursued for their own sakes by a relatively small number of students. In time this ideal began to clash with the requirements of modern, industrialized society, and the nature of studies changed to become almost exclusively job-focused. Numbers of students also rose dramatically. Whereas in 1960 in the west of the country only 8 per cent of the qualifying age group took up academic studies, in 1991 33 per cent sought a university place, with total student numbers of more than 1,700,000.

Staff at universities tend to be better qualified academically than their polytechnic counterparts, but the latter have more practice-related experience. Moreover, university staff must teach and pursue research, whereas polytechnic staff must teach and are entitled to research, but research work is not an obligation placed upon them.

Finally, as already indicated, university courses are of greater duration than their polytechnic equivalents. The average length of diploma studies for university graduates is 6.5 years. Though a longer period of study does not in itself imply a higher standard in the final diploma, there is a general consensus that the university award is higher than that from a polytechnic. This is also reflected in the fact that a polytechnic diploma entitles the holder to entry into the **gehobener Dienst** (middle ranks) of the civil service, but a university diploma to the **höherer Dienst** (higher ranks).

University graduates in general, and business economics graduates in particular, have been the subject of criticism on the grounds that their learning is too theoretical in nature. There was a most acrimonious debate on the topic in the 1960s, which served in the end to promote the value of the polytechnic courses. Today the consensus among companies would appear to be that university graduates are good, abstract thinkers but require a two-year 'apprenticeship' in the business before they become really useful. Polytechnic graduates, however, possess more practical experience on entry, and as a consequence are up and running from the outset of their company careers. This may well be the reason why so large a percentage of polytechnic graduates find employment in small and medium-sized companies, where induction training is rare.

The average age of university students on graduation at diploma level is 28 years.

If a university graduate aspires to the topmost ranks of management in Germany, he or she – it would almost inevitably be he – would be well advised to take a doctorate in a relevant subject. Whereas German universities awarded some 6971 doctorates in 1965, rising to 11,418 in 1975, the figure reached 18,103 in 1991. What is more, the extra effort seems to pay off in German industry and commerce. According to a study in the mid-1980s, 36.7 per cent of management board members in all the AGs possess the title of doctor; 41.5 per cent of management board members in the AGs quoted on the stock exchange also possess the title; and 53.8 per cent of the management board members of the 100 largest AGs have the right to be addressed as 'Herr Doktor' (Figure 9.2).

One apparently glaring omission from German higher education would appear to be the presence of any American-style business schools or MBA (Master of Business Administration) courses in the official system. The German situation presents such a contrast to the rest of Europe that this topic is worthy of brief examination.

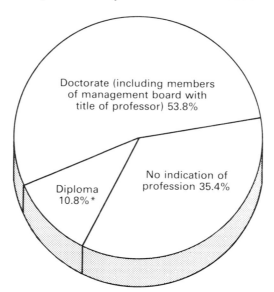

*Includes 5.4% engineers and 4.5% economic scientists

Figure 9.2 *Educational qualifications of management board members of the 100 largest German companies. Source: Dr Frank Grütz Unternehmensberatung, Bergisch Gladbach*

In 1990 approximately 10,000 MBA graduates emerged from about 120 business schools in Europe. None of these schools formed part of the official German education system. Moreover, the number of MBAs turned out each year in Europe is forecast to double by the turn of the millennium. Again there are no official plans in Germany to contribute to this particular form of inflation.

What are the reasons for German resistance to business schools on the American model? Why do German educators eschew the most famous product of these schools? What is the attitude of German students in the 1990s? How do German companies view the MBA? Above all, can any changes be detected?

Part of the German reluctance to embrace business schools and the MBA can be accounted for by the history of business teaching and research in Germany. The country looks back on a long and successful tradition of erudition in economics and business economics, with the first **Handelsschule** (commercial college) established in Leipzig in 1898. Thus there have been few sustained initiatives emanating from the ministries of education in the individual states. Moreover, post-war prosperity in the west has reinforced the attitude: 'If it isn't broken, don't fix it'. This notion has combined with the NIH (Not-Invented-Here) Syndrome, which is widespread in German business and not always inappropriate, to frustrate the introduction of the MBA.

The official German education system would appear, however, to be ignoring a substantial demand for the MBA among students. There is mounting evidence that Germans are becoming more visible on MBA programmes in other parts of Europe, with one estimate claiming that they represent some 12 per cent of all European MBA students.

The only way in which a German institution in the official system could offer an MBA at present is through co-operation with a partner abroad. Thus the **Universität der Bundeswehr** (University of the German Army) at Neubiberg, near Munich, is making available the Henley Management College distance-learning package to its students. Other German institutions have concluded partnerships with MBA providers in the rest of Europe and in the United States of America.

The cause of the MBA in Germany is not helped by a predominantly bad press. Horror stories relating to bogus business schools providing the MBA abound even in the most serious journals. Nor have German academics been slow to criticize the MBA in print. It has been unfavourably compared with both the German diploma and the **Vordiplom** (part I of the diploma). Indeed one academic has even gone so far as to claim that the MBA title stands for **Mediocre But Arrogant**!

Yet the attitude of German companies to the MBA appears to be changing in its favour. A study dating from 1990 found that 53 per cent of top managers in industry and commerce preferred graduates with the MBA, while only 17 per cent expressed a preference for those with the doctor title. What these managers found particularly appealing in MBAs was their international perspective, their willingness to take decisions, and their pronounced task-orientation.

Attitudes to the MBA in Germany are changing, but only slowly. The demand among students is growing. Partnership agreements are on the increase. The MBA is held in higher esteem by companies. But how long it will take for these forces to compel the German educational establishment to introduce a real MBA 'Made in Germany' is still a matter that is open to conjecture.

Management development in the west

Large companies in western Germany conduct approximately 80 per cent of their **Weiterbildung** (management training) programmes in-house. They are fully committed to the training and development ethos and are convinced that few can develop their managers more effectively than they can. Moreover, many of them possess their own lavishly-equipped continuing-studies centres and are resolved to make maximum use of them. In addition, they perceive their own programmes as a means of emphasizing their particular corporate culture and thus encouraging the individual manager to identify more closely with this culture. In other words, one of the spin-offs of in-house development is its usefulness as a management retention tool.

The pattern in large companies is for lower management to receive more development than middle or senior managers. Among the lower managers might also figure the Industriemeister, Fachwirte and Fachkaufleute who have emerged from the shopfloor. Continuing-studies programmes at this level would be function-specific or product-specific. Typical examples for Industriemeister would be courses on quality assurance or safety at work. Programmes for middle managers would be more company-specific and have a high management information content. Senior managers tend to concentrate on objective management techniques, subjective management behaviour and, ever increasingly, on the company and its physical environment (see pp. 177–181).

Medium-sized companies, possibly lacking the appropriate human, physical and financial resources, look for the most part outside the company for their management development courses. Open courses are available at such locations as the Universitätsseminar der Wirtschaft at Erfstadt/Liblar, near Cologne, and the Akademie für Führungskräfte der Wirtschaft at Bad Harzburg.

The cost of management development starts to become significant for small companies and those at the lower end of the medium-sized scale. Here programmes run by the IHKs are particularly attractive. Since all companies paying trade tax must be members of their local IHK and must therefore pay membership fees, these value-for-money courses are particularly popular.

The IHKs, either singly or severally, offer an impressive range of development programmes for all levels of management, from entrepreneurs to lower and even middle managers. Teaching staff are brought in from large companies, polytechnics or universities. Programmes are taught either in the IHKs' own short-course centres or in hotels. The management development programmes organized by the IHKs should not be regarded in any way as inferior to those run by the large companies. In fact the IHKs have very sensitive radar for company development needs because of their many contacts with firms of all sizes. They are ideally placed to identify the latest development trends in the large companies and subsequently to provide similar, or even better, programmes for other large, medium-sized and small companies.

As was noted earlier (see pp. 140–142), the IHKs play a key role among the associations in Germany. In addition, they and the craft chambers are central in training and development for so much of business activity. The IHKs themselves play a large part in initial vocational training and in higher vocational training, and the natural progression of their activities into the field of management development in the 1980s met with almost universal acclaim.

If management development in western Germany can be faulted at all, criticism would have to focus on its heavy emphasis on functionality. The whole system is geared to producing functional specialists to such an extent that there is little or no room for the generalist. Nor perhaps were such courses necessary in the past, when German companies were operating mainly within their own business culture. But in the light of the globalization of business, and of increased outward investment by western German companies (see p. 28), a more generalist approach to management development has now become desirable.

Lifelong learning

Initial vocational training, higher vocational training and management development should be viewed against the background of a concerted attempt in the west of the country to promote the concept of lifelong learning. It is claimed that 25 per cent of the population in the west between the ages of nineteen and sixty-five take part every year in some form of continuing education. Participation rates are, however, disproportionate. Only 10 per cent of unskilled workers took part in

1991, and in the same year participants having the tertiary level entrance qualification outnumbered those with the general school-leaving certificate by six to one.

To rectify at least some of these imbalances, the concept of **Bildungsurlaub** (extra paid holidays for self-improvement) has been mooted. Six of the western states have legislated in favour, and Bildungsurlaub has formed part of a few tariff agreements between trade unions and employers' associations. While welcoming the notion of lifelong learning and actively supporting the process of adaptation to new technologies, the vast majority of companies in the west oppose the concept of extra paid holidays. They argue that their employees already work the shortest number of hours in Europe, enjoy the longest holidays, retire as pensioners at the lowest age, and receive the best education, training and development in the world. Despite certain, perhaps trifling, reservations relating to the latter point, it is difficult to disagree with them.

School education in the east

It is perhaps in the area of education that the business culture of former East Germany was most deeply inculcated into its citizenry. Since many managers and specialists educated within the old system are still active in business there, it is worth casting a backward glance at how they were taught, trained and developed. Only then can many of the changes currently being made to the system be appreciated fully.

The whole of the education system in the east was predicated on the state's claim to the right of the education of children within the socialist world order. The education of children was not a parental right. Since the state was defined as 'The political organization of workers led by the working class and its Marxist-Leninist Party', the nature of the education to which all children were exposed, including future managers, was heavily influenced by the tenets of socialism.

The state also claimed the unity of education and the economy, and this led, *inter alia*, to a system of ideological homogenization in all schools, colleges and universities. There were no confessional schools, nor was there any religious education in schools.

Ideological homogenization began even in pre-school education in the state or state-company-run Kindergärten, which, in 1987, were attended by 93 per cent of suitable age. One of the aims of pre-school instruction was 'To prepare for learning in school and to make initial acquaintance with socialist life and the activities of working people'; another 'To educate children to love their socialist home and to love peace'. These aims were achieved in the pre-school curriculum by learning about feast days and holidays, especially those relating to the birthdays of the founders of Marxism–Leninism and leading politicians, and by promoting contacts to state-owned companies, party represen- tatives, and the **Deutsche Volksarmee** (German People's Army).

Indoctrination continued in the **Polytechnische Oberschule** (poly- technic school), attended by all children from the age of six to sixteen (Figure 9.3). This school was viewed throughout the country as a pre- selection stage for the trade or profession to be chosen. Closely linked to its godfather company, with 80 per cent of pupils doing voluntary work in the factory during school holidays, one of the main aims of the school was to contribute to the development of the rounded socialist personality.

In the polytechnic school special emphasis was placed on the com- munication of work virtues and the particular socialist attitude to work. One of the ways in which it was hoped to achieve these aims was through the system of work instruction, which permeated the whole curriculum. In classes one to three all pupils were required to work in the school garden; in classes four to six they were expected to acquire knowledge of work materials and gain their initial experience in technical modelling; in classes seven to eight technical drawing was introduced, accompanied by regular light work in the godfather factory; in classes nine to ten, the final two years of obligatory school attendance, theoretical instruction in economic socialism and socialist production methods was complemented by actual manufacturing work in the factory.

Other features of the Polytechnic School designed to inculcate the work ethic and its relationship with socialism were the six-day week for school children (214 days per annum), and the insistence throughout on Russian as the first foreign language.

Entry to the **Erweiterte Oberschule** (extended school), the equivalent of the Sixth Form in England and Wales, was restricted by the state to only 8 per cent of the appropriate age group. The Abitur was taken at the age of eighteen or nineteen. The subjects studied were German language and literature; Mathematics; Russian; Sport; and Physics, Chemistry or Biology.

Vocational training in the east

Very few youngsters in former East Germany failed to take an appren- ticeship. According to the state, 'All young people have the right and duty to learn a profession'. Thus, after completing the tenth class in the Polytechnic School, 87 per cent of the age group went through a two-year apprenticeship, with 85 per cent of these young people signing an apprenticeship contract on first application, usually with the school's

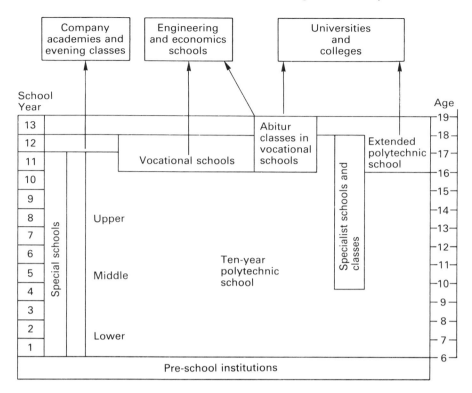

Figure 9.3 *Structure of the education system in former East Germany. Source: Vergleich von Bildung und Erzielung in der Bundesrepublik Deutschland und in der Deutschen Demokratischen Republik*

godfather factory. Not only was the practical learning done in this factory, but the vocational school where the theory was taught actually belonged to the godfather factory.

It was possible for the more gifted to embark upon a three-year apprenticeship after the tenth class, leading to the twin qualifications of skilled worker and Abitur, and 6 per cent of all pupils took this route, which could lead to university or one of the eighty-eight engineering schools, or alternatively one of the seven economics schools, both termed **Fachschulen**. The final qualification at these schools was the approximate equivalent of technician.

Higher education in the east

Studies at the six universities and nine technological universities, the nine engineering colleges and two economics colleges, called

Hochschulen, all of which were controlled by the state, were held to be a high social distinction and the personal duty of the student to the working class and the state. Access to higher education was, on the one hand, structurally determined by the economic and social needs of the state, i.e. study places at universities and colleges were allocated according to state economic plans, and, on the other hand, by the aspiring student in the form of political loyalty, e.g. membership of the Free German Youth movement, and by readiness to defend East German society. University and college studies were therefore much facilitated by males 'volunteering' for three years' military service in the German People's Army, instead of eighteen months, which was the regular conscription period. The ratio of tertiary-level places to applicants in the 1980s was 1:1.4.

All studies at university or college, except medicine, lasted four to four and a half years. Common to all, including medicine, was a three-year compulsory study of Marxism–Leninism, with even a fourth-year elective on offer! Two years of further instruction in Russian and one in another foreign language, usually English, were also compulsory, as were sports studies for males and females, military studies for men, and civil defence training for women.

By the end of the 1980s a twin-track system had established itself in tertiary education in the east: the universities and technological universities provided the people for the top management functions of all aspects of the state; the engineering and economics colleges furnished the technical or back-up staff. Expressed in quasi-Marxist terms, then, most engineers formed the middle layer between the intelligentsia and the working class.

Management development in the east

It was therefore the members of the intelligentsia who took over not only the running of the state, the SED (Communist Party), and its central planning institutions, but also its combines and their associated companies. Indeed the strict, closed hierarchy of the *Nomenclatura* system was even extended to the system of development for all managers in former East Germany (Figure 9.4).

Nomenclatura I received their management development at the élite **Zentralinstitut für sozialistische Wirtschaftsführung** (ZSW) (Central Institute for Socialist Economic Management) of the Central Committee of the SED, which was founded in 1965. *Nomenclatura II* had to be content with what the **Institute für sozialistische Wirtschaftsführung** (ISWs) (institutes for socialist economic management), attached to the fourteen different industry ministries, had to offer. These ministries

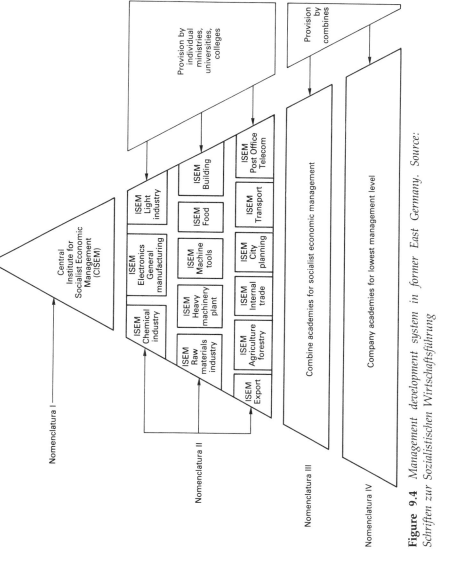

Figure 9.4 *Management development system in former East Germany. Source: Schriften zur Sozialistischen Wirtschaftsführung*

often worked in close association with the universities and the engineering colleges in the provision of management development. The universities and colleges were thus responsible for approximately 20 per cent of management development. *Nomenclatura III* were catered for by the 150 **Akademien für sozialistische Wirtschaftsführung der Kombinate** (combine academies for socialist economic management) and *Nomenclatura IV* by the **Betriebsakademien** (company academies). The latter institutions furnished some 60 per cent of management development.

Reorganization of education and training in the east

It is for all the above reasons that education, training and development are being reformed in the east of the country. The states there now enjoy the same autonomy in matters of education and culture as their western counterparts.

In the schools the curricula are being depoliticized, but it has still to be decided whether some elements of the old system should be retained, e.g. the school period of twelve years. The eastern states are at present adopting various school models from the west. However, the state governments there are predominantly CDU-controlled, and currently the selective system is being taken over lock, stock and barrel, with the **Gesamtschule** (comprehensive school) representing very much a minority experiment. Although the teachers from the old system in the east were kept on after unification, they have not automatically been made Beamte, like many of their counterparts in the west. Whether they will remain in the school system will be decided on a case-by-case basis. Such people are said to be, like aircraft in a stack above a busy airport, **in einer Warteschleife** (on hold).

As we have seen, a dual system of sorts for vocational training had been established in East Germany, but it was more centralized, and training standards were usually based on a lower level of technology. The former system of vocational training in the east is now being reformed strictly along the lines of the western model. By 1991 all 140,000 young people seeking an apprenticeship found one. This was made possible by massive efforts on the part of all concerned – industry, federal and state governments, the Federal Institute of Employment and the Trust Agency. In addition, 10,000 places were offered in the public service, and all small firms (with up to twenty employees) who took on an apprentice in 1991 received a grant of DM 5000. The first inter-company training centres were established. But apprenticeship examinations will have to be made easier to pass, since mass failures in the east would reflect badly, given the 90 per cent first-time pass rate in the west.

Training remuneration for apprentices in the east had, by 1991, not reached the levels encountered in the west. Apprentices in the chemical industry were receiving only 39 per cent of their western counterparts' remuneration, but apprentice thatchers had already succeeded in taking home 75 per cent of their western German equivalents.

The universities in former East Germany are being reorganized in line with the recommendations of the **Wissenschaftsrat** (Science Council). Greater participation rates at the tertiary level have led to a deterioration in the staff:student ratio, which at the time of unification was 1:4 (compared to 1:14 in the west). Some of the research carried out at academies is being integrated into the universities or being transferred to extramural research establishments financed jointly by federal and state governments. Staff in universities and colleges have had to re-apply for their posts, in competition with candidates from both parts of Germany. Some staff who were officially employed by the Stasi have been purged, and in the many cases outstanding there are allegations of unofficial collaboration with the former security service. Suitable professors and lecturers with an untainted political past are being incorporated in the public service. The reorganization process is due to be completed by the mid-1990s, and is being financed to the tune of DM 2.4 billion from a fund for the renewal of higher education, which runs until 1996.

Conclusion

No less a personage than Chancellor Kohl has frequently referred to the reform in education, training and development in the east as a crucial prerequisite for the growing together of society as a whole in the two parts of Germany. So many of the beliefs, attitudes and values grow out of education at school and training and development in the company.

The full integration of the former state-dominated model with the western model will not happen overnight, nor even by December 1994 (the date of the second pan-German elections), nor even by the turn of the millennium − so great was the gulf between the two systems. Perhaps full integration might take even until 2020, one generation after unification, or even longer.

It is by no means idle to speculate how long the integration process will last because education, training and management development exercise such vital influences, not only on academic or technical standards but also on modes of behaviour and core values, and not least on the business culture at large.

10 Business and the environment

Introduction

Once again, the situations in western and eastern Germany present marked contrasts. While the business culture in the west of the country has been increasingly concerned with issues associated with the environment for the past thirty years, the response in the east has been one of almost total indifference. With unification, however, the western view has prevailed, as in so many aspects of the business culture. Indeed the main thrust of environmental policy for the united country in the foreseeable future will be the clean-up in the east. The task will not be completed before the end of the millennium, so great was the damage wrought in forty years of neglect. What is more, it will cost billions of DM.

Yet eastern Germany is fortunate, compared with other former Communist, and similarly polluted, countries in central Europe. Not only is the federal government willing to spend vast sums of money to rectify the situation, eastern Germany also enjoys ready access to much of the world's leading-edge technology in the fields of pollution-monitoring and control equipment. The technology was researched and designed in western Germany. In 1990 this part of the country also registered the world's largest share of patents in environmental technology (29 per cent) and enjoyed annual sales of goods amounting to some DM 22 billion.

Moreover, while manufacturing companies in the west of the country were in the past never exactly ecstatic about the massive investments they were forced to make to clean up their act, they now appreciate that this capital expenditure has put them at a competitive advantage *vis-à-vis* many of their neighbours in Europe. Green issues are likely to increase in significance throughout the continent, and companies in other European countries will be obliged to match the equipment that many German companies have already installed, and almost certainly at much greater cost.

The origins of the problem

Germany as a whole is one of the most densely-populated countries in the EC (222 people per square kilometre), with only Belgium and the Netherlands having a higher population density. The western part of Germany is much more densely populated (252 citizens per square kilometre) than the five states in the east (152 inhabitants per square kilometre). Current forecasts indicate a rise in Germany's population from 79,790,000 in 1990 to some 81,000,000 by the year 2000 (see also pp. 93–94).

In the west, after the Second World War, industrial reconstruction progressed at a rapid pace. Economic growth rates in the 1950s and up to the mid-1960s were phenomenal; more and more manufacturing facilities were established; and an increasing number of people moved from the land into the new conurbations. The economic miracle duly occurred. But the miracle was built on the steel, steel-processing, machine-tool, chemical, pharmaceutical, and electrical industries.

In addition, the **Wohlstandsgesellschaft** (affluent society) created in the west enabled the citizenry to indulge in a love affair with the motor-car, and the high-performance car in particular, mirroring the **Leistungsgesellschaft** (high-performance society) in which they were living. One of the results is that even now, in the days of the **Freizeit-gesellschaft** (leisure society), there is no general speed limit on the motorways; another is that there are some 30 million private cars on the roads.

The origins of the problems are different for the east:

- Many years of maintaining an energy and structural policy based on the large-scale use of lignite, or brown coal (in 1989 consumption of lignite was in the order of 320 million tonnes, the highest for any country in the world); inefficient power stations (every kilowatt-hour of electricity generated produces twenty-five times as much sulphur dioxide as in the west); unsafe nuclear reactors (two were closed down shortly after unification); high per-capita energy consumption (25 per cent greater than in the west); heavy industry with intensive use of energy and raw materials; and outdated production processes in light manufacturing industry.
- Long-term neglect of environmental precautions and excessively low funding for environmental-protection measures.
- An underdeveloped industry for the research, development and production of environmental-protection technology unable to meet the demand.

Environmental damage

Air pollution

In the west air pollution caused after the combustion of coal, heating oil and petrol, when sulphur dioxide and nitrogen oxides combine to descend as an acidic precipitation on the leaves and needles of trees, began in the 1960s to affect woods and forests. By 1972 approximately 8 per cent, by 1983 approximately 34 per cent, and by 1990 approximately 50 per cent of the west's woodlands were either damaged or suffered from reduced vitality as a result of the effects of acid rain. In the east it was estimated in 1989 that 54 per cent of the country's forests were severely damaged.

But **Waldsterben** (dying forests) in the east betray only part of the problem there: air pollution is of a different order of magnitude than in the west. Between the Baltic coast and the Erz Mountains approximately six million tonnes of sulphur dioxide are emitted every year by three dozen inefficient, large-scale, lignite-burning power stations and more than 300 smaller plants. In 1989 emissions of sulphur dioxide and dust affected 36 per cent and 30 per cent of citizens respectively. In certain areas, classified as suffering from extremely high air pollution, respiratory diseases among children rose between 1974 and 1989 by 111 per cent. Indeed doctors in Halle issued a statement in 1990 declaring 'Of the three possible types of illness caused by environmental air pollution – eye infections, respiratory diseases, skin disorders – almost every local inhabitant has one'.

Water contamination

Air pollution has contributed in its turn to water contamination. In the west precipitations have deposited phosphates, heavy metal and halogen compounds in rivers and lakes. The nitrates used in intensive farming and present in factory effluents have only served to exacerbate the problem. The worst-affected areas are in the Northern Black Forest, the Fichtel Mountains and the Bavarian Forest. In some of these areas the water has become so acidic that the ph-value has fallen by one or two degrees since the 1950s, which corresponds to a ten- to twenty-fold rise in acidity.

After air pollution, water contamination is the second most significant environmental problem in the east. Of the 17.7 billion cubic metres of water available each year, 19 per cent cannot be used for drinking, or even for irrigation, on account of contamination. Moreover, in 1988 approximately 450,000 inhabitants of former East Germany were drinking water, over sustained periods, with a nitrate content above the World Health Organization (WHO) limit value. By the end of 1989 the figure had risen to 1,200,000.

The water-contamination capital in the east is the town of Bitterfeld. When added together, the liquid waste produced by Bitterfeld's factories and chemical plants amounts to an annual total of 70 million cubic metres of poisonous by-products, containing dangerous salts and acids, phenol, chlorohydrocarbons and mercury, all mixed up together. This toxic cocktail then meanders in streams and rivers, past enormous rubbish dumps piled high with chemical spoil, until it finally reaches the Elbe. And the lethal flow from Bitterfeld is only one of many such in the east: every year, approximately 8 billion cubic metres of water waste flow, usually untreated, into the east's 9000 rivers and lakes.

Waste

Every inhabitant of western Germany produces annually 375 kilograms of waste that have to be disposed of, with domestic refuse accounting for approximately 32 per cent of the west's total waste of 250 million tonnes per year. The 365 domestic refuse-disposal sites can no longer cope with such quantities, and many towns and cities have begun to incinerate on a large scale, using the excess energy for district-heating schemes. The disposal of industrial waste is, however, more problematical. The construction of incineration plants for special industrial waste has led to vociferous protests from the citizens most immediately affected. Even environmentally-conscious western Germany is not immune to the NIMBY (Not-in-My-Back-Yard) syndrome, which has frustrated the building of dozens of much-needed industrial waste-burning facilities.

In the east, there were few plants to reduce the volume of waste or to provide the preliminary treatment necessary to eliminate pollutants, and even those that did exist failed to meet international standards. In 1989 there were 121 regulated dumps, 4870 registered tips and 7437 unregistered tips. The situation in the east was exarcerbated, before unification, by the import of five million tonnes of waste per annum, including 650,000 tonnes of toxic waste and in excess of 200,000 tonnes of sewage sludge, from western Germany.

Harm to wildlife

The damage done to the woods and forests in the west by air pollution and water contamination is largely responsible for the extinction of large numbers of species. In the west it is estimated that 25 per cent of the 45,000 different species of animals, and 33 per cent of the 27,000 types of plants have died out. In the opinion of many experts, up to 50 per cent of the bird species in the Central Uplands are threatened with extinction.

The ecological dangers to the natural environment in the east as indicated above have also led to the extinction of many animal and bird species. Nonetheless, certain types of animals and birds have flourished more successfully than in the west, e.g. beavers, otters, sea-eagles, cranes and storks. All the same, the number of animal species threatened with extinction increased between 1970 and 1985 from 203 to 296, and the number of endangered species from 347 to 619.

The political response

The first voices were raised in protest at the damage being done to the environment in the west in the mid-1950s, but they were ignored. The initial, faltering response came from the legislators in the mid-1960s:

1965 First Clean Air Act passed by the Federal Parliament. Fears about the effect that more radical legislation might have on western Germany's industrial competitiveness were still widespread.

1969 Protection of the environment included for the first time in a federal government declaration in Bonn.

1971 First comprehensive environmental programme published by a federal government. In the course of the 1970s a whole series of Acts were passed for the protection of the environment. The lead content of petrol was reduced, refuse disposal was placed under legal controls, and the use of certain additives in detergents was restricted.

1975 Environmental consciousness began to spread rapidly through large sections of the population. The number of citizens' initiatives increased considerably.

1980 The Greens established themselves as a political party.

1983 The Greens entered the Federal Parliament for the first time.

1986 The **Bundesministerium für Umwelt** (BMU) (Federal Environment Ministry) was founded.

1990 The BMU introduced the **Verpackungs-Verordnung** (Packaging Ordinance) (see p. 176).

1990 The Greens failed to clear the 5 per cent hurdle into the first all-German parliament.

1992 Petra Kelly and Gert Bastian, two of the most prominent members of The Greens, committed suicide.

Environmental agencies

The BMU

Germany's BMU has a multiplicity of tasks to perform. At the international level it co-operates with all the important world agencies. It acts as a particularly strong lobbying force in the EC, in an attempt to achieve agreement on its desire for more stringent, statute-based standards than prevail at present. This was the case, for example, in Germany's 1988 initiative to impose a ban on leaded petrol throughout the EC. At the national level Acts and ordinances are drafted or updated for all fields of environmental protection. This is particularly essential in the light of the clean-up required in eastern Germany. Moreover, the BMU considers it to be part of its brief to continue to strengthen the citizenry's environmental awareness. At the local level vital decisions have to be taken by the BMU for specific on-site environmental protection measures, and for projects entailing research and development. The organization of the BMU is shown in Figure 10.1.

The BMU's budget of approximately DM 1,822 million in 1992 was modest in comparison with that of many other ministries. But this does not in any way represent the total money allocated to environmental protection in any year in Germany. The BMU's spend is augmented by:

- DM 1394 million earmarked for basic research into environmental protection.
- DM 566 million for environmental improvements in structural measures in agriculture, and coastal protection.
- DM 1257 million for environmental protection work undertaken by the Federal Ministry of Defence.
- DM 1399 million for environmental co-operation with developing countries.
- DM 750 million for structural aid and reduced interest rates on loans for environmental-protection measures.
- DM 3990 million for loans targeted at environmental-protection measures in the fields of air-pollution reduction, waste-water treatment, rational use of energy, waste avoidance and waste disposal.
- DM 729 million for other environmental protection measures, e.g. in the fields of urban redevelopment and energy saving.

In 1992, a total of DM 11,897 million was also spent from the federal budget on environmental protection and improvement.

The BMU does not of course act alone in the introduction of new Acts, laws or ordinances on the environment. At a higher level, EC

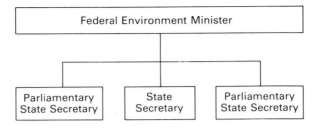

Areas of activity

Guidelines and strategies of environmental protection
Ecological clean-up and development in the new Länder
International co-operation
Protection of the earth's atmosphere
Protection of inland water bodies and seas
Protection of groundwater
Waste-water treatment
Soil protection and clean-up of contaminated sites
Avoidance, recycling, re-use and disposal of waste
Noise pollution abatement
Protection of human health against hazardous substances
Prevention of hazardous incidents in industrial plants
Public information on environmental questions
Environmental technologies
Nature conservation
Landscape protection and planning
Safety of nuclear installations
Radiological protection
Disposal of nuclear waste

Figure 10.1 *Political administration of the Federal Environment Ministry (BMU). Source: Bundesministerium für Umwelt*

directives are handed down. Within Germany responsibility for environmental protection is shared between the BMU, the sixteen individual states, and the local authorities.

The fundamental tenet of German environmental legislation is that the individual states have the right to legislate unless the GG says no, though there are some exceptions to this principle. The exceptions, where the federal government alone can act, are in international affairs, the internal development of the EC, and bilateral and multilateral agreements. There are also some cases where legislative power is shared between the federal government and the states, i.e. concurring legislation. The following areas are subject to such legislation: air-pollution control, waste management, noise-pollution abatement, and radiological protection.

German local authorities are also responsible, under the prin-ciple of self-administration enshrined in the GG, for planning and implementing local environmental policy. Particular responsibilities rest on the local authorities for construction and 'green planning', urban renewal, waste-water disposal, clean-up of old sewage networks, and expansion of waste management facilities.

A practical example of how the system works is quoted by the BMU in its publication *Das Bundesumweltministerium (The Federal Environment Ministry)*. According to an EC directive, lawn-mowers may be sold in the member states only if they adhere to the noise limit values prescribed in the directive and bear the corresponding EC-wide label. The directive was enacted into national law in Germany through the **Rasenmäherlärm-Verordnung** (Ordinance on Lawn-Mower Noise).

This means that all lawn-mowers offered for sale in Germany must comply with EC provisions. At the national level the ordinance regulates, in addition, the times when lawn-mowers may be used. There is a general ban on lawn-mowing between 7 am and 7 pm on weekdays, including Saturdays. Only particularly quiet lawn-mowers may be used on weekdays, including Saturdays, between 7 pm and 10 pm. The individual states are at liberty to prescribe even more stringent controls. Nor does the process finish here. The local authorities are also able to place further restrictions on lawn-mowing through local by-laws. For example, lawn-mowing is banned during the midday rest period between 12 am and 3 pm on Sundays in many local authorities.

The BMU has a staff of 850, of whom 130 work in its Berlin Office.

The UBA

The BMU is supported in its work by the **Umweltbundesamt** (UBA) (Federal Environmental Agency). Founded in 1974, the UBA has an annual budget of DM 87 million. But it also administers other funds totalling over DM 300 million. Its expertise is required at the scientific and technical levels in the fields of air-pollution control, noise reduction, waste and water management. Its tasks include:

- The inclusion of scientific and technical know-how in environmental legislation.
- Public enlightenment and sensitization in environmental issues.
- Operation of the environment information and documentation system (UMPLIS).
- Co-operation in the award of the **Blauer Engel** (Blue Angel). By 1990, 3200 products in some sixty product groups had been awarded the Blue Angel seal of environmental approval (Figure 10.2).
- Participation in the biological monitoring of the North Sea.
- Work associated with implementing the soil-protection programme and cleaning up former pollution areas, e.g. dumps and old industrial sites.

The UBA has a staff of 850, located in Berlin.

Figure 10.2   *The Blue Angel. Source: Bundesministerium für Umwelt*

The BFANL and the Bfs

The work of two other federal bodies should be highlighted in the field of environmental protection. These are the **Bundesforschungs-anstalt für Naturschutz und Landschaftsökologie** (BFANL) (Federal Research Centre for Nature Conservation and Landscape Ecology) and the **Bundesamt für Strahlenschutz** (BfS) (Federal Office for Radiological Protection).

The BFANL has three institutes: nature conservation and animal ecology, landscape protection and landscape ecology, and phytosociology. Their tasks are geared largely towards landscape planning, the drawing up of regulations governing intervention in the natural environment, and the protection of designated areas and species.

The BFANL has a staff of 200, of whom twenty-seven work at its academy on the small island of Vilm, near Rügen, in the Baltic Sea.

The BfS supports the federal government and the BMU in issues relating to nuclear safety, the transport of radioactive substances, the disposal of such substances, and radiological protection. Its staff of 550 are based in Salzgitter.

Green police

Statistics from the UBA reveal that crimes against the environment are responsible for some DM 20 billion of damage every year. The most common environmental offence is water contamination. The statistics recorded 11,827 offences of this type in 1989. The largest increase in environmental crime has been in environmentally-harmful waste disposal, from 1165 offences in 1983 to 8559 in 1989. Here not only large companies that introduce poisonous effluent into a river or stream are to blame, but those drivers sneaking off into the woods to change the oil in their cars and tipping the waste on to the ground are equally culpable. In 1990 the total number of known environmental crimes fell for the first time − 21,412 compared with 22,816 in 1989 − and thanks in no small extent to an alert public, the clear-up rate in 1990 was some 73 per cent.

The first and only German police department dealing with environmental offences has been operating in Eschborn, near Frankfurt, since 1985. The department has a staff of ten officers. Typical of their work was a case in 1988, which arose after ramblers had reported seeing a film of oil on the surface of a stream. The source of the oil was identified as a manufacturing company pouring a poisonous liquid into the public sewers. However, under German law, it is not enough to identify a company: only so-called 'natural persons' can be prosecuted, and not a firm. The manufacturer's records showed that the company's internal environmental officer had presented proposals for the prevention of water pollution to his superior, who had rejected them on grounds of cost. As a result, this manager had rendered himself liable for prosecution. The court sentenced him to a fine of DM 60,000 to be paid out of his own pocket. The company had to upgrade its waste-disposal facilities and bear all the costs of taking probes and carrying out laboratory tests.

Apart from reacting to reports of environmental offences, part of the Green police's work is to be pro-active. This they try to be, particularly in the field of the transport of dangerous loads. Here the law is most complex, because there are not only thirteen different categories of hazard but also countless special markings that have to be observed. Every year almost 400 million tonnes of dangerous cargoes are transported in western Germany alone, two-thirds of them by road. In 1991 83 per cent of the vehicles transporting these dangerous loads were found wanting in some respect.

The first successes in the west

Air

The most spectacular successes in western Germany have been achieved in the field of air pollution. Since 1970 sulphur dioxide emissions have fallen constantly from 3.7 million tonnes to 1 million per year in 1989. Mainly responsible for this improvement are some 170 so-called desulphurizer plants, which had been installed at the approximately seventy coal-burning power stations by 1988.

Nitrogen oxides have proved to be more difficult to eliminate. From 1970 to 1986 they rose from 2.4 million tonnes to just below 3 million. The reason for this rise was largely the increase in road traffic. In 1987 and 1988 emissions stabilized at 3 million tonnes but fell back to 2.7 million in 1989, mainly as a result of the introduction of the three-way catalytic converter for motor cars (Table 10.1).

Carbon monoxide emissions dropped from 14.5 million tonnes in 1970 to 8.25 million in 1989. Carbon dioxide emissions also fell, after a temporary rise in the 1970s, from 730 million tonnes in 1970 to 690 million in 1989. At the Earth Summit in Rio de Janeiro in June 1992 Chancellor Helmut Kohl confirmed the federal government's decision to reduce Germany's carbon dioxide emissions by a further 25 to 30 per cent by the year 2005. Carbon dioxide is held to be one of the gases contributing to the **Treibhauseffekt** (greenhouse effect).

Dust emissions reduced considerably from the 1.1 million tonnes in 1970 to 0.5 million in 1980. The reasons for this particular success lie in the dust-removal filters fitted at power stations, the reduced use of solid fuels by industry and private households, and the electrification of the railway network. Emissions fell even further in the 1980s, down to 0.3 million tonnes in 1989.

In March 1992 Germany signed the EC agreement to cease the production and consumption of **Fluorchlorkohlenwasserstoffe** (FCKWs) (chlorofluorocarbons) (CFCs) as from 1996, though great progress had already been made in this direction (see Figure 10.3). CFCs are held to be some of the gases contributing to the **Ozonloch** (hole in the ozone layer) in the earth's atmosphere.

Water

The average annual amount of rainfall in western Germany is 837 millimetres per square metre, or 207 billion cubic metres in all. The largest water-users are power stations (26 billion cubic metres), manu-

Table 10.1 *Western Germany's cleaner air (emissions in million tonnes)*

Emissions	1970	1989
Sulphur dioxide	3.7	1.0
Nitrogen oxides	2.4	2.7
Carbon monoxide	14.5	8.2
Dust	1.1	0.5
Total	21.7	12.4

Source: Bundesministerium für Umwelt

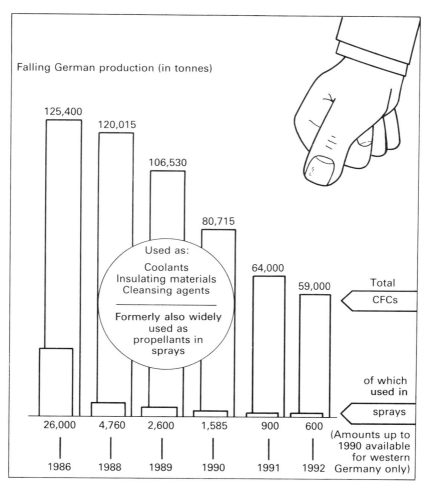

Figure 10.3 *Germany's self-imposed ban on CFCs. Source: Bundesministerium für Umwelt*

facturing industry and mining (11 billion cubic metres), and households (5 billion cubic metres).

From 1970 to 1989 over DM 90 billion were spent on measures to improve water quality. Of this sum, DM 23 billion went on sewage plant and DM 67 billion on sewers. The expenditure has led above all to a marked amelioration in the biological health of rivers, with the Rhine, Danube, Neckar, Main, Weser and Leine profiting in particular from raised oxygen levels.

One of the most impressive success stories relates to the Rhine.

Not only has the oxygen content returned to the saturation limit of approximately 10 milligrams per litre, but mercury and cadmium traces have been reduced by 99 per cent since the 1970s. As a result, certain species of algae, snails and crabs have returned to the Rhine. Moreover, forty different species of particularly resistant fish have now made the river their home. Yet it will not be generally accepted that the Rhine has recovered until the **Salm** (Rhine salmon) has returned in significant numbers. Even here there is hope: in December 1990 a salmon swallowed an angler's bait in the Rhine for the first time since the mid-1950s. Its markings indicated than it was one of the parr released two years earlier, which had returned to the river in an attempt to spawn.

Waste

Before 1989 environmental successes in the field of waste disposal had proved to be among the most elusive. A decision was therefore taken by the Federal Environment Minister, Dr Klaus Töpfer, to tackle the problem at source. This he did in April 1990 by publishing the Packaging Ordinance, in an effort to combat the throw-away society.

The ordinance prescribed that, as from 1 December 1991, companies had to take back and recycle the 'primary packaging' used during transport of the product, or to arrange for someone else to do it for them. One of the effects of this first stage of the ordinance was that 1.6 million tonnes of cardboard are now collected annually, of which 70 per cent is recycled. On 1 April 1992 the second stage of the ordinance came into force, with prescriptions extended to cover 'secondary packaging'. Customers are able to leave, for example, the box round a tube of toothpaste in the shop where it is bought. Shops now contain special receptacles for paper, plastic foil, polystyrene and other waste. From 1 January 1993 it also became possible to return sales packaging such as cans and disposable bottles. Two of the more exotic repercussions of this third stage are that potato chips are now being served on edible waffles, and popcorn is replacing polystyrene as a packaging material.

From 1 July 1995 80 per cent of packaging waste must be collected, with 90 per cent of glass and metals, and 80 per cent of plastics, laminates, cardboard and paper having to be recycled.

Initial projects in the east

Since 1990 six major environmental initiatives have been launched in the east:

- The installation of a smog early-warning system.
- The establishment of a heating plant for untreated brown coal in Magdeburg.
- The construction of a small heating plant in Staaken.
- The building of several plants to recover chlorohydrocarbons and mercury in Buna.
- The incineration of pharmaceutical residues at high temperatures in Dresden.
- The establishment of a plant for the production of chlorine in Buna.

By late 1991, the first of these major undertakings was well under way. Three new air-pollution monitoring units and thirteen container stations fitted with automatic surveillance equipment were set up between the Baltic Sea and the Thuringian Forest. The monitoring unit at Zings was opened in September 1991. Other units are operating at Neuglobsow in Brandenburg and Auf der Schmücke in Thuringia. The aim of the project is to permit long-term forecasts of atmospheric pollution and the travel-range of pollutant particles caught by high-altitude airstreams. These data are of great importance for the smog alarm system in the winter months. A similar system, providing early warning of elevated ozone levels in summer − 'summer smog' − is currently undergoing trials. To keep the public informed, arrangements are in hand to screen the latest environmental data on BTX, the Bundespost's interactive videotex system.

The reaction of business

Even as late as the early 1980s protection of the environment was considered by both trade unions and employers' associations to be hostile to employment. It was presumed that the additional costs of measures for the protection of the environment would lead to reductions in the incomes of employees, if not actually to job losses. But there has now been a change of heart on both sides. Protection of the environment is no longer regarded as a job-killer but as job-neutral, and latterly even as job-creating.

In 1985 it was calculated that approximately 300,000 employees were engaged, either directly or indirectly, in work connected with protection of the environment. The sector of the economy associated with environmental protection was growing, in 1985, at 14 per cent per annum above the average for all other sectors. Even back in 1980 gross sales of goods to the value of DM 13 billion had been achieved, and 25 per cent of those goods were exported.

In March 1985 the DGB presented its programme on protection of the environment. It demanded for the years up to 1990 environmentally-effective investments of DM 50 billion. The aim of these demands was to avert further stress on the environment and to bring about a drastic reduction in existing pressures. Protection of the environment was, according to the DGB, to be achieved by 'quality growth', and not by a virtual renunciation of industrial society, as proposed by sections of the Greens.

In 1988 the BDI signed the Tutzing Declaration, pledging that only environmentally-friendly corporate strategies would in future be pursued by its member companies.

The myth that protection of the environment destroys jobs, because of the expense, was finally laid to rest in western Germany by 1989 at the latest. It was disclosed then that the immediate production of goods for environmental protection accounted for 190,000 jobs. The production value of goods and services connected with the environment was estimated at DM 18 billion annually. Again in 1989, 27.2 per cent of total investments by industry was earmarked for investments in environmental measures. A total of 440,000 jobs were associated either directly or indirectly with protection of the environment. Growth estimates for further employment in this sector of the economy were approximately 16 per cent per annum.

Since December 1990 German companies have had to come to terms with the Packaging Ordinance. To comply with this apparently draconian piece of legislation, companies have established the **Duales System Deutschland** (DSD) (Germany's Dual System), a non-profit-making organization that operates its own waste-collection system. About 400 companies have taken a nominal share in DSD. Producers of consumer goods have to pay at least two pfennigs per packaged item, which allows their goods to sport a DSD green dot. Firms that do not join DSD have to make their own collection arrangements.

Companies in western Germany have been finding the system frustrating, partly because the costs and benefits of the green dot system are distributed rather arbitrarily from sector to sector. Plastic, for example, is more difficult to recycle than aluminium. Companies exporting to Germany have found the system even more exasperating, and foreign goods have been turned back at the borders for non-compliance with the Packaging Ordinance. Small exporters have been particularly affected by the extra costs. DSD maintains that it is up to the import companies, who often repackage goods anyhow, to apply for the green dot. Yet exporters argue that some of their products enter Germany without the need for repackaging, and the green dot system is just one more invisible barrier to trade.

Germany has been accused of breaking ranks with the EC over the question of waste disposal and recycling, but domestic companies are gradually finding ways to accommodate to the tough rules and regulations. Some of the industries that have made the most progress are the following.

Paper

The paper industry in Germany was long regarded, as elsewhere, as one of the largest environmental polluters. The cellulose used in the production of paper was separated from the wood by sulphur compounds and then bleached by means of chlorine. The latter process gives rise to dioxin, a carcinogenic compound. As environmental awareness grew throughout the west of the country, pressure was put on the paper-makers to change over to the more environmentally-friendly oxygen bleaching process. Today all the manufacturers have stopped using chlorine. Yet the new process is not entirely pollution-free either, which is why all the companies are interested in three new 'Organosolv' processes. One of these, which has been tested at Kelheim on the Danube, allows all the chemicals used to be re-extracted.

Chemicals

One of the main reasons for the clean-up of the Rhine, to which reference has already been made (see p. 176), is that Bayer, BASF and numerous smaller companies have made huge efforts to reduce the amount of waste produced in total and to bring down pollutants to tolerable levels. The name of the most successful process used here is 'integrated environmental protection'. An example from Bayer will illustrate what happens. A compound by the name of dimethyl siloxane is necessary for the manufacture of silicone. But the use of traditional technology gives rise to contaminated hydrochloric acid, which is very expensive to dispose of. In a new process devised by Bayer the hydrogen chloride forming the hydrochloric acid when dissolved in water now reacts with methanol. This produces methyl chloride, which can then be used in the production of siloxane. Thus the cycle is closed.

Textiles

At the beginning of 1992 Brinkhaus, a textile company located at Warendorf in Lower Saxony, became the first manufacturer in the world to produce its bed linen without creating a single litre of waste water. Before this, the textile mill had generated 145,000 tonnes of waste water annually. The new process leaves behind 200 tonnes of solid waste. This material is pressed into cylinder-shaped pellets, which can easily be incinerated, and which produce more energy than the equivalent amount of lignite. At the heart of the new process are two gas turbines, which can each generate 1.2 megawatts of electricity. The turbines provide both energy and heat, which has reduced energy needs by 28 per cent. The excess heat is used to evaporate the waste water, which then condenses and can be returned immediately to the production cycle because it is virtually residue-free.

Motor-cars

The German car industry has made great advances in reducing air pollution, *inter alia*, through the development of the three-way catalytic converter and more economical engines. A diesel engine designed by Audi can produce 115 bhp and accelerate a car up to 195 kph, with a fuel consumption of only 4.4 litres per 100 kilometres. VW's 'Eco-Golf' is even more revolutionary. When the accelerator pedal ceases to be depressed, the engine cuts out but the car continues to move on under its own momentum. In urban driving conditions the new car reduces fuel consumption by up to 22 per cent.

In recent times, the industry has concentrated on obviating the need for **Autofriedhöfe** (motor-car mortuaries), which so disfigure the landscape. Moreover, it claims with some justification to be a world leader in the field of recycling car components. The VW Golf and the Opel Astra were the first cars to be designed in such a way that they can be disassembled easily and a large number of the components re-used. At the end of 1991 six disassembly plants went into operation. These plants had been established in a joint project by the seven German car-makers. Beginning in 1993, BMW started to disassemble 500 cars per day at its vast recycling plant in Wackersdorf, and VW has shown that 30 per cent of the recyclable plastic in a Passat can be dismantled in just twenty minutes. Mercedes-Benz is already fitting to its cars twenty-five components that are made from recycled materials. The aim is to recycle 30 to 50 per cent of all plastic components. Pilot processes have recycled protective plastic side panels into components such as floor matting, wheel-arch stone protectors or under-bonnet parts. The engineers in the German car companies maintain that even if the approximately 600 different materials in a car cannot all be taken back into the vehicle-manufacturing process, they can be recycled in other industries.

Retail

The German government hopes that by the year 2000 environmentalism in the high street will not merely be confined to **Reformhaüser** (health-food shops). Leading supermarkets are being urged to stock more ecologically-farmed products (up to at least 20 per cent of their range), and to reduce substantially the number of environmentally-harmful goods on their shelves. The organization that has taken up the leading role in this campaign is the **Verbaucher-Initiative** (Consumer Initiative), a non-profit-making association with some 8000 members throughout the country.

In an effort to make the market more transparent, the consumer lobby is launching a two-pronged attack. First, it has published a 'green checklist' against which consumers can rate their local super-market in terms of the detergents, cleansing agents, foodstuffs, paper and packaging it stocks. Second it has brought out a book containing the results of a survey conducted among Germany's fifty-three largest trading companies, department stores and supermarket chains. As could be expected, the beauty parade of retailers as evidenced by the survey drew sharp criticism from the ten retailers that had refused to take part. The book also contains useful information aimed at enabling the consumer to spot misleading product descriptions. It comes complete with an appendix providing data on chain stores, their recycling systems, and addresses for complaints and eco-tests.

Two-thirds of consumers in western Germany are receptive to the environmentalist message, but only half of them are convinced of the practicality of ecologist doctrine. Nonetheless, in 1989 in the west companies with a green image rose by 17–21 per cent in the environmentally-aware shopper's estimation.

Conclusion

Some sceptics argue that Germany has stricter environmental laws than other countries in Europe because, thanks to its size, wealth and level of industrialization, it produces more pollution than fellow members of the EC. Others maintain that even the west of the country still presents at best a 'mixed picture' in terms of environmental pollution. But no one could doubt the effort that has been made in the west, which is now being extended to the east, to restore the natural balance of the environment.

In 1993 almost 50 per cent of company capital expenditure in western Germany was devoted to protection of the environment, and to safety. Moreover, this part of the country has some of the highest standards of ecological awareness in the EC. As environmental legislation throughout the EC is harmonized, this is one area where standards will not be allowed to fall to the level of the lowest common denominator. On the contrary, environmental standards will be forced to rise as the degree of environmental consciousness common to the citizenry of western Germany spreads throughout EC countries and beyond.

11 Business and enterprise

Introduction

Much that has been written in the first ten chapters has dealt with the 'harder', factual or institutional aspects of business culture, such as business and the law or business and finance. Thus cultural perceptions have, of necessity, been present by implication almost as much as in any other form. However, in the final three chapters of the book, attention is focused more on the 'softer', human aspects of culture, beginning with consideration of the German entrepreneur. In this way it is hoped that, towards the end of the book, cultural insights can be made more explicit than perhaps hitherto.

Western Germany's business culture has been enriched since the Second World War by many entrepreneurs. Celebrated names such as Grundig, Neckermann and Bauknecht immediately spring to mind. Without them and their ilk there would have been no **Wirtschaftswunder**. But 'Where is the next generation of entrepreneurs coming from?' is the oft-repeated cry in western Germany in the 1990s. The answer is that the entrepreneurs are already there. Yet they are less flamboyant, more discreet, than their predecessors, and running some of the world's most successful medium-sized companies.

Moreover, the medium-sized companies in western Germany are complemented by a whole legion of small companies, again quietly going about their business and making very little fuss. The small and the medium-sized companies constituting the **Mittelstand** are also aided in their activities by a vast array of financial support specially geared to their needs.

As could be expected, the picture is completely different in the east of the country. Here the legacy of the command economy has rendered it enormously difficult for both small and medium-sized businesses to establish themselves. Nevertheless, valiant efforts are being made in both sectors, yet whether they will be crowned with success is open to question for a whole variety of reasons.

The entrepreneur in the west

It is idle to speak of business and enterprise without referring to entrepreneurs themselves. Often it is the energy, expertise and business acumen of one man, or one woman, or one family, that is responsible for the prosperity of small or even medium-sized companies.

Typical of western Germany's modern entrepreneurs is Hans Peter Stihl. He runs the Stihl family group of companies, the world's largest manufacturers of chainsaws. The group had a turnover of DM 1.15 billion in 1991, up from DM 935 million in 1987, and a workforce worldwide of 5600. In 1992 Peter Stihl was also president of the DIHT (see pp. 140–143).

The family company was founded by his father, Andreas Stihl, in Waiblingen-Neustadt, Baden-Württemberg, in 1926. Today the group embraces seven manufacturing plants in western Germany; production and distribution companies in Brazil, the USA, Switzerland and Austria; and distribution companies in the United Kingdom, France, Spain, Belgium, the Netherlands, Sweden, Norway, Canada, New Zealand and Japan. Among its latest subsidiaries are two in eastern Europe – one in Budapest, Hungary, and the other in Modrice, the Czech Republic (both established in 1991).

Hans Peter Stihl joined the company in 1960 as a management assistant. Today he is the managing director of the company. His sister is responsible for financial control and his brother-in-law for marketing and distribution, his brother is the firm's lawyer, and his second sister is on the company board.

He was born in nearby Cannstadt, in 1932, the oldest of four children, and recalls his father as possessing a great talent for Technik (see also pp. 203–204). Andreas Stihl first successfully sold saws in America in 1930, then returned from Russia in 1931 with several hundred orders.

The Second World War and the immediate postwar period had a great effect on the young Hans Peter: the nightly bomber raids, and the corpses the following morning all left their mark on him. This time of adversity impressed upon him the need for hard work and the application of all the talents he possessed. Moreover, the end of the war marked a completely new departure for the whole family: Andreas Stihl was interned, and the company was placed under Allied control but eventually returned to the Stihls.

Hans Peter Stihl inherited his father's gift for most things technical. After leaving school, he studied mechanical engineering and received his university diploma as an engineer. Studies were followed by a period of practical experience as a designer with Bosch and a series of posts as a management consultant.

Both his technical and commercial training have stood him in good stead. The Stihl company has recently diversified its product range, and now, in addition to chainsaws, it also manufactures lawn-trimmers and hedge-clippers as well as other garden, landscape and forestry equipment. This diversification was facilitated by the company acquiring a holding in Viking GmbH (horticultural equipment) in 1991.

Hans Peter Stihl realized early in his career with the family company that the success and image of a firm depend to a large degree in modern Germany on how environmentally friendly its production processes and products are (see also pp. 176–181). In the autumn of 1992 a special supply and waste-disposal centre went into operation in Waiblingen-Neustadt, which cost DM 6 million to build. The company also developed the first catalytic converter for high-performance, two-stroke engines. Protected by five patents, it appeared on the market in 1988 after years of expensive R & D work. The Stihl catalytic converter reduces carbon emissions by 70 to 80 per cent.

Part of Hans Peter Stihl's business philosophy is his belief in a committed workforce. He is proud of the fact that over 60 per cent of the workforce has been with the company for more than ten years. One incentive among many is the Stihl staff share participation scheme. Each year a member of the workforce can acquire annual dividend rights up to DM 2700. To qualify, he or she must pay only DM 936 marks, and the rest is made up by the company. The fund is invested for ten years, and the interest is paid on the basis of the company's performance. If a member of staff takes up this offer every year, with a personal investment of just under DM 10,000 in all, a yield totalling approximately three times this amount can be expected. Apart from binding the employee closer to the company, the scheme also helps to increase staff motivation.

In 1992 Hans Peter Stihl's oldest son, Nicholas, aged thirty-two, started work at the firm as an engineer, after studying mechanical engineering and spending a number of years in the development department at Mercedes-Benz and as a management consultant. Nicholas will succeed his father as managing director 'when appropriately qualified'.

Other, mainly older, entrepreneurs in Germany have not been so clever, or so fortunate, as Hans Peter Stihl. In western Germany today the older entrepreneur in particular is sometimes regarded as an old-time capitalist, ruining the environment, exploiting workers, and bribing politicians. Nevertheless, many older entrepreneurs still exist, and their businesses thrive. These are mainly the entrepreneurs who started their businesses after the Second World War. Some of them now wish to retire completely or at least enter semi-retirement.

Here they have a problem: sometimes there are no members of the family willing to continue their businesses because the younger relations have taken up different careers. But what distinguishes so many of these entrepreneurs, at least from their British counterparts, is that the Germans wish to see their businesses survive as private companies. They do not wish to float them on the equity market and celebrate 'pay-day'. Not that they would not like the money: they just want their companies to live on, preferably incorporating their own or the family name. If they sold out to the equity market, their companies might be merged or subjected to a friendly takeover, and the company name could be changed. Immortality beckons, at least in the sense of the continuation of the name of the family firm. Thus opportunities present themselves for domestic or even foreign companies to acquire these firms, with the probable proviso that the family name is retained (see pp. 219–221).

The attitudes of the western German manager are quite different from those of his entrepreneur boss (see pp. 195–196). Being a manager means belonging to the workforce and enjoying the same privileges of security. Moreover, contemporary German society often values the social standing of a senior manager more highly than that of an entrepreneur. A position as a member of the management board of a large company can be more prestigious than being the owner of a medium-sized company.

He — and it is predominantly he — would hardly ever dare ask the owner if he wanted to sell the company to him, because this might be construed as disloyal and could constitute grounds for dismissal. Management buyouts (MBOs) are thus relatively rare in western Germany, though they have become more prominent in the east of the country since unification (see pp. 192–194). The reasons usually cited for the scarcity of MBOs in western Germany are, apart from the lack of ambition of senior managers, the high levels of borrowings by some western German companies.

Medium-sized companies in the west

All the same, western Germany's medium-sized companies count among their number thirty-nine firms that have been identified by Professor Hermann Simon, probably the country's second most-celebrated management guru, as 'hidden champions'. These are not companies that regularly make headlines in the newspapers nor enjoy such worldwide renown as BASF, Bayer and Hoechst, Mercedes-Benz or Volkswagen, Siemens or Bosch. But they do have world market shares of between 70 and 90 per cent, and when their exports are combined, they account for a considerable part of western Germany's much-vaunted trade surplus in normal times.

Simon calls them 'hidden champions' for two reasons. First, most of their products form part of the manufacturing process but are often subsumed in the end product. Examples are sunroofs for cars or labelling machines for bottles, or cans, of beverages. These products are therefore not immediately obvious to the end consumer. Second, western Germany's medium-sized companies relish their obscurity. They make a point of not courting the media, because they are wary of revealing their winning formulae to potential competitors.

The hidden champions pursue a policy of technical excellence combined with worldwide marketing. They focus on niche markets and marshal all their resources to staying in the top position in that niche. Diversification without a high degree of synergistic effects is a notion that is abhorrent to them.

In addition, for many of these companies the global market place is not a recent phenomenon. They began to internationalize their market presence in the 1950s or 1960s. Today the thirty-nine champions own a total of 354 foreign sales and service or manufacturing subsidiaries (not including agents, importers or other forms of company representation). Each company has, on average, 9.6 foreign subsidiaries — a large number for companies of such size.

Once abroad, the hidden champions prefer to retain full control of their operations, perceiving their relationship with the customer as something too important to be left to third parties. Here the firms' commitment to continuity of their own management pays off, since their customers are quick to realize that they will probably be dealing with the same manager ten years hence.

Even western Germany's most successful medium-sized companies do not have the wherewithal to beat the competition at every turn. Thus they concentrate on what they have identified as the issues most valued by the customer. These are, according to their calculations, product quality, proximity to the customer, service, quality of staff, technological leadership and innovation.

As for product quality and innovation, the hidden champions place their reliance in their own capabilities. They are firmly convinced that they can tackle any manufacturing and R & D problems independently. Self-reliance in these fields guarantees control over standards and prevents precious technological know-how from seeping out of the company. Another of their features in this area is their tendency to 'make it themselves' rather than 'buy it in'. One of the champions even operates its own foundry!

Simon's study is not uncritical of medium-sized companies in western Germany. He fears that they might have to change some of their practices if they are to continue to flourish. For example, though the hidden champions are close to their customers, they do lack formal marketing skills. Few employ marketing specialists or have marketing departments, or even pursue formal market research. Indeed many of their pricing strategies are founded on a cost-plus basis, an approach that would be frowned upon by most marketing experts.

A further possible weakness of the thirty-nine champions identified by Simon is their tendency to 'overshoot the mark technologically', i.e. to overengineer their products. This means that such products can be too sophisticated and expensive. While acknowledging that German machines are often the best in their field, some customers prefer cheaper alternatives with fewer features.

Among the hidden champions ranking at position number one in the world, in terms of relative market share, are Baader (fish-processing machines), Bamberger Kaliko (bookbinding textiles), GKD (metal-fitters and fabrics), Heidelberger Druckmaschinen (offset printing machines), Haidenhain (measuring and control instruments), Körber/Hauni (cigarette machines), Krones (labelling machines for bottles and cans), Leybold (vacuum technology), Märklin & Cie (model railways), Starck (special plastics products), Stihl (chainsaws), Trumpf (bending and punching machines), Webasto (sunroofs for cars), and Weinig (automatic moulding machines).

Finance for small companies

Calculating levels of aid for small firms is difficult because of Germany's bewildering array of programmes. However, figures published by the Anglo-German Foundation for the Study of Industrial Society show that western Germany pumped DM 4.5 billion a year into small-business support in the late 1980s.

Finance for small business in Germany comes from three principal sources: the federal government; the state governments; and specialist banks, some of which are the legacy of the Marshall Plan. Backing from the federal government includes 18 per cent of the start-up costs of any manufacturing company establishing itself in a depressed region, grants for specific sectors, training handouts, and tax breaks. The individual states often have an even wider selection of subsidies. North Rhine-Westphalia, for example, runs a technology fund to encourage a shift away from heavy into light industry.

Hans Hermann Jürgensmann, who is responsible for small business at the DIHT, has gone on record as stating: 'A firm can receive more than 60 per cent of its start-up costs in the shape of grants and soft loans if it can meet the right criteria'. Indeed Germany's generous support for small business at government levels actually prompted an investigation by the EC. There was a suspicion abroad that government aid might have amounted to unfair competition, but the investigation concluded that it was within permitted limits. Many German business people are convinced that they got away with it only because their government systems are so complex at both federal and state levels.

Quite apart from government sources, small and medium-sized German companies can call upon a number of specialist banks for funding. Among them figure the IKB Deutsche Industriebank (IKB), the Deutsche Ausgleichsbank, and the powerful Kreditanstalt für Wiederaufbau (KfW), which enjoys a Standard & Poor's AAA rating.

Founded in the late 1940s with dollars from the Marshall Plan, KfW's task is essentially to pass on the low interest rates at which it can borrow in international markets to the country's small and medium-sized company sector. The German government's role only extends to being a KfW guarantor and owner of the majority stake. Apart from a modest cash injection at the time of its creation, the federal government has never had to pay an additional pfennig towards its operating costs.

An institution like the KfW is especially important in a period of relatively high interest rates, such as Germany experienced after unification. Though it is not allowed to offer interest at levels below short-term market rates, the KfW can ensure that a possibly vulnerable sector of the economy, i.e. small and medium-sized companies, is relieved from paying an undue rate margin on top of an already high base.

The financing ruse employed by the KfW is to exploit its good credit rating to make capital available to companies that would otherwise not have a chance of attracting loans. Thus the KfW can be held to be a development bank for this company sector, by allowing small and medium-sized companies access to loan capital on terms similar to those which large companies can command, on their own merits, on international markets. The crucial point about the KfW is not that it permits access to capital that would otherwise not be available, but that it levels the interest rate gap between small and large companies, thereby removing one of the greatest disadvantages for small companies.

The system works through the commercial banking network. The bank lends to the client and the KfW refinances the loan. This means a guaranteed, though limited, profit to the commercial bank. KfW avoids direct competition with such banks, and the service for customers is quick and unbureaucratic.

In 1991 the KfW's commitments were approximately DM 40 billion of investment loans for small and medium-sized companies. As the KfW does not finance more than two-thirds of any single investment, and often much less, the total amount mobilized by its loans is invariably much higher.

Start-ups in the west

The number of **Existenzgründungen** (businesses start-ups) in western Germany has been rising steadily over the 1980s and early 1990s, though some businesses quickly fail. In 1980 start-ups numbered approximately 160,000; in 1985, 290,000; and in 1990, 320,000, of which one in three companies was founded by a woman (cf 1975, when one in ten had a female founder). Western Germans, it would appear, still possess an entrepreneurial spirit, but it manifests itself in start-ups rather than MBOs.

Some start-ups are still based on the German fascination with Technik. In 1993, at a plant in Wakefield, West Yorkshire, Coca-Cola cans flashed round the factory at a rate of 120,000 per hour. Then a man-size robot arranged them in two rows for packing. A few years earlier this robot was still the dream of an ageing German scientist and his partner, a postgraduate philosophy student. They were convinced that their machine would revolutionize the drinks industry. Beside high-speed packing, it would test the content level of bottles in a millisecond and sort out returnable empties from disposable bottles.

The company manufacturing the robot, Centro Kontroll-Systeme, was established in 1986 at Siegen, ninety kilometres west of Cologne. The two men painstakingly assembled their first robot by hand. It was sold to an American bottling firm for $14,000, and Centro has never looked back. The company had sold more than 400 machines worldwide by mid-1993, and employed twenty-two people.

Centro thus joined a thriving army of small capital-goods manufacturers in western Germany employing between twenty and 200 people each. These small firms accounted for 46 per cent of the country's wealth in 1993.

Start-ups in the east

There are several sources available for statistics on start-up firms in the eastern states, and those produced by the **Bundeswirtschaftsministerium** (Federal Ministry of Economics), the **Statistisches Bundesamt** (Federal Statistical Office), and the commercial banks, are among the most accurate. Yet agreement on precise numbers appears to be difficult to achieve. For some time the Ministry claimed a figure of 300,000 start-ups in 1991 alone, but subsequently it had to acknowledge that for every two start-ups there was one firm that had to close down. For 1992 the Federal Statistical Office claimed 500,000 new start-ups in the east of the country. Yet doubt was cast on both these sets of figures by Kurt Kasch, head of the Deutsche Bank in Berlin, who claimed in

1993 that though the statistics may reflect the number of company registrations, whether these companies are actually alive and operating, and not merely registered, is quite a different question. He put the combined total in the east for 1991 and 1992 at some 300,000 real start-ups.

Whatever the exact figures, eastern Germans are attempting to put into practice what they have been urged to do by western politicians. At the beginning of 1990 Helmut Haussmann, Federal Economics Minister at the time, proclaimed that in the east a 'market economy from below' would be built up, and he went on to predict the establishment of 1 million small businesses there.

Small business people in the east were, however, struggling by 1993. Though they had thrown themselves into the task with great optimism and energy, they were finding out how unforgiving the market economy can be if mistakes are made. A typical example was provided by Wolfgang Krüger, an economics graduate who established an office furniture business in 1991, together with two partners from western Germany. Initially he was successful in recruiting a well-known office furniture manufacturer from western Germany as a supplier that even granted him generous credit terms. Orders came in quickly, and instead of the anticipated DM 500,000 in takings in the first year, turnover was actually DM 2.4 million. Krüger expanded quickly, with staff numbers increasing to eighteen. Each of the seven salesmen was furnished with his own company car. He even established his own advertising agency, with four employees, to provide his office furniture company with a new image.

Matters began to go downhill from the beginning of 1992. The expensive office furniture on offer from Krüger became a luxury item for many of his customers. Those who did actually purchase then insisted on large discounts, because Krüger's competitors in West Berlin had discovered the potential of the eastern market in the meantime. He diversified into furnishings for doctors' and dentists' surgeries, but could only pursue this line as a loss-leader. In 1993, he was frantically looking for a credit of DM 500,000 to save his company from bankruptcy.

The mistakes made by Krüger were typical of failing small businesses in eastern Germany. Young entrepreneurs were often dazzled by initial high turnover figures, expanded too quickly, diversified rashly, and then ended up with cashflow problems. Their plight was not helped either by the absence in the east of the country of a burgeoning large, or even medium-sized, company sector, or by the recession from 1993 onwards.

Small companies in the east

Undeterred by such experiences, political figures and economic experts in the country were determined to replicate in the east what had proved successful in the west, viz. a dynamic Mittelstand. Indeed, on 20 June 1992, the Treuhandanstalt held a conference in Berlin to find ways of speeding up the privatization of small firms in the east. This is ironic because, despite its oft-declared enthusiasm for small companies, the Treuhand's own bureaucracy was one of the major obstacles to western German entrepreneurs trying to gain control of the many small firms still on its books.

Wolfgang Karrte, head of the Federal Cartel Office in Berlin, complained twice between April and June 1992 that the Treuhand had been doing too little to promote small business and concentrating instead on the sale of large companies, thus failing to create a Mittelstand in the east. Stung by such criticism, Birgit Breuel, president of the Treuhand, pointed out that it was indeed keen to attract entrepreneurs from the west. In August 1992 the Treuhand actually changed some of the rules requiring competitive bids, which were more appropriate to large concerns, in an effort to ease the sale of many of the 4800 companies it still had in its portfolio. Many were of Mittelstand size.

But farther down the Treuhand bureaucracy there seemed to be little interest in dealing with western Germany's small business people. A Treuhand advertising campaign in 1992, aimed at attracting western entrepreneurs to buy an eastern firm, appeared to have been a great success, prompting 1600 enquiries. But these were quickly whittled down to 300 candidates with both the money and the experience to run a company. By mid-June 1992 not a single deal had been completed.

Most of the blame was placed on petty officials at the Treuhand unit in Berlin. It is said that they failed to provide individual bidders and small western firms with enough information on the eastern companies available. When the Treuhand's regional offices were approached for more information, letters and telephone calls went unanswered. The root of the problem lay in the fact that the local offices were being pressed to sell eastern German companies as quickly as possible. Thus, the easiest way to do this was to sell them to their existing managers.

Even if a western entrepreneur had managed to acquire a business in the east, it was unlikely that he or she would have wanted to venture into the retail trade, especially not in the larger cities. Crime soared once the fall of the Berlin Wall in 1989 had removed the omni-present Stasi police and allowed in criminals from the west. Though the small entrepreneur may be the federal government's big hope for economic recovery, the law in the eastern states afforded little security against criminals, attracted by easy pickings in what business people referred to as the 'Wild East' (see p. 55).

Leipzig, with a population of 550,000, and known as the **Heldenstadt** (city of heroes), where demonstrations helped to bring down East Germany's Communist leaders in 1989, and home to the 828-year-old trade fair, was known in 1993 as eastern Germany's crime capital. Extortion was rife. Shopkeepers, bar and casino-owners, and tradesmen either paid up anything between DM 50 and 500 per week or saw their businesses wrecked. In 1992 the Samson Gang was reputed to be in control of Leipzig's protection racket.

Management buyouts in the east

Though the management buyout (MBO) has hardly figured prominently in the business culture in the west for reasons already indicated (see p. 185), one of the ways in which the Treuhand attempted both to privatize eastern German industry and establish a viable small and medium-sized company sector at the same time was through the **Initiative Mittelstand** (small and medium-sized company campaign). By the end of 1992 approximately 1500 companies had been privatized by means of the MBO technique.

Acquirers were allowed three years to pay, but they were not obliged to purchase the real estate immediately. This meant that the managers of the former state-run companies could become the owners, earn money, and then pay up from what they had earned. To deter speculation, the Treuhand insisted on certain conditions for future investment and employment from its purchasers. Each bidder for a company had to furnish a business plan that included investment figures, job forecasts, and sources of finance, and these figures were included in the sales contract.

Some MBOs were quick and promising. In March 1992 Hendrikus Reineke, managing director of Mitteldeutsche Industrie-Ofenbau GmbH & Co KG (Mioba) of Böhringen, near Rosswein, Saxony, signed an agreement to purchase his company from the Treuhand. Under the settlement, Reineke agreed to take on all of Mioba's old debts. The company, which manufactures a wide range of industrial furnaces, employed 150 people. Mioba was also starting to make its presence felt in the west, boasting small orders from Volkswagen, Saab and Scania. Annual turnover stood at DM 12 million in 1993. To improve profitability, Reineke was attempting to co-operate with partners in Poland and the Czech Republic.

In March 1993 Rotkäppchen (Little Red Riding Hood), the sparkling wine that was once the toast of East Germany's Communist élite, went private in an MBO. Five managers and a small western German distiller applied to buy the firm. Before the Berlin Wall came down, Rotkäppchen and the even sweeter Crimean sparkling wine were almost the only champagne-like drinks East Germans could buy. Yet the company's 70 per cent market share disappeared with the Wall, as erstwhile customers began to prefer the drier bubbly from the west. Subsequently, Rotkäppchen changed the taste of its product, modernized its plant, and even started selling in western Germany. Annual sales, once 17 million bottles per annum, or one for every East German, rose from a post-unification low of 3 million to 5 million in 1992.

Other MBOs took longer to arrange. In September 1992 Deutsche Binnenwerften GmbH (DBG) (Eastern German Inland Shipyards) was privatized retroactively from 1 July 1992. Under an MBO, the Treuhand sold the equity to a new holding company, which in turn was controlled by management and staff. The group consisted of five yards with 450 employees. After the Treuhand had agreed to cover old debts of DM 11.5 million, the new shareholders promised investment of up to at least DM 8 million in the following three years. DBG's predecessor had 1365 staff in sixteen plants. Five yards remained in 1992, at Berlin–Stralau, Genthin, Tangermünde, Dresden–Laubegast and Malz (Oranienburg). They were concentrating on pusher tugs, passenger ships, ferries and other specialized inland vessels. The Dresden yard was the only one in Europe able to repair steam vessels and steam engines.

Other MBOs still proved virtually impossible to set up. In April 1993 the Treuhand decided to postpone the privatization of the Rostock-based Neptun-Werft GmbH (Neptun Shipyard). The reason for the latest delay was that a German investment group had suddenly shown an interest. Originally, the only interested party was Bremer Vulkan AG, which had planned to acquire an 80 per cent stake in Neptun via Hansa Schiffe- und Maschinenbau of Rostock, which it owns. Under this plan the remaining shares would have been offered to the Neptun employees in the form of an MBO.

According to a not-entirely disinterested party, Wolfgang Finkbeiner, a member of the board of the **Bundesverband Deutscher Unternehmensberater** (BDU) (German Management Consultancy Association), eastern German companies privatized through MBOs were facing serious management and financing problems as early as 1992. However, only 55 per cent of the companies acquired by MBOs were taking advice from consultants. He also alleged that the Treuhand's management buyin (MBI) programme had been a flop. By September 1992 fewer than ten western German managers had been prepared to put their own capital into an eastern German company.

Again in September 1992, the **Arbeitsgemeinschaft zur Förderung der Partnerschaft in der Wirtschaft, e.V.** (AGP) (Association for the Advancement of Partnership in Industry and Commerce) criticized the Treuhand for overburdening MBO companies with legally-suspect and unrealistically-formulated sales contracts. AGP called for all such contracts to be rewritten.

Conclusion

These criticisms of specific policies pursued by the Treuhand had been overshadowed to a certain extent by more general and weighty reproaches to the federal government by the summer of 1992. Elmar Pieroth, head of the CDU's Small Business Forum, told a news conference that Bonn should continue tax reforms and trim bureaucracy. He called for federal and state authorities to agree investment tax credits in the east more quickly, even if all the conditions for such credits were not met immediately. He maintained that new business ventures in the east often failed because they did not fulfil extensive legal requirements that were not always necessary. Pieroth urged the federal government to continue with reforms of corporation tax, and he suggested that new companies should be exempted from profit taxes for the first two years.

The federal government wishes to reduce both corporation taxes and inheritance taxes on medium-sized companies. In 1993 it was considering cutting the top corporation tax and top income tax rates to a uniform 46 per cent from the existing 50 per cent and 53 per cent levels.

12 Business and business people

Introduction

It is appropriate, in this the penultimate chapter, to continue to focus attention not on the impersonal determinants of business culture such as those treated in the earlier parts of the book but on the more human influences on culture, e.g. business people. By so doing, we can perhaps access further the 'softer', less tangible, aspects of culture than has been possible hitherto. At the same time, our insights into the business culture in Germany will become more rounded and more meaningful.

Business people come of course in various guises, from the entrepreneurs in the west and east who were written about in the previous chapter (see pp. 182–192), to male and female managers in the west, male and female managers in the east, engineers throughout Germany, and many more. Should the balance of this chapter be tilted slightly more towards the east than the west, and more towards females than males, then this, too, is most appropriate, since so many of the previous chapters have been tilted the other way.

Male managers in the west

The vast majority of managers at the various levels in western German companies are men. What is more, they are usually older than their counterparts in many other countries. Germans firmly believe that a manager should be a 'man-ager', i.e. have the age of a man, not of a boy!

As has already been revealed (see pp. 144–156), managers at all levels in western Germany are highly educated, even to the extent of many of them in the topmost ranks possessing doctorates. Indeed 'academization' of management at all levels is a clearly discernible trend. In 1974 58 per cent at the managing director level had completed studies to diploma standard, and ten years later it was 62 per cent. The figure for managers with a diploma at the 'first' level, e.g. head of division, was 36 per cent in 1974, and 55 per cent in 1984. At the 'second' level, e.g. head of department, the percentages were 28 and 44 respectively. This means that fewer managers are reaching the upper echelons of management via the apprenticeship route, unless of course they had taken an apprenticeship before embarking on tertiary-level studies – a growing trend, given the relatively high percentage of graduate unemployment in the west (see pp. 99–100).

As was also noted earlier (see p. 156), the managers at these top three levels reach their positions on the management ladder through their functional specializations. Generalist managers do not begin to emerge from the system until the uppermost level, i.e. board of management, is reached. Here, in the largest companies at least, a somewhat belated effort is made to broaden the vision of top managers by assigning to them, in addition to their functional role, responsibility for a geographical area. Thus, apart from a vertical role down the organization as finance director, a member of the management board might also assume horizontal accountability across the company for the performance of, for example the territory of northern Europe or South America.

A further characteristic of managers in western Germany, as is implied in the above, is their strict adherence to traditional, fairly steep hierarchies. Although experiments with flatter hierarchies have been tried out in certain companies in the west of the country, particularly in American multinationals, they have not been emulated to any significant extent in real German firms. Here the traditional three levels of management have for the most part been retained.

Below the 'second level', in a large number of companies, would figure the **Prokuristen** (persons to whom the power of procuration has been granted by the company). As such, they have the right to bind the company legally towards third parties (see also p. 52). The presence of their signature, or that of one of their superiors, together with the signature of the person who has actually done the work, on a letter from a German company has contributed to the reputation of western German managers as being legalistic. A further factor contributing to this notion is the existence in German management of a surprisingly high percentage of ex-law graduates, who make sure that neither the companies themselves nor their trading partners break any of the rules and regulations.

Finally, on the commercial side of management as opposed to the industrial side, would figure the **Handelsbevollmächtigter** (a person to whom limited powers of procuration have been granted) and a whole array of **Sachbearbeiter** (specialists or experts), more about whom below (see p. 204).

Female managers in the west

Western Germany has at its disposal a large, highly-educated female workforce, some 40 per cent of all employed persons being women. Approximately 48 per cent of school-leavers with the Abitur qualification are female, and women represent about 41 per cent of the student population at universities and polytechnics. But females are very much conspicuous by their absence in top jobs in general. Only 4 per cent of all professors at universities and polytechnics are female. In addition, there are very few women in senior management, and they are strongly under-represented in middle and lower management.

Exactly what happens to the large cohorts of highly-intelligent women after completion of their education at university and polytechnic is something of a mystery. Of course some of them marry but not many begin to bear children. Western Germany, with 1.3 children per woman, has one of the lowest fecundity rates in the world (see p. 93).

Some of the most reliable statistics on women in management are still to be found in a survey published in 1986 by FIDA, the society for the promotion of scientific research into the position of women in international co-operation. In the mid-1980s this organization sent out 4000 questionnaires to a representative sample of companies − large, medium-sized and small − in manufacturing industry and in the services sector. Fewer than 10 per cent of the questionnaires, i.e. 398 in total, were returned and completed. Crushing indifference to the issue of women in management is therefore the first inference that might be drawn from the evidence of the response rate alone.

Most of the responses came from the chemical and food industries (13 per cent each). Next followed the services sector in general, including financial services with 11 per cent. The average number of women in the companies responding was slightly lower, at 33 per cent, than the average for female employment throughout western German companies as a whole (37 per cent).

The findings of the survey show that the percentages of women in management positions at the individual levels of the hierarchy assume the form of a pyramid. The higher the level of hierarchy, the lower the percentage of females (Figure 12.1).

The main reasons given for the low number of women in management positions are, first, the traditional role perception of women in western German society − that of the three Ks (**Kinder, Kirche, Küche**, i.e. children, church, kitchen) − is changing only slowly (48 per cent of responses). Second, the nature and scope of a woman's professional life take second place to her family duties (31 per cent). Third, there are too few female applicants for management positions (28 per cent). Fourth, too few women are professionally and vocationally qualified (17 per cent). Finally, women interrupt their working life for too long in order to bear and rear children (16 per cent).

It is perhaps worth recording here that, in a random sample of interviews conducted by the author with female managers one year

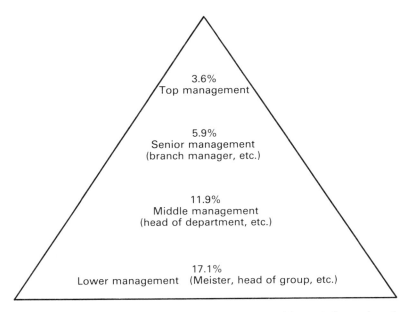

Figure 12.1 *Percentages of women in management positions at the various levels of the western German hierarchy. Source: FIDA, 1986*

after the survey, the most frequently-voiced opinion for the low numbers of females in management positions at all levels was that a woman had to be twice as good at her job as a man before she became a manager. The same criterion holds good, it was claimed, for promotion further up the management ladder.

What should be done about the situation was examined by the FIDA survey. The most-favoured solution was an improvement in the vocational counselling of female school-leavers (38 per cent of responses); the creation of better conditions for working parents (31 per cent); abolition of anti-female prejudice by information and enlightenment in the company (23 per cent); experimentation with new career patterns, i.e. a second course of training after the child-rearing phase (20 per cent); private industry should implement its own promotion programmes targeted at women (18 per cent).

What should *not* be done is perhaps the most revealing finding of all, after the disappointing response rate. The highest degree of rejection was met by the following suggestions: an Office of Equality should be established, with powers of intervention similar to those of the Federal Cartel Office (36 per cent of responses); an Anti-Discrimination Act should be passed (35 per cent); employment quotas for women should be established in companies (34 per cent); equality commissions should be set up in organizations (22 per cent); special employment programmes for women should be instituted by the federal government (17 per cent).

The survey separates some of the replies by male respondents from those by females, and male chauvinism is not difficult to detect in several of the former. Two will suffice as illustrations: 'Mothers just don't belong in a factory or office but with their children, because children have to be brought up, and our society needs new generations with good, bourgeois values'. 'Do women really want to be equal with men? Leave the weaker sex as it is. As they are now, women are just fine for us men.' Both these responses came from owners of companies, and as long as such attitudes are prevalent among the decision-makers, women in western Germany will have to wait some considerable time before they achieve anything like equality of representation at any of the levels of management, let alone the uppermost ranks.

Male managers in the east

It is ironic in the extreme that, in the egalitarian society that former East Germany was purportedly attempting to achieve, the management system was strictly of the one-man, but hardly ever one-woman, variety. This is nowhere better typified than by the overwhelmingly male directors general of the approximately 300 state-owned combines. These directors general had arguably more power than the presidents of large corporations in the United States. Eight of the economic overlords sat on the SED's central committee from 1986. They were thus even more influential than the industry ministers to whom they reported, because some of these ministers were not members of the central committee.

The elevated position of the directors general enabled them to influence the economic plan in favour of their particular combine. It also gave them the freedom to break many of the stultifying rules and regulations, and to cut red tape. Above all, however, their membership of the central committee afforded them priority in the allocation of precious resources and access to hard currency.

In addition, the directors general of the combines were personally responsible for everything in the combine, from plan fulfilment through to the combine academy and the protective equipment worn by the company firemen. They could remove middle-level managers, create new divisions in the combine, shift the manufacturing site from one company in the combine to another, or effect inter-combine transfers of plant and machinery. Although they were obliged to present a monthly progress report to all employees at the parent plant, and had to meet regularly with the trade union and SED party officials (the Holy Trinity of director general, the trade unions and the Party), it was

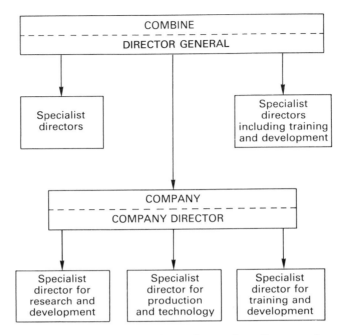

Figure 12.2   *The management hierarchy in former East Germany. Source: Schule und Berufsbildung in der DDR*

usually not in the interest of the latter two bodies to probe too deeply into the actions of the director general (Figure 12.2).

Although they enjoyed great social prestige within the country, not only on the basis of their positions but also by dint of their personal achievements and their membership of the **nichtsozialistischer Reisekader** (personages allowed to travel to non-Socialist countries), some of the directors general could astonish observers in the west by their pronouncements. One example will suffice. Reporting on the zero defects drive within his combine, Wolfgang Jacob stated: 'Step by step, we want to make EAW-Electronic into a name familiar all over the world: a watchword for quality everywhere. Like Zeiss, Coca-Cola, or Lada'(!)

The 'middle managers' in the former East German system (Nomenclatura II) are perhaps best defined as a substantial layer of professionally-qualified, but for the most part ideologically-detached, officials. They had sought relatively high positions in order to fulfil personal ambitions and to receive the perquisites of life on the Nomenclatura ladder (see pp. 160−161).

The term 'middle managers' in fact is probably inappropriate for this stratum of society: in reality they were nothing but higher industrial functionaries. Their power was constrained, not only by the one-man management practices of their directors general, and by the trade unions and party officials, but also by the realities of commercial life within the system. Profits were only regarded as genuine if earned within the framework of the state-determined economic plan; profits could only be made by cutting costs and not by raising prices, unless sanctioned by the economic plan; profits were retained partly by the companies and partly by the combines. The rest went to the state.

These functionaries were usually not permitted to shop around in order to reduce costs: raw materials had to be bought in at prices laid down by the state; and semi-finished products, possibly from another company within the combine, had to be purchased at cost levels determined outside their sphere of influence. In other words, these people did not manage, but functioned by taking orders from above, executing them, and working to the rule-book. They had just one boss — their immediate superior.

Post-unification, companies in eastern Germany are suffering from a severe shortage of professional managers. However, there are not sufficient western German managers to go round, and it would be politically insensitive to fill too many management positions with them even if they were available. All the same, many older managers from the west have been brought back out of retirement. Experienced managers deprived of the possibility of becoming top managers, for whatever reason, are now being put into the most senior posts in the east. In addition, a few young line managers just a year or two after qualification are being presented with an opportunity to become assistant managers.

Most of the top positions are, however, being filled by native eastern Germans. The vast majority of the top managers of the old state companies have been removed from their positions in the meantime, either because they were too closely connected with the SED party or with the Stasi, or with both. Now it is the second-, or even third-level managers, the former industrial functionaries, that have been moved into the top positions.

Yet even they are unhappy with post-unification developments. They claim that they 'must have done something right' from 1945 to 1990. Besides helping to build the so-called showcase of the Eastern bloc countries, they protest that former East Germany was the best of the CMEA countries in automation, robotics and microelectronics. They met their targets in the past, and now the Wessis are coming along, closing down many of their companies, and/or telling them that they have been doing it all wrong!

There is a widespread lack of confidence among the former 'middle managerial' strata. Like the former top managers in the east, many of them have been dismissed or demoted by Western firms taking over companies in eastern Germany. But the reasons for dismissal or demotion are slightly different. There have been wholesale removals of personnel managers, who were widely regarded by the workforce as local SED party spies. Accountants have suffered similarly, but because of their ignorance of market economy techniques. Yet some sales managers have been retained on account of their deep knowledge of, and contact with, markets in eastern European countries, despite the fact that many of their acquaintances have in the meantime disappeared from the commercial scene.

The very nature of management has naturally changed in eastern Germany. Now managers have to manage not to fulfil plans but to make profits, and this is proving to be a difficult task. According to a report by Professor Horst Albach, probably Germany's most eminent management guru, managers formerly had to fulfil plans that were totally unrealistic. To meet production targets that were illusory, given the state of productivity in the country's factories, managers were more than economical with the truth about the available capacity at their plant when putting together their production plans. 'They lied about inventories in formulating delivery requirements for supplies and raw material. They lied about capital requirements for replacement investment and yet did not get enough money for necessary modernization. They were forced against their will to invest heavily in totally uneconomical projects that had high political priority like chips and computers.'

Their first challenge now is to start telling the truth. The second is to adapt from commanding a highly-skilled workforce with obsolete machinery, who were unbeatable in improvising, and repairing ancient plant and machinery, to managing a team of workers who can operate modern equipment effectively and efficiently. While all of the new managers are keen to improve their professional and technical expertise, according to a survey by the **Stiftung Industrieforschung** (Industry Research Foundation) only one-third wish to update their commercial skills. Most disappointing of all is the finding that very few of them perceive any necessity to rethink or to change their former behaviour.

In the years since unification, over 500,000 citizens of former East Germany have emigrated to western Germany. Not many of them are managers.

In 1990 Mülder & Partner, management consultants, tried to ascertain whether, despite all the fragmentary evidence to date, there was an untapped pool of top management talent in the east of the country, and 250 former East German managers were surveyed for their suitability as management board members in western German companies. The finding was that only seven would qualify.

The other 243 would fail in the west on account of their lack of market knowledge, lack of confidence, lack of creativity, lack of initiative, and lack of mental flexibility. Although some of the candidates possessed positive qualities, the most outstanding of which were intelligence, motivation and a talent for improvisation, far too many had been scarred by the system.

Even the successful candidates, however, would face an uphill task, not least from their peers in the west. They would encounter an acceptability problem because of the widespread conviction in western Germany today that 'Ossis are all turncoats: yesterday Karl Marx; tomorrow Ludwig Erhard'.

Female managers in the east

Despite the fact that women in former East Germany represented a very high portion of the active labour force (some 47 per cent), and although the country had most generous provisions for working mothers before unification (see p. 98), the scant evidence available to date would suggest that female representation in management ranks was even lower than for western Germany.

One of the reasons lies in the career choice for highly-intelligent females. These women were directed by the state to opt in large numbers for positions in medicine and teaching. Although a small percentage studied economics, law and engineering at the most respected universities and colleges, very few indeed penetrated the ranks of management after graduation.

Engineers in west and east

Engineers in both parts of Germany share a common heritage: their profession enjoys high esteem throughout the length and breadth of the land. This esteem derives from a peculiarly German **Weltanschauung** (view of the world) and is thus worthy of some detailed consideration.

Whereas man's achievements are classified in English-speaking countries in terms of the arts and sciences, the Germans adopt a fundamentally-different approach. They distinguish between **Kunst** (the performing and fine arts), **Wissenschaft** (all knowledge, science and some of the arts), and **Technik** (the art and science of making useful artefacts). The advertising slogan for Audi cars, **Vorsprung durch Technik** (in the lead through engineering) is not idly chosen, because the word Technik is imbued with so many, varied and affirmative connotations for the German mind (Figure 12.3).

The position of Technik as a main category of man's accomplishments

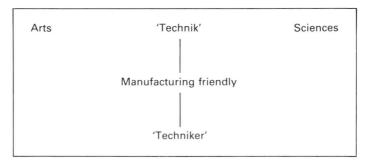

Figure 12.3   *German classification of man's achievements. Source: Lawrence, 1980*

in its own right has significant implications for the German economy and for the set of values cherished by the citizenry of the country. The pre-eminence of Technik gives rise to a manufacturing-friendly environment, with the result that neither part of Germany has moved too far down what is commonly held in the country to be the dreaded slope towards the service economy (see p. 19). Over 30 per cent of GNP is still furnished by manufacturing industry, in which higher value is more often added than in the service sector, and from which exports frequently come more easily.

The high esteem in which Technik is held not only dignifies the engineers, the designers and the actual makers on the shopfloor, but one of its derivations, **Techniker** (technician), possesses overwhelmingly positive overtones in the German language. To say of someone, **'Er ist ein guter Techniker'** or **'Sie ist eine gute Technikerin'** would be to pay the sincerest of compliments to either the chairman of the management or to the car-park attendant. This is not to imply, by any stroke of the imagination, that car-park attendants are all women, but to indicate that almost all those engaged in business in Germany like to regard themselves, and be regarded by others, as technicians, specialists or experts.

This mindset contrasts sharply with the British attitude, where the amateur, the Corinthian ideal, is still held up as the model which should be aspired to. As a consequence, the British are uncomfortable with the notion of technicians or specialists. 'Too clever by half' is the damning criticism most often heard. As for experts: an 'ex' is a has-been and 'spurt' is a drip under pressure! This sort of thinking, or lack of it, leaves Germans cold.

Engineers in the west

Engineers still enjoy high status in the west of the country. They were the people who helped to rebuild a land destroyed by war, their skills were responsible for bringing about the economic miracle and the affluent society that accompanied it, and it is on their shoulders that responsibility rests for ensuring continued prosperity in the future.

But the engineers in the west have not just sat back and rested on their laurels: they have taken certain active steps to protect their profession and its associated status. First, they have seen to it that **Ingenieur** (engineer) is a legally protected title, as is **Mechaniker** (mechanic). Thus nobody without the correct qualifications can assume such titles. Again, the comparison with the United Kingdom is unavoidable, where plumbers call themselves heating engineers, fitters maintenance engineers, and window-cleaners vision-enhancement technicians!

Second, the engineers have seen to it that their professional body, the **Verein Deutscher Ingenieure** (VDI) (Association of German Engineers), remains one united organization. As such, it can act as a powerful lobby for the interests of engineers and engineering in general, and can protect status. Yet again, it would be remiss not to point out the contrasting situation in the United Kingdom, where there are no less than seventeen professional institutions for engineers, each of them having the right to bestow chartered status.

Third, the German **Diplom-Ingenieur** does not need to become chartered. His, or less frequently her, education has been long and thorough, with the average length of diploma studies for electricals lasting 6.2 years and mechanicals 6.4. It has also been expensive, with average costs to the students for the former courses being estimated at some DM 70,000 and DM 73,000 for the latter, with no grants and very few loans being available.

In addition, the education of the average engineer emerging from university has been of a high quality. Professors of engineering at the various universities are recruited from a broad spectrum of engineering functions, especially the design function, and not predominantly from research and development, as happens in certain other countries. Theoretical knowledge from the lecture theatres has been complemented with practical, hands-on experience gained in probably the best-equipped university laboratories and workshops in Europe. It has then been topped off with compulsory, mentored study periods in manufacturing companies.

The newly-qualified engineer enters a company as a fairly raw recruit, but his or her education does not cease at this point. Attendance at regular in-company courses, which update the knowledge young engineers originally gained at university, or familiarize them with new technology, can be anticipated. He or she will, in the fullness of time, inevitably specialize in one of the engineering functions within the company and possibly enter the ranks of management.

If the engineer is very successful, he, but most probably not she, will finish his career on the management board of a company. In fact there is a preponderance of engineers on such boards throughout manufacturing companies in western Germany. The advantage here is that engineers have an excellent technical grasp of their company's product range. The disadvantage is that in some cases they can become too product-oriented and not sufficiently market-oriented. The result is that some German companies tend to overengineer their products: 'making nails with heads on' is one of the most common criticisms, and even self-criticisms, of German companies (see p. 187). In the late 1980s the dominance of engineers within Siemens actually prompted the chairman of the management board at the time, Karl-Heinz Kaske, to proclaim to *Der Spiegel*: '**Wir brauchen mehr Marketing-Leute: wir brauchen mehr Spinner**' ('We need more marketing people: we need more fibbers'), an utterance that says as much about the German attitude to marketing (see pp. 186–187) as it does about the decision-takers within Siemens.

The social standing of engineers, their status within society, and their long and thorough education, have significant repercussions for pay. Engineers in western Germany are rewarded handsomely. In 1993, in a joint project at Bristol between German and British personnel, the engineers from BMW were being paid twice as much as their counterparts from Rolls-Royce.

Engineers in the east

Since unification, many eastern German engineers have been recruited by companies from the western part of the country in an effort to meet skills shortages. Yet the recruiting companies are often disappointed with their new staff. Complaints abound that their technical competence is the equivalent of only eight-bit technology (in 1981, IBM introduced a sixteen-bit computer). Moreover, the training of these engineers, it is claimed, was too narrow because it was specifically related to the immediate needs of their former combines. Finally, the engineers tend to see only production problems and fail to heed the needs of the market.

Interpersonal skills are reported to have been hardly developed at all among former East German engineers. Their attitude to their superiors was one of blind obedience. They commonly assumed that the boss *must* be better informed: power is knowledge, therefore the boss was always right. Moreover, it is often alleged that engineers from the east are unable to work successfully in teams because they are incapable of motivating people. Motivation was not regarded as a management task in former East Germany, where orders came from the top down. According to one of the personnel managers of Germany's largest electrical company, these engineers are 'totally unsuited to management tasks'.

Conclusion

Business in Germany is taken very seriously, and so are business people. Many of business's foremost exponents appear regularly on television and radio, and are called upon to give frequent press interviews. Indeed a measure of the seriousness with which both business and business people are taken is provided by the large number of journals and newspapers devoted to business. Prominent among them are *Handelsblatt*, a daily newspaper; *Wirtschaftswoche*, a weekly magazine; and *Capital* and *manager-magazin*, both monthly journals. In addition, the daily newspapers *Frankfurter-Allgemeine*, *Die Welt* and *Süddeutsche Zeitung*, and the Sunday *Die Zeit*, all contain substantial business sections or supplements, as do many of the regional and local newspapers.

A more macabre measure of the significance of business in Germany is furnished by the thirty-two prominent business people and public figures who were murdered by terrorists in the 1970s, 1980s and early 1990s. The late Hanns-Martin Schleyer, chairman of the management board of Daimler-Benz at the time; Karl-Heinz Beckurts, director of research at Siemens; Alfred Herrhausen, chairman of the management board of the Deutsche Bank; and Detlev Rohwedder, head of the Treuhandanstalt, all fell victims to terrorism during this time. Now that there is no bolt-hole for terrorists, such as was provided for them by former East Germany, where the Stasi not only gave succour to fleeing members of the **Rote Armee Fraktion** (RAF) (Red Army Faction) but also trained them in long-range shooting and the use of explosives, it is devoutly to be wished that this period of fear and anxiety for western Germany's leading business people has finally passed into history.

13 Penetrating the German business culture

Introduction

The student of German business culture might be content to stop reading at the end of the previous chapter. The 'harder', factual and institutional aspects of the culture were treated in the earlier parts of the book, then attention was switched to the 'softer', less tangible, beliefs, attitudes and values. The practitioner, however, might justifiably feel frustrated if the book were to end without some thoughts on how this facinating business culture might be penetrated.

In the final chapter we shall consider just two potential penetration scenarios – marketing to Germany and acquiring a German company. These scenarios should bring together many of the issues emerging from what has gone before and point up others inherent in the business culture in Germany.

There are many ways in which foreign business people come into contact with their German counterparts. Buying products or services from German companies, or attending conferences, fairs and exhibitions represent just some of these encounters. Much that has already been written should help to interpret the different facets of the German business culture that will be witnessed on such occasions. But actually penetrating the business culture in a more active manner is a task requiring separate consideration.

Active penetration of the German business culture is not easy. It is a mission that should be embarked upon only after much deliberation and planning. As we have already seen, business people in Germany hold certain beliefs, adopt certain attitudes, cherish certain values and evidence certain behaviours that are unique to their culture, and these must be respected on all occasions if penetration is to be successful.

Penetrating by marketing

The nature of the market

With imports totalling some DM 526 billion, western Germany alone boasted the world's largest import market back in 1987. Since unification in 1990, the value of imports into the enlarged country has risen to a staggering DM 750 billion per annum. On the evidence of these figures it would appear logical to conclude that marketing to Germany is child's play. Nothing could be farther from the truth.

Germany is a buyer's market. It is one where the private consumer or the industrial buyer is seeking to purchase products or services of a high standard, and at German prices. Germans, especially those in the west, where the main purchasing power currently lies, have been educated to be quality-conscious because they have constantly been told that **Deutsche Wertarbeit** (high-value German work) is the unique selling proposition for the goods and services they themselves produce. At the same time, the German purchaser is a sophisticated 'value engineer', extraordinarily adept at making subconscious value/price trade-offs when buying.

Yet the potential supplier to Germany should not be put off. Though difficult to penetrate, the market in Germany is lucrative. It is also open, and one where there has never been a 'Buy German' campaign since 1945. But Germans have no shortage of goods and services to choose from, because domestic industry provides almost universal coverage, and foreign suppliers have not been slow to discover the rich potential of the market. At the same time, however, it must be stated that both individual German consumers and industrial buyers do express a preference for products and services 'Made in Germany' (see p. 143).

A well-organized, long-term marketing plan is thus an indispensable prerequisite for success. Such a plan would embrace some or all of the following features, and probably many more.

Product/service strategy

To be successful in the German market, the foreign supplier must be not only as good as the German competitor but better. Only in very exceptional cases does the German market provide a suitable outlet for excess or non-recurring lines of production. This means that the foreign supplier must excel in terms of product or service quality, new product technology, general technical competence, customer orientation, commercial competence, delivery performance, and after-sales service. In other words, the foreign supplier must emulate those virtues the small and medium-sized German companies treasure so highly and to which they attribute their success in their own export markets (see p. 186).

To select just one industrial product area, the German market for finished and semi-finished products, particularly labour-intensive products, is especially attractive. This is on account of Germany's own high labour costs in both the western and the eastern states (see pp. 120−124). In the case of technically-sophisticated items the guarantee terms, a qualified repair service and compliance with regulations laid down by the **Deutsches Institut für Normung** (DIN) (German Standards Institute) are essential prerequisites for business success.

Though the advent of Europe's Single Market from 1 January 1993 was intended to establish Europe-wide technical standards, which had hitherto been regarded as invisible barriers to trade, some foreign companies were still experiencing problems with German standards institutions half way through 1993. It is often not enough merely to gain DIN apporval. Further standards for specific areas are worked out, for example, by the **Verein Deutscher Ingenieure e.V.** (VDI) (Association of German Engineers), the **Deutscher Verein des Gas- und Wasserfachs e.V.** (DVGW) (German Association of Gas and Water Engineers), the **Verband Deutscher Elektrotechniker e.V.** (VDE) (Association of German Electrical Technicians), the **Abwassertechnische Vereinigung e.V.** (ATV) (Waste Water Technology Association), and the **Luftfahrt Bundesamt** (Federal Aviation Office).

Special attention should be paid to the **Technische Überwachungsvereine** (TÜV) (Industrial Safety Surveillance Associations). The TÜV associations, which are organized regionally throughout Germany, are unified under an umbrella organization, the **Vereinigung Technischer Überwachungsvereine e.V.** (VTÜV) (Federation of Industrial Safety Surveillance Associations). The Federation and the individual associations prepare and publish codes covering, for example, safety inspection of steam boilers, lifts and other systems requiring technical surveillance, as set forth under Section 24 of the HGB (see p. 45).

As far as consumer products are concerned, the market in Germany is influenced by the rising average age of the population (see pp. 93–94). As a result of an extremely low birth rate, a relatively small share of disposable income is devoted to satisfying basic needs. This sets free a considerable amount of buying power in the country, which is then devoted to more distinctive, individual needs (education, travel, skin and body care, sport, information, fashion, entertainment, etc.). As a consequence, the focal point of marketing efforts has shifted slightly, away from basic market research (identifying existing needs) and towards market initiation (creating new needs) (see Figure 13.1).

The development of a new range of consumer products (travel accessories, sporting goods items, cosmetics, games, etc.) makes it necessary for the foreign supplier to devote considerable creative sensitivity to new trends. Although international design trends and fashion items certainly appeal to the younger generations, the more general German market continues to be characterized by a preference for functional styles and colour tones. This basically conservative attitude is augmented to an ever-increasing extent by the demand for environmental soundness in terms of production techniques, in the consumer

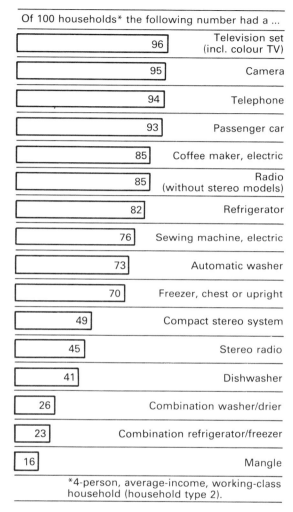

Of 100 households* the following number had a ...

96	Television set (incl. colour TV)
95	Camera
94	Telephone
93	Passenger car
85	Coffee maker, electric
85	Radio (without stereo models)
82	Refrigerator
76	Sewing machine, electric
73	Automatic washer
70	Freezer, chest or upright
49	Compact stereo system
45	Stereo radio
41	Dishwasher
26	Combination washer/drier
23	Combination refrigerator/freezer
16	Mangle

*4-person, average-income, working-class household (household type 2).

Figure 13.1 *Selected consumer durables in private households in 1990. Source: Statistisches Bundesamt*

goods themselves, and in their packaging (see pp. 176 and 178). Several new markets have opened up in connection with the German sensitivity to the environment, and foreign manufacturers have an opportunity to profit here, in terms of processes, products and packaging innovations.

In general, when marketing to Germany, the foreign supplier would be well advised to think product or service first, second and third, before considering any of the other elements of the marketing mix.

Pricing strategy

Yet any marketing strategy must also embrace serious considerations of pricing. Products or services which command premium prices in the home country will probably not be able to command these same premiums in Germany, on account of the tough competition in virtually all market sectors there.

Thus it is not enough to convert domestic prices into DM prices. Nor should the DM price of the product or service be allowed to drift upwards as a result of own-country devaluations or German revaluations. An exporter to Germany faced with rising costs might be advised to bite the bullet and trim profit margins rather than risk losing market share through unrealistic price increases. Imported inflation is, in German eyes, the very worst form of inflation, a phenomenon all Germans abhor (see pp. 57–59).

Conversely, pitching prices too low on the German market will not meet with success either. In the past some foreign companies unable to meet German quality standards have entered the market with prices much lower than German price levels. The outcome has usually been unsuccessful, because the German purchaser has a habit of looking upon prices which are too low as indicative of inferior quality product. With so much disposable income, the German domestic consumer will not purchase what is perceived as low quality. In the long term there is no alternative to take what the market defines as quality as a given, and to pitch prices accordingly.

Only products or services which are truly competitive, and offered in Germany within the framework of a realistic pricing strategy, will hold out any promise of substantial orders over the long term.

Place strategy

There is obviously no simple recipe available for successful distribution strategy in Germany. First, the size of the united country is huge. Second, regional tastes within Germany vary enormously. Third, circumstances differ from one supplier company to another, and from one product or service to another. The foreign supplier must conduct studies to determine which distribution channel best suits his or her products or services. The length of the distribution chain is not the criterion for sales success: this is determined by the nature, range and prices of goods or services on offer.

Depending on the supplier company's strategy, the size and make-up of its own-country operation, the nature of the product or service concerned, there is a choice between selling into Germany through an importer, appointing a German agent or distributor, operating from one or more warehouses in Germany, or setting up a manufacturing facility there.

Owing to the continuing diversity and complexity of customs laws, technical regulations and other specialist legislation, such as that affecting pure food or packaging, it is often advisable for a foreign supplier to seek to establish long-term business relations with a qualified German importer. The specialized import traders, and the retail and wholesale firms that import direct, are familiar with all the rules and regulations and can inform foreign suppliers accordingly. In addition, they may take care of warehousing and some financing of the imported goods. Many also have their own distribution organizations and networks of representatives.

The distribution channels mentioned above are those in which foreign suppliers conclude contracts direct with German importers. There is, in addition, the option of using an intermediary in the shape of a sales representative or agent. The sales representative is of particular importance to those foreign suppliers that wish to work the German market intensively but do not wish to use a direct importer or to set up their own warehouse or manufacturing subsidiary.

If it is decided to appoint an agent or distributor, great care should be taken in the final choice. The agent or distributor should not be given the contract just because he or she is available. Is he/she a quality agent? Who else does he/she represent? (In Germany it is common for the sales representative to work with several companies whose products are complementary.) Is the quality of the other products commensurate with that of the foreign supplier? Where does the agent operate now? A German agent might agree to a franchise to sell throughout Germany when in practice his/her real trading area is merely one of the smaller states. In fact different agents might be needed for different states or regions to cater for their distinctive and individualist tastes. Indeed the HGB recognizes this by allowing a supplier to appoint geographically-exclusive agents for different regions. The **Centralvereinigung Deutscher Handelsvertreter- und Handelsmakler-Verbände** (CDH) (Central Federation of German Sales Representatives' and Sales Agents' Associations) will arrange contact with qualified representatives. A sample of a sales agency contract can also be acquired from the Federation.

In practice it is often advisable to consult the IHK in the exporter's own country (see p. 140), the home-country supplier's promotion agency, or the **Bundesstelle für Außenhandelsinformation** (BfAI) (Federal Office for Foreign Trade Information), when selecting the distribution channel for a particular product or service.

Promotion strategy

Any commercial advertising for foreign consumer products or services must proceed from the standpoint that the German market is already saturated. It may prove successful where the foreign supplier manages to conform to local advertising techniques or attempts to gain a foothold for a product through 'forced' competition. Foreign suppliers would, however, enhance their opportunities if they were to locate, and direct their advertising, towards areas of unfulfilled needs.

Indeed the most difficult task for foreign suppliers is to find new market niches for their products or services. This may be done by segmenting the market into several consumer groups, and then by directing the advertising towards the segment identified. For example, the German economy employs numerous foreign workers, all of whom have special culturally conditioned consumer needs (see pp. 100–106).

Commercial advertising in Germany must adapt to the prevailing marketing concepts. It should be based not on the marketing suppositions in the home country but on the special circumstances in Germany. There are a number of market research companies and advertising agencies whose services are available to the foreign supplier, and these should be used. Information relating to such organizations can be obtained from the **Zentralausschuß der Werbewirtschaft e.V.** (ZAW) (Central Office of the German Advertising Association).

A league table of Germany's ten leading brand names, compared with the top ten in Europe and the world, speaks for itself. Germans think most highly of technological brands such as Mercedez-Benz, Volkswagen, Bosch, BMW, Siemens and AEG – yet another reflection of the German fascination with Technik (see pp. 19–31 and 203–204). Half the top brands in Europe are produced in Germany. Though Mercedez-Benz comes third in both the European and world league tables, Coca-Cola is clearly unbeatable (Table 13.1).

Department stores, supermarket branches, and independent chains of retail stores sometimes give preference to foreign products in their own advertisements. To participate in the **Werbewochen** (promotion weeks) that are frequently sponsored by the various types of stores, it is necessary to display a sufficiently large range of foreign products. At other times, however, the stores will offer a whole series of products under a special theme, e.g. the fashions for a particular season, or consumer preferences on certain holidays and feast days.

For marketing industrial products in particular, a **Messe** (trade fair) or **Ausstellung** (exhibition) is often a useful entry point to the German market. Just one glance at the schedule of German trade fairs indicates a comprehensive programme of international and national fairs and exhibitions staged annually throughout the country. In fact 60 per cent

Table 13.1   *Leading brand names by esteem in Germany, Europe and the World*

Germany's top ten		Europe's top ten		The World's top ten	
1	Mercedes-Benz	1	Coca-Cola	1	Coca-Cola
2	Volkswagen	2	Sony	2	Sony
3	Bosch	3	Mercedes-Benz	3	Mercedes-Benz
4	ZDF	4	BMW	4	Kodak
5	BMW	5	Philips	5	Disney
6	Siemens	6	Volkswagen	6	Nestlé
7	ARD	7	Adidas	7	Toyota
8	Aldi	8	Michelin	8	McDonald's
9	AEG	9	Nivea	9	IBM
10	Adidas	10	Porsche	10	Pepsi Cola

Source: First Landor Image Power Survey 1992

of all international trade fairs are held in Germany, and there are more than 100 international fairs for use by the business world, touching on every sector of consumer and capital goods.

Participation in a fair can be of help in introducing a product to the market. Indeed a fair should be used to exhibit those products an initial market survey has shown to be of interest to the German market. It should be noted, however, that a display of goods is not designed primarily as a means of direct marketing. Though transactions concluded at the fair are a useful indicator, it is often post-fair sales that prove to be the more reliable yardstick. Trade-fair participation is actually used by German companies both to launch new products and to keep an eye on what competitors, especially those from abroad, are doing in the fields of product enhancement and innovation.

Careful preparation for a fair is decisive for success. Applications to participate must be submitted on time, and requests for technical equipment and back-up personnel should not be left till the last minute. Goods for display should be carefully selected with an eye to the German market. Company personnel on the stand must be capable of providing specific counselling and answering any technical and commercial questions posed by visitors. Therefore company employees present should possess the appropriate technical and linguistic competencies.

A word of warning about trade fairs and exhibitions would appear appropriate at this stage. Ever since the mid-1980s Germany has been suffering from **Messe-Müdigkeit** (trade-fair fatigue). There are perhaps too many trade fairs and exhibitions in the country, with the result that attendance figures at certain of these events have been declining. It is very important therefore for the foreign supplier to focus his or products on the most successful fairs. Information about fairs and hibitions in Germany can be obtained from the **Ausstellungs- und Messe-Ausschuß der Deutschen Wirtschaft e.V.** (AUMA) (Confederation of German Exhibition and Trade Industries).

No matter how good the marketing strategy, instant results should not be expected from initial forays into Germany. A medium-term commitment to the market is required, one that will embrace strategic thinking, hard work and tenacity, before rewards are forthcoming in this demanding culture. German companies feel that they have had to work long and hard to nurture their own export markets. They perceive little reason to make life easy for foreign suppliers to penetrate Germany.

Penetrating by acquiring

To date, public takeovers in the Anglo-American sense have not in any way formed a significant part of the German business culture. Hostile takeovers are virtually unknown, and no firm ground rules exist to cover them. This is due to what might be regarded by British and American corporate lawyers as a lack of sophistication in German corporate structures. It is also due to the fact that many substantial businesses are still closely controlled or family owned, e.g. Siemens, BMW, Henkel and many more. In addition, the substantial equity stakes held in large companies by the private commercial banks, either for their own account or as proxies (see pp. 63−66), have restricted takeover activity.

Recently, however, businesses in Germany, quite apart from those in eastern Germany on offer by the Treuhandanstalt, have increasingly become targets for takeovers and acquisitions by foreign companies. Among the factors responsible for this trend are the new second-tier market for German companies on the eight regional German stock exchanges (see pp. 69−70), pressure on banks to reduce their influence on non-financial companies, and general efforts to 'internationalize' the German market. Another increasingly important factor is that many Mittelstand companies formed after the Second World War are now facing succession issues (see pp. 184−185).

In general, foreign companies may act as offerors in the German market on the same footing as German companies, whether in public or private transactions. Thus, it is not necessary for reasons of corporate law for an offeror to act through a wholly-owned subsidiary incorporated in Germany. For statistical purposes, acquisitions must be notified to the Bundesbank.

Public takeovers

In the context of a public acquisition the target encountered will be an AG (see pp. 50–53). Although stock-exchange takeovers have not been significant to date, the second-tier market segment has awakened new interest in this area.

There are no statutory rules affecting takeovers, although general corporate law as stipulated in the HGB does cover such areas as transfer of shares, anti-trust issues and filing requirements. There is no regulatory authority like the Panel on Takeovers and Mergers in the United Kingdom. Nor are the eight regional stock exchanges obliged to suspend trading in the shares of a company that is the target of an agreed or hostile takeover, although this has occurred in practice.

Such rules as do exist are purely voluntary guidelines, as promulgated by the Stock Exchange Committee of Experts in 1979. These guidelines apply to public offers to shareholders of an AG for the purchase of shares, stock options or transfer rights from convertible bonds and option bonds. In this sense the guidelines are similar to the City Code on takeovers and mergers in the United Kingdom.

There is no tradition of statutory insider dealing rules, although such rules were approved by the federal cabinet in November 1993 following the EC Insider Trading Directive (see pp. 72–73). There is, however, a voluntary code, which AGs listed on the stock exchanges tend to sign, although they are not obliged to do so.

The principal points covered by the guidelines are as follows:

- Strict confidentiality must be observed by any person participating in negotiations until such are made public or abandoned.
- The offeror must inform the target of any offer and must solicit its comments.
- During the offer period the offeror must refrain from any action that may have a negative effect on the target's share price.
- All shareholders of a particular class of share must receive equal treatment.
- An offer must be open for at least twenty-one days and not more than sixty days. If the offer is revised, it must be open for at least fourteen days even if such exceeds the sixty-day limit.

For a whole variety of reasons, a public takeover in Germany, and particularly a hostile takeover, is surrounded by difficulties. The principal impediments stem from lack of information and from specific legal hurdles.

Listed AGs are required by the Stock Exchange Act to give additional information beyond that in their statutory accounts (see pp. 77–87), which could substantially affect the value of their shares. But markedly less information has to be filed than in the United Kingdom or in the United States of America.

A further problem is that it is often difficult to identify the shareholders in an AG, since in many cases shares are issued in bearer, rather than registered, form (see p. 50). Moreover, a shareholder is not required to disclose an interest in an AG until this reaches 25 per cent, and again on exceeding 50 per cent. Similarly, the target does not have to provide the offeror with information on its shareholders and their holdings, or any other information unless the offeror is already a shareholder and can exercise statutory rights to such information. Even in the capacity as a shareholder, the offeror may face difficulties, since the target's management is required by law, subject to criminal sanctions, not to disclose secret information.

One of the principal legal hurdles in the path of an offeror is the necessity to acquire at least a 75 per cent voting stake in the target. Although this is not dissimilar to the 75 per cent limit in the United Kingdom to pass a special resolution, the subsequent link between a 75 per cent shareholding and control over the target is not so strong. Here the supervisory board can present a further difficulty (see p. 51). Although an offeror may replace members of the supervisory board once 75 per cent of the votes have been acquired, since the members of this board are normally appointed for five years, there will be some delay before the offeror's nominees constitute a majority on this board.

It is not possible for the offeror compulsorily to acquire the shares of minority shareholders who do not accept an offer. Thus the offeror may be left with a rump of non-accepting shareholders.

In principle, the target may take any action permitted by the Stock Exchange Act and its own articles to defend against a hostile offer. Thus, in addition to the myriad of hurdles inherent in German law, some 'poison pill' tactics as used in the United Kingdom and the United States of America may be used in Germany to discourage offerors. One difference worth noting is that under German law management may not grant itself excessive termination payments. Thus an offeror should not have to anticipate unreasonable 'golden parachutes'.

Other defences common in Germany relate to the fact that many AGs have provisions in their articles restricting the maximum voting rights exercisable by any one shareholder, regardless of the size of shareholding. Similarly, it is not uncommon for large numbers of non-voting shares to be listed, while the voting shares are concentrated in a small number of 'friendly' hands.

The absence of statutory rules regulating takeovers, the dearth of information on target companies, and the intricacies of German commercial law all combine to render hostile takeovers virtually impossible for potential foreign acquirers. Thus the most that they can realistically hope for is an agreed takeover. This situation will not be resolved until EC directives covering the acquisitions area are published and enacted into national legislation. Even then, it should not be beyond the wit of clever German managements and company lawyers to frustrate unwanted suitors.

Negotiated acquisitions

The vast majority of successful negotiated acquisitions in Germany concern GmbHs or GmbH & Co. KGs (see pp. 48–50). The basic information on such companies, e.g. share capital, articles, directors' names, is contained in the Commercial Register at the local court (see p. 47). There is no central register of companies and partnerships.

Particularly in the early stages of an approach to a Mittelstand company, a potential foreign acquirer must search for that inestimable German quality of **Fingerspitzengefühl** (tact and sensitivity). A factor of entirely disproportionate importance in acquiring a small to medium-sized company in Germany is the etiquette that is expected by the selected target. It is vital for the acquirer to remember that he or she is dealing in the main with owner-drivers, people who have themselves built up the company or watched their own parents do so. There will almost inevitably be a strong family tradition to respect.

Imagine the culture shock if the owner were to learn that the family company was being considered as an acquisition. It is just not possible, as in other business cultures, to telephone the owner out of the blue and say 'We're interested in buying your company. Can we talk?' German business people are in business for the long term. They think long term, and anyone wishing to acquire them with an essentially short-term approach could be in serious trouble.

One consideration in the acquisition process should be the recognition that owner-drivers do not like to become passengers. They should not be confused with employees, and very early in any acquisition it is important to identify someone in top management as a future managing director. Yet the owner will probably have built a company in which he or she was entirely in charge. A cadre of competent senior managers may well be left behind, but they will probably be unused to accepting ultimate responsibility (see p. 85).

A further consideration in the acquisition relates to the thorny issue of asking for financial details. Vendors will be extremely reluctant to hand over financial data until they are completely sure of the acquirers (see p. 90). Acquiring practitioners have encountered many cases in which the audited figures were not tabled until the due diligence stage had been reached. The reason for this is that the figures produced were mainly intended to minimize the tax liability rather than reveal the true worth of the company (see p. 77).

The different business cultures permeate the whole process of acquisition, from the delicacy of the approach through the valuation to the final structuring of the deal. One of the most important cultural factors that can cause trouble between German small and medium-sized companies and their potential foreign acquirers is the preference of the former for debt rather than equity. German businesses are much less capitalized than, for example, British businesses. This is perhaps because most Mittelstand businesses have spent a long time building up assets from their own strength, i.e. from their own cashflow. There is comparatively little external equity capital in such companies. Thus the acquirer must be prepared to see a balance sheet from the target which is apparently undercapitalized, and which is seeking to sell at a high multiple of book net worth.

The general advice on valuation given by professional acquirers is to use the technique that is most familiar to the foreign acquirer, and not to attempt to 'Germanize' the valuation calculations themselves. This means using a capitalized earnings basis, discounted cashflow analysis, discounted net assets, or a combination of these. In the end future cashflow is crucial to all the respectable and workable valuation techniques.

Yet appreciation of any future earnings stream requires very subjective analysis, and the essence of the early negotiations is to determine the likelihood of the vendor's projections bearing much resemblance to reality. In discussions with vendors, at this stage of the valuation, frequent references will be heard to **Zukunftsmusik** ('jam tomorrow'). Though any estimate of future cashflows must begin with an examination of the past, the potential acquirer must find out whether past earnings have been dressed up or, more likely, dressed down to avoid tax. A potential foreign acquirer must also wonder how much the company's earnings picture would have been improved if none of the owner's family had received either salaries or fringe benefits, such as Mercedez-Benz cars, or even yachts berthed in the Mediterranean.

The data a foreign acquirer is given will need substantial adjustment before they can be fed into any valuation model. They will not be reliable because they were not produced for the acquirer. So the acquirer must examine the scope for silent reserves in the real estate; the equipment must be carefully appraised to see whether there has been exaggerated use of the depreciation rules (see pp. 81–82), and the stock must be estimated to see what is really there; and what the market and replacement values are. Thus the most important task before detailed valuation calculations can commence is to clean up the data.

One technique to be avoided is the Stuttgart valuation. It may sound well established, and it is widely used in Germany, but caution is advised. The Stuttgart technique is a method generated by the Stuttgart taxation authorities. It is essentially for taxation purposes. As a generalization, it is based about one-third on the substance value of the company according to net asset value and two-thirds on yield. Yet its real pitfall is that it uses historical data, and it is neither meaningful nor useful in the context of company valuation. If vendors try to use this method, they may be reluctant to speak about future profits.

Structuring the acquisition is a subject of endless complexity. In general, Mittelstand companies show an aversion to anything other than cash. Most vendors are still very unwilling to accept shares as part of the price because the German stock market is relatively weak in international terms and because the companies themselves possess so little external equity. Some Mittelstand owners are, however, prepared to consider an earn-out: either an active earn-out where they work for a few years and continue to run the company and to instruct the new management; or a passive earn-out where they sell the company, disappear after a month or so, but are paid over a period of a few years.

The best advice for would-be foreign acquirers is to engage an adviser. He or she will assist in approaching the vendor correctly, usually by means of someone the vendor trusts. Once friendly contact has been established, financial data can be asked for. Such data will then be reconstructed before a valuation is made, probably by means of a discounted cashflow technique. A cash offer usually follows. Throughout the whole process it is vital for the acquirer to remember that he or she is dealing with a private company. Hostile bids are out of the question, and a hostile or aggressive approach is almost certainly doomed to failure.

Conclusion

Considerations of marketing to Germany, public takeovers and negotiated acquisitions indicate just how difficult it is to penetrate the German business culture. Yet suppliers and managements in other countries will be obliged increasingly to come to terms with this culture as the German economy develops further into the powerhouse of Europe. With the largest population and the dominant economy in the EC, Germany, many believe, is also set to re-exert a massive influence on its erstwhile economic hinterland in central Europe, after the not-inconsiderable problems in eastern Germany have been solved.

Once this fascinating business culture has been penetrated, at whatever level, foreign suppliers and managers will find that their efforts have been worthwhile. Not only should the financial rewards be considerable but they will also discover that German business people make firm and loyal business partners. To reach this point, however, the beliefs, attitudes and values making up the business culture in Germany must be understood and respected at all times.

It is to be hoped that this book has made a contribution, no matter how minor, to the appreciation of the business culture in Germany.

Sources and suggestions for further reading

Albach, H. (1992), 'Upswing with brakes', in *WHU-Nachrichten*, Koblenz, Vol. 2.

Ambrosius, G. (1984), *Der Staat als Unternehmer*, Göttingen: Vandenhoeck and Ruprecht.

Ardagh, J. (1987), *Germany and the Germans*, London: Hamilton.

Banker, The, various issues between 1982 and 1993.

Berghahn, V.R. and Karsten, D. (1987), *Industrial Relations in West Germany*, Oxford, New York and Hamburg: Berg.

von Beyme, K. (1980), *Challenge to Power: Trade Unions and Industrial Relations in Capitalist Countries*, London: Sage.

Böhler, W. (1984), *Betriebliche Weiterbildung und Bildungsurlaub*, Cologne: Centenarius.

Bundesumweltministerium (1992), *Unweltschutz in Deutschland*, Bonn: Economica-Verlag.

Bundesumweltministerium (1992), *Das Bundesumweltministerium*, Hausen: Verlag Druck-Service E. Böhm.

Burda, M. (1990), 'The Consequences of German Economic and Monetary Union', in *INSEAD Research and development of pedagogical materials working papers*.

Bundesverband der Deutschen Industrie e.V. (1992), *BDI-Bericht 1990–92*, Cologne: Industrie-Förderung GmbH.

Bundesverband der Deutschen Industrie e.V. (1992), *Der Betriebliche Umweltschutzbeauftragte*, Cologne: Heider.

Bundesverband der Deutschen Industrie e.V. (1992), *Eine gute Verbindung*, Cologne.

Bildung und Wissenschaft, various issues between 1982 and 1993, Bonn: Inter Nationes.

Bundesvereinigung der Deutschen Arbeitgeberverbände (1992), *Der Arbeitgeber*, Cologne.

Bundesvereinigung der Deutschen Arbeitgeberverbände (1993), *Jahresbericht 1992*, Cologne.

Bundesvereinigung der Deutschen Arbeitgeberverbände (1992), *Organisationsplan*, Cologne.

Business International Ltd (1992), *Control from Brussels*, London: The Economist.

Capital, various issues between 1982 and 1993.

Carl, M. and Zahn, P. (1982), *The German Private Limited Company*, London.

Childs, D. (1992), *Germany in the Twentieth Century*, London: Batsford.

Childs, D. and Johnson, J. (1981), *West Germany – Politics and Society*, London: Croom Helm.

Cowling, K. and Tomann, H. (1990), *Industrial Policy after 1992: An Anglo-German Perspective*, London: Anglo-German Foundation for the Study of Industrial Society.

Deutsche Angestellten-Gewerkschaft (1992), *Zur wirtschaftlichen und sozialen Lage in den neuen Bundesländern im Frühherbst 1992*, Hamburg.

Deutscher Beamtenbund (1992), *Mainzer Beschlüsse*, Bonn.

Deutscher Industrie- und Handelstag (1987), *Herausforderung Außenwirtschaft*, Bonn.

Deutscher Industrie- und Handelstag (1988), *Wegweiser zum EG-Binnenmarkt*, Bonn.

Economist, The, various issues between 1982 and 1993.

European Industrial Relations Review, various issues between 1992 and 1993.

Facts about Germany (1992), Frankfurt/Main: Societätsverlag.

FIDA (1986), *Frauen als Führungskräfte der Wirtschaft*, Hamburg.

Financial Times, various editions between 1982 and 1993.

Fritsch-Bournazel, R. (1992), *Europe and German Unification*, New York, Oxford: Berg.

Globale Umweltpolitik tut Not (1992), Bonn: Inter Nationes/Economica Verlag.

Grund-und Strukturdaten 1992/93, Der Bundesminister für Bildung und Wissenschaft, Bonn.

Handy, C. et al. (1988), *Making Managers*, London: Pitman.

Harvard Business Review, various issues between 1982 and 1993.

Heidensohn, K. (1984), *Fachhochschulen and Polytechnics*, Bristol.

Issing, O. (1993), *Unabhängigkeit der Notenbank und Geldwertstabilität*, Stuttgart: Franz Steiner Verlag.

Jäkel, E. and Junge, W. (1988), *Die deutschen Industrie- und Handelskammern und der Deutsche Industrie- und Handelstag*, Düsseldorf: Droste.

Jürgens, U., Klinzing, L. and Turner, L. (1993), 'The Transformation of Industrial Relations in Eastern Germany', in *Industrial and Labor Relations Review*, Volume 46, No. 2, January.

Kloss, G. (1989), *West Germany: An Introduction*, Basingstoke: Macmillan.

Koch, K. (1989), *West Germany Today*, London: Routledge.

Lafferty, M. (1975), *Accounting in Europe*, Cambridge: Woodlands-Faulkner Ltd.

Lawrence, P. (1980), *Managers and Management in West Germany*, London: Croom Helm.

Locke, R.R. (1985), 'Business Education in Germany; Past Systems and Current Practice', in *Business History Review*, Summer 1985, Harvard.

Manager-Magazin, various issues between 1982 and 1993.

Markovitz, A. (1986), *The Politics of the West German Trade Unions*, Cambridge: Cambridge University Press.

Nobes, C.W. (1992), *Accounting Harmonization in Europe*, London: *Financial Times*.

Petit, M. (1991), *L'Europe Interculturelle – Mythe ou Réalité*, Paris: Les Éditions d'Organisation.

Price Waterhouse (1992), *Doing Business in Germany*, London.

Randlesome, C. (1990), 'Making Middle Managers?', in *Journal of European Industrial Training*, Volume 14, Number 4, MCB University Press Ltd.

Randlesome, C. (1992), 'East German Managers — From Karl Marx to Adam Smith?', in *European Management Journal*, Volume 10, Number 1, March.

Randlesome, C. *et al.* (1993), *Business Cultures in Europe*, Oxford: Butterworth-Heinemann.

Report, various issues between 1982 and 1993.

Scala, various issues between 1982 and 1993.

Schuster, D. (1977), *Der Deutsche Gewerkschaftsbund*, Düsseldorf: Droste.

Seitz, K. (1991), *The Japanese — American Challenge — Germany's High-Tech Industries Battle for Survival*, Munich: Verlag Bonn Aktuell.

Simon, H. (1992), 'Lessons from Germany's Midsize Giants', in *Harvard Business Review*, March—April.

Smith, G. (1992), *Democracy in Western Germany*, Aldershot: Gower.

Smith, P. (1981), *The Administration of Justice in the Federal Republic of Germany*, Limburg/Lahn: Hemmelsbach-Verlag.

Smyser, W.R. (1992), *Economy of United Germany: Colossus at the Crossroads*, Boston: C. Hurst.

Spiegel, Der, various issues between 1982 and 1993.

Sunday Times, The, various issues between 1982 and 1993.

Thelen, K. (1991), *Union of Parts: Labour Politics in Postwar Germany*, Ithaca, New York: Cornell University Press.

Times, The, various editions between 1982 and 1993.

Touche Ross, (1992), *Harmonizing Accountancy in Europe*, London.

Walter, N. (1991) 'The Heyday of German Trade — Past, Present, or Future?', in *Meet United Germany*, Bonn: Atlantik-Brücke.

Watson, A. (1992), *The Germans: Who are they now?*, London: Thames Methuen.

Wegen, G. (1990), *Forms of Doing Business in Germany*, Stuttgart: Gleiss, Lutz, Hootz, Hirsch & Partner.

Williams, K. (1988), *Industrial Relations and the German Model*, Aldershot: Avebury.

Witte, E., Kallmann, A. and Sachs G. (1989), *Führungskräfte der Wirtschaft*, Cologne: Poeschel.

Zeit, Die, various issues between 1982 and 1993.

Index

Aachener und Münchener (AMB), 66
Abitur (A-level certificate), 147
Abs, Hermann, 63
Abwassertechnische Vereinigung
    e.V. (ATV) (Waste Water
    Technology Association), 210
Accountants, training of, 88
Accounting harmonization, 89–92
Acid rain, 166
Acquisitions, see takeovers
Adenauer, Konrad, 1, 56
Administrative courts, see
    Verwaltungsgerichte
    (administrative courts)
Advanced technology, export of, 26
Advertising, commercial, 214
Agents, German, 213
Agriculture, 33–5
Air pollution, 166, 177
    successes against, 173–4
Airports, 36
Akademien für sozialistische
    Wirtschaftsführung der
    Kombinate (combine academies
    for socialist economic
    management), 162
Aktiengesellschaft (AG) (stock
    corportation/limited liability
    public company), 50–3, 217–19
Aktiengesetz (AktG) (Stock
    Corporations Act) 1965, 50, 77
Albach, Horst, 202
Allfinanz (all-inclusive financial
    services), 66
Allgemeiner Deutscher
    Gewerkschaftsbund (ADGB), 123
Allgemeinverbindlich (generally
    binding), 113
Altersübergangsgeld (old-age
    transition payments), 97
Amtlicher Handel (full listing), 69
Amtsgerichte (local courts), 40

Angestellte (white-collar workers),
    110
Appeal courts, see
    Oberlandesgerichte (appeal
    courts)
Apprentices, see Lehrlinge
    (apprentices)
Arbeiter (blue-collar workers), 110
Arbeitgeberverband Eisen- und
    Stahlindustrie, 131
Arbeitgeberverbände (employers'
    associations), 129
Arbeitsämter (labour offices), 53
Arbeitsbeschaffungsmaßnahmen
    (job-creation measures), 96, 97
Arbeitsdirektor (personnel director/
    manager), 51, 131
Arbeitsgemeinschaft zur Förderung
    der Partnerschaft in der
    Wirtschaft e.V. (AGP), 194
Arbeitsgericht-Gesetz (Labour Courts
    Act) 1954, 41
Arbeitsgerichte (labour courts), 41
Arbitration, 118
Articles of association, see
    Gesellschaftsvertrag (articles of
    association)
Assets, valuation of, 81–3
Association for the Advancement of
    Partnership in Industry and
    Commerce, 194
Association of the Chemical Industry,
    24
Association of Communications
    Technology, 138
Association of German Chambers of
    Industry and Commerce, 129
Association of German Electrical
    Technicians, see Verband
    Deutscher Elektrotechniker
    (VDE)
Association of German Engineers,

see **Verein Deutscher Ingenieure e.V.** (VDI)

Association of German Machinery and Plant Manufacturers, 23−4

Association of Thuringian Industry, 139−40

Associations of Nationally-Owned Enterprises of GDR, 130

Asylanten (asylum-seekers), 93, 104−6

Asylum-seekers, *see* **Asylanten** (asylum-seekers)

Audit procedures, 87−8

auditors' report, 78

Aufschwung Ost (upturn in the east), 12

Aus- und Umbildungsmaßnahmen (training and retraining measures), 96

Ausbildung (initial vocational training), 149

Ausbildungsvergütung (training remuneration), 148−9

Ausländerfeindlichkeit (hatred of foreigners), 106

Ausländerkriminalität (crime by foreigners, 106

Aussiedler (returnees), 93, 102−3

Ausstellung (exhibition), 214−16

Ausstellungs- und Messe-Ausschuß der Deutschen Wirtschaft e.V. (AUMA), 216

Auszubildende (Azubis) (trainees), 148

Autofriedhöfe (motor-car mortuaries), 180

Automobile industry, 23, 180

Automobilwerk Eisenach, 23

Bachmann, Heinz, 90, 91

Baden-Württemberg, 15, 16

Balance sheet, 81−6

Bargaining autonomy, *see* **Tarifautonomie** (bargaining autonomy)

BASF, 24, 64

Basic human rights, 39

Basic Law, *see* **Grundgesetz** (GG) (Basic Law)

Baumgartl, Wolf-Dietel, 66

Bayer, 24, 64, 179

Beamte (civil servants), 42

Beckurts, Karl-Heinz, 207

Berufsschulen (vocational schools), 148

Bessis (besserwissende Wessis), 17

Betriebsakademien (company academies), 96, 162

Betriebsrat (works' council), 114

Betriebsverfassungsgesetz (Works Constitution Act) 1972, 114, 115

Betriebswirtschaftslehre (BWL) (business economics), 147

Biedenkopf, Kurt, 16, 98

Bildungsurlaub (extra paid holidays for self-improvement), 157

Bitterfeld, 167

Blauer Engel (Blue Angel) award, 171

Blue Angel award, *see* **Blauer Engel** (Blue Angel) award

Blue-collar workers, *see* **Arbeiter** (blue-collar workers)

Blühende Landschaft ('blossoming landscape'), 11

BMW, 29, 121, 180

Bonds, 71

Börsenumsatzsteuer (stockmarket turnover tax), 70

Breuel, Birgit, 13, 191

Brinkhaus, 179−80

Budget deficits, public-sector, 17−18

Bulgarians, 106

Buna AG, 24

Bund der Steuerzahler (BdSt) (Taxpayers' Association), 9

Bundesamt für Strahlenschutz (BfS) (Fed. Off. for Radiological Protection), 173

Bundesanstalt für Arbeit (Federal Labour Office), 96

Bundesbank, 56−62

Bundesforschungsanstalt für Naturschutz und Landschaftsökologie (BFANL), 173

Bundesgerichtshof (Federal Court of Justice), 40−1

Bundeskartellamt (Federal Cartel Office), 63, 66

Bundesminister für Arbeit und Sozialordnung (Federal Min. of Labour and Social Affairs), 113, 131

Bundesministerium für Umwelt (BMU) (Federal Environment Ministry), 168, 169−71

Bundesnotarordnung (Federal Notary Act) 1961, 45
Bundesstelle für Aussenhandelsinformation (BfAI), 213
Bundesverband der Deutschen Industrie e.V. (BDI), 129, 130−2
branch activity, 137−8
in east, 138−40
Bundesverband Deutscher Unternehmensberater (BDU) (German Management Consultancy Association), 193
Bundesverband Druck (Printing Employers' Federation), 121
Bundesvereinigung der Deutschen Arbeitgeberverbände (BDA), 129, 130−2
Bundesverfassungsgericht (Federal Constitutional Court), 40
Bundeswirtschaftsministerium (BWM) (Federal Ministry of Economics), 189
Business associations, 129
Business crime, 55
Business press, 207
Business start-ups, 189−90

Capital, balance sheet display, 81
Car production, *see* Automobile industry
Carbon monoxide emissions, 174
Carl Zeiss Oberkochen, 14
Cash subsidies, 4
Central Authority for the Allocation of Study Places, 147
Central Federation of German Sales Representatives' and Sales Agents' Associations, 213
Central Office of the German Advertising Association, 214
Centralvereinigung Deutscher Handelsvertreter- und Handelsmakler-Verbände (CDH), 213
Centro Kontroll-Systeme, 189
Chairman, management board, 51
Chamber of Accountants/Auditors, 91
Chambers of industry and commerce, *see* **Industrie- und Handelskammern** (IHKs) (chambers of industry and commerce)

Chemical industry, 24, 179
Chemical-Workers' Union, *see* **IG Chemie** (Chemical-Workers' Union)
Chlorofluorocarbons, *see* **Fluorchlorkohlenwasserstoffe** (FCKWs) (chlorofluorocarbons)
Christian Democrats (CDU), 2, 3, 6, 8, 33, 108
Christian Socialists (CSU), 2, 6, 8
Christian Trade Union Federation, *see* **Christlicher Gewerkschaftsbund Deutschlands** (CGB)
Christlicher Gewerkschaftsbund Deutschlands (CGB) (Christian Trade Union Federation), 110
Civil servants, *see* **Beamte** (civil servants)
Civil Servants' Federation, *see* **Deutscher Beamtenbund** (DBB) (German Civil Servants' Federation)
Clean Air Act 1965, 168
Cleanliness, cost of, 29
Co-determination, 116
Co-determination Act for the Iron, Steel and Coal Industries 1951, 131
Co-op, 111, 112
Co-operative principle, *see* **Gemeinwirtschaft** (co-operative principle)
Co-operatives, agricultural, 34
Coal-Miners' Union, 127
Coca-Cola, 14, 214
Collective Agreements Act 1949, *see* **Tarifvertragsgesetz** (Collective Agreements Act)
Collective bargaining, 112−14, 131−2, 133−4
Collective Bargaining Association of German States, 131
Colleges, *see* **Hochschulen** (colleges)
Commercial Code, *see* **Handelsgesetzbuch** (HGB) (Commercial Code)
Commercial paper, DM, 71
Commercial Register, *see* **Handelsregister** (Commercial Register)
Commerzbank, 63−7
Communes, *see* **Gemeinden** (communes)
Communist Party, *see* **Sozialistische**

Einheitspartei Deutschlands (SED) (Communist Party)
Communist rule, East Germany, 38
Company:
  limited liability private, *see* **Gesellschaft mit beschränkter Haftung** (GmbH)
  limited liability public, *see* **Aktiengesellschaft** (AG)
Company academies, *see* **Betriebsakademien** (company academies)
Company performance, 92
Company wage agreements, *see* **Firmentarifverträge** (company wage agreements)
Comprehensive school, *see* **Gesamtschule** (comprehensive school)
Conciliation procedures, 118
Confederation of Communal Employers' Associations, 130–1
Confederation of Employers' Associations, 128, 129
Confederation of German Exhibition and Trade Industries, 216
Confederation of German Industry, 129
Confederation of German Trade Unions, 109
Consumer Initiative, *see* **Verbaucher-Initiative** (Consumer Initiative)
Consumer products, 210–11
Contingencies, disclosure of, 83
Continuing education, 156–7
Costs allocation, 82
Council for Mutual Economic Assistance (CMEA), 10, 31, 201
Craft chambers, *see* **Handwerkerkammern** (craft chambers)
Currency reform, 57

Daimler-Benz, 15, 27
Debt instruments, 71
Demographic trends, 6, 93–4
Depreciation, 82–3
Deregulation commission, 33
Deutsche Angestellten-Gewerkschaft (DAG) (German Union of Salaried Employees), 109, 114, 127
Deutsche Ausgleichsbank, 188
Deutsche Bank, 14, 62–7

Deutsche Binnenwerften GMbH (DBG) (East German Inland Shipyards), 193
Deutsche Börse (German Stock Exchange), 70
Deutsche Bundesbahn (DB), 3, 35
Deutsche Bundespost POSTBANK (banking services), 32
Deutsche Bundespost POSTDIENST (postal services), 32
Deutsche Bundespost TELEKOM (telecommunications), 9, 32
Deutsche Demokratische Republik (DDR) (German Democratic Republic), 10–12
Deutsche Mark (DM), 57, 73
  Balance Law, 54
Deutsche Reichsbahn (DR) (German Imperial Railways), 35, 123
Deutsche Siedlungs- und Landesrentenbank (DSL Bank), 7
Deutsche Termin-Börse (Options and Futures Exchange), 69
Deutsche Verkehrs-Kredit-Bank (DVKR), 7
Deutsche Volksarmee (German People's Army), 158
Deutsche Wertarbeit (high-value German work), 209
Deutscher Aktienindex (DAX) (German Share Index), 71
Deutscher Bauern-Verband (German Farmers' Association), 33
Deutscher Beamtenbund (DBB) (German Civil Servants' Federation), 109–10
Deutscher Gewerkschaftsbund (DGB) (Confederation of German Trade Unions), 109–10, 123, 127
Deutscher Industrie- und Handelstag (DIHT), 129, 140
Deutscher Verein des Gas- und Wasserfachs e.V. (DVGW) (German Assn. of Gas and Water Engineers), 210
Deutsches Institut für Normung (DIN) (German Standards Institute), 210
Deutsches Institut für Wirtschaftsforschung (DIW) (German Institute of Economic Research), 25
Diplom-Betriebswirt, 152
Diplom-Ingenieur, 152, 205

Diplomprüfung (diploma
    examination), 152
Distribution strategy, 212−13
Diversification, banking, 67
DM Balance Law, *see* **DM-
    Bilanzgesetz** (DM Balance Law)
DM-Bilanzgesetz (DM Balance Law),
    54
Doctorates, 153
Dresdner Bank, 14, 63−7
Duales System Deutschland (DSD)
    (Germany's Dual System), 178

Early-retirement measures, *see*
    Frühpensionierungsmaßnahmen
    (early-retirement measures)
East German Inland Shipyards, 193
East−west divide, *see* **Ost−West
    Gefälle** (east−west divide)
Eastern Germany, 8, 10−12, 26−7
    agriculture, 34
    automobile industry, 23
    banking operations, 67
    BDI in, 138−40
    business start-ups, 189−90
    chemical industry, 24
    education, 157−8, 159−60
    electrical industry, 25
    employment opportunities, 13,
       95−8
    environmental problems, 164−6,
       177
    female workers, 98
    food, beverages and tobacco
       industry, 25
    guest workers, 102
    investment in, 14, 27
    legal reorganization, 53−4
    management buyouts, 192−3
    management development, 160, 162
    management role, 199−203
    manufacturing industry, 21
    mechanical engineering industry,
       24
    small companies, 191−2
    start-ups, 189−90
    state co-operatives, 34
    structural adjustment, 13
    universities, 159−60
    vocational training, 158−9
Economic indicators, 2, 3
Economic miracle, *see*
    Wirtschaftswunder (economic
    miracle)

Economic statistics, manufacturing,
    20−2
Economic turnround, *see*
    wirtschaftliche Wende
    (economic turnround)
Education:
    continuing, 156−7
    in east:
       higher, 159−60
       school, 157−8
    in west:
       higher, 151−5
       school, 145−7
Einigungsstelle (arbitration
    committee), 118
Einigungsvertrag (Unification
    Treaty), 39
Einzelkaufmann (sole trader), 46
Elections, pan-German, 11
Electrical engineering industry, 24−5
Employers' Association of the Iron
    and Steel Industry, 131
Employers' associations, 129
Employers' organizations, 128−9
Employment opportunities, eastern
    German, 13
Endangered species, 168
Engineering Employers' Federation,
    see **Gesamtmetall** (Engineering
    Employers' Federation)
Engineers:
    in east, 203, 206
    in west, 203−6
Entrepreneurial union activity,
    111−12
Environmental agencies, 169−72
Environmental problems, 164−5
    business response, 177−81
    political response, 168
Environmental protection:
    export of technology, 26
    green shopping checklist, 181
    trade-union concerns, 125
Equity market, 68−71
Erhard, Ludwig, 1, 56
Eröffnungsbilanz (opening balance),
    54
Erweiterte Oberschule (extended
    school), 18
European Association of
    Manufacturers of Security
    Technology (EURALARM), 138
European Central Bank, 61−2, 72
European Community (EC), 4, 31

agricultural quotas, 33
environmental legislation, 181
Fourth Company Directive
  (company accounts), 89–91
Insider Trading Directive, 217
Seventh Company Directive
  (consolidated accounts), 89, 91
trade-union concerns, 126
European Monetary System (EMS),
  60–2
European Monetary Union (EMU), 18
European Telecommunications and
  Professional Electronics
  Industries (ECTEL), 138
Exchange Rate Mechanism (ERM),
  60–1
Exhibition, *see* **Ausstellung**
  (exhibition)
Existenzgründungen (business
  start-ups), 189–90
Export market, German, 25
Export marketing, to Germany,
  208–16

Fachhochschulen (polytechnics), 99,
  150, 151–2
Fachkaufleute examinations, 150
Fachoberschule (higher technical
  school), 147
Fachschule (technical school), 147
Fachspitzenverbände (branch
  associations), 130
**Fachverband
  Kommunikationstechnik**, 138
Fachverbände (trade associations),
  138
Fachwirte examinations, 150
Familiengerichte (family courts), 40
Family courts, *see* **Familiengerichte**
  (family courts)
Feast days, *see* **Feiertage** (feast days)
Federal Aviation Office, *see* **Luftfahrt
  Bundesamt** (Federal Aviation
  Office)
Federal Cartel Office, *see*
  Bundeskartellamt
Federal Constitutional Court, *see*
  Bundesverfassungsgericht
  (Federal Constitutional Court)
Federal Court of Justice, *see*
  Bundesgerichtshof (Federal
  Court of Justice)
Federal Environment Agency, *see*
  Umweltbundesamt (UBA)

  (Federal Environment Agency)
Federal Environment Ministry, *see*
  Bundesministerium für Umwelt
  (BMU) (Federal Environment
  Ministry)
Federal Labour Court, 133, 134
Federal Labour Office, 96
Federal Minister of Labour and Social
  Affairs, 113
Federal Ministry of Economics, *see*
  Bundeswirtschaftsministerium
  (BWM) (Federal Ministry of
  Economics)
Federal Ministry for Research and
  Technology, 30
Federal Notary Act 1961, *see*
  Bundesnotarordnung (Federal
  Notary Act)
Federal Office for Foreign Trade
  Information, 213
Federal Office for Radiological
  Protection, 173
Federal Research Centre for Nature
  Conservation and Landscape
  Ecology, 172
Federal Statistical Office, *see*
  Statistisches Bundesamt (Federal
  Statistical Office)
Federation of Industrial Safety
  Surveillance Associations, 210
Fee-charging system, lawyers', 44
Feiertage (feast days), 29
Female managers:
  in east, 203
  in west, 196–9
Female workers, in east, 98
FIDA research, 197, 198–9
Finance courts, *see* **Finanzgerichte**
  (finance courts)
Financial markets, 68–71
Financing, small-company, 187–8
Finanzgerichte (finance courts), 42
Finanzplatz Deutschland (Germany
  as a financial centre), 68, 70
Fingerspitzengefühl (tact and
  sensitivity), 219
Finkbeiner, Wolfgang, 193
Firmentarifverträge (company wage
  agreements), 113
Fluorchlorkohlenwasserstoffe
  (FCKWs) (chlorofluorocarbons),
  174
Food, beverages and tobacco
  industries, 25

Footnote disclosure, balance sheet, 83, 85

Foreign investment, in eastern Germany, 14

Foreign workers, *see* Guest workers

Forschung und Entwicklung (Research and Development), 19

Fortbildung (higher vocational training), 150

Fossa Carolina (Charlemagne's Ditch), *see* Rhine–Main–Danube Canal

Framework agreement, 113

Franke, Heinrich, 107

Free Democrats (FDP), 2, 9

Free German Trade Union Federation, 110–11, 123

Freier Deutscher Gewerkschaftsbund (FDGB) (Free German Trade Union Federation), 110–11, 123

Freizeitgesellschaft (leisure society), 26, 119, 165

Friedenspflicht (peace obligation), 117

Fringe benefits, 121

Frühpensionierungsmaßnahmen (early-retirement measures), 96–7

Gastarbeiter (guest workers), 36 in east, 102 in west, 100–102

GATT (General Agreement on Tariffs and Trade), 33, 35, 137

Gefahrengemeinschaft (mutual aid fund), 135

Gemeinden (communes), 142

Gemeinschaftsausschuß der Deutschen Gewerblichen Wirtschaft, 129

Gemeinwirtschaft (co-operative principle), 111–12

Gemu (German economic and monetary union), 9, 11, 59–60, 89, 93, 123

Geographical location benefits, 31

Geregelter Freiverkehr (regulated free market), 69

Geregelter Markt (regulated market), 69

German Association of Gas and Water Engineers, *see* **Deutscher Verein des Gas- und Wasserfachs e.V.**

German Democratic Republic, *see* **Deutsche Demokratische Republik**

German economic and monetary union, *see* Gemu

German Electrical and Electronic Manufacturers' Association, 137–8

German Farmers' Association, 33

German Institute of Economic Research, 25

German Management Consultancy Association, 193

German People's Army, 158

German Share Index, 71

German Standards Institute, *see* **Deutsches Institut für Normung** (DIN)

German Unity Fund, 71

Gesamtmetall (Engineering Employers' Federation), 120, 122, 134

Gesamtschule (comprehensive school), 162

Gesamtverband der Metallindustriellen Arbeitgeberverbände (Gesamtmetall), 132

Geschäftsführer (managing director), 49

Gesellschaft des bürgerlichen Rechts (GbR) (civil law partnership), 46

Gesellschaft mit beschränkter Haftung (GmbH) (limited liability private company), 48–50, 219–21

Gesellschaftsvertrag (articles of association), 49

Gesetz über die Deutsche Bundesbank (Bundesbank Act) 1957, 56–7

Gesetz zur Regelung offener Vermögensfragen (Law on the settlement of Open Questions Relating to Assets), 54

Gesetz zur vorläufigen Regelung des Rechtes der Industrie- und Handelskammern (IHKG), 142

Gessler Commission, 63

Gewerbeordnung (Trading Regulations), 122

Gewerbesteuer (trade tax), 129

Gewerbliche Wirtschaft (trading economy), 142
Gewerkschaft der Polizei (GdP) (Police Trade Union), 109
Gies, Helmut, 66
GmbH (limited liability private company), 48–50, 219–21
GmbH & Co KG (special limited partnership), 48
GmbH-Gesetz (Limited Liability (Private) Companies Act), 48–9
Gohlke, Rainer, 13
Goodyear, 121–2
Graduates, *see* Universities
Grammar school, *see* **Gymnasium** (grammar school)
Green checklist, shopping, 181
Green issues, *see* Environmental problems
Green police, 172–3
Greenhouse effect, *see* **Treibhauseffekt** (greenhouse effect)
Greens, the, *see* **Die Grünen** (the Greens)
Gross National Product (GNP), 4, 19–20, 204
Growth, economy, 2, 6, 7–8
Grundgesetz (GG) (Basic Law), 9, 38–9
Grundschule (primary school), 145
Grundstudium (foundation course), 151
Grünen, Die (the Greens), 6, 9, 168
Guest workers, *see* **Gastarbeiter** (guest workers)
Gymnasium (grammar school), 147

Handelsbevollmächtigter, 196
Handelsgesetzbuch (HGB) (Commercial Code), 45, 213, 217
Handelsregister (Commercial Register), 47, 50, 54, 219
Handelsschule (commercial college), 154
Handwerkerkammern (craft chambers), 148
Harmonization:
accounting, 89–92
working conditions, 123
Hauptschulabschluß (general school leaving certificate), 146
Hauptschule (general school), 145

Hauptstudium (main studies section), 151
Hauptversammlung (HV) (shareholders' meeting), 51
Hausbank-Prinzip (house-bank principle), 63
Haussmann, Helmut, 190
Health-food shops, 180
Heereman, Baron Constantin, 33
Heldenstadt (city of heroes), 192
Henkel, 97
Herrhausen, Alfred, 32, 207
'Hidden champions', 185–7
High-performance society, *see* **Leistungsgesellschaft** (high-performance society)
Historical costs, 81
Hochschulen (colleges), 159–60
Hoechst, 24
Holiday agreements, 121
Honecker, Erich, 11
Hubert, Jürgen, 30
Human rights, 39

IBM, 121
IG Chemie (Chemical-Workers' Union), 122, 127
IG Medien (Print-Workers' Union), 121, 122
IG Metall (Metal-Workers' Union), 109, 120–1, 122, 124, 134
IGM-Ost, 124
IKB Deutsche Industriebank (IKB), 188
Immigration, 102, 106
Imports, 208–9, 213
Industrial policy, 2–5, 165
Industrial relations, 114–15, 118–22
conflict, 117–18
democracy, 115–17
Industrial Safely Surveillance Associations, *see* **Technische Überwachungsvereine** (TÜVs)
Industrie- und Handelskammern (IHKs) (chambers of industry and commerce), 129, 140, 142, 148, 156, 213
Industriemeister examinations, 150
Industriestandort Deutschland (Germany as a location for industry), 5–6, 28, 29, 31
Industry Research Foundation, *see* **Stiftung Industrieforschung**

(Industry Research Foundation)
Inflation, control of, 2, 57−8
Ingenieur (engineer), 205
Initiative Mittelstand (small company campaign), 192
Insider dealing rules, 217
Institut der Deutschen Wirtschaft (IDW) (Institute of the German Economy), 31, 129−30
Institut für Arbeitsmarkt- und Berufsforschung (Institute of Labour Market and Vocational Research), 99
Institute of Economics and Social Science, 130
Institute für sozialistische Wirtschaftsführung (ISWs) (institutes for socialist economic management), 160
Institute of the German Economy, *see* **Institut der Deutschen Wirtschaft** (IDW)
Institute of Labour Market and Vocational Research, 99
Insurance market, 66
Inter-city express (ICE) service, 35
Inventory valuation, 82
Investment, 28
  abroad, 28
  in eastern Germany, 14, 27
  foreign inward, 28
  Japanese, 28
Investment grants, 83
ius sanguinis (law of the blood), 106
IVG, 5

Japanese investment, 28
Job-creation measures, *see* **Arbeitsbeschaffungsmaßnahmen** (job-creation measures)
Joint Committee of German Trade and Industry, 129
Joint Finance and Economics Council (German/French), 61
Judges, *see* **Richter** (judges)
Jürgensmann, Hans Hermann, 187
Justice administration, 39−42

Kartte, Wolfgang, 63
Kasch, Kurt, 189−90
Kaske, Karl-Heinz, 24−5, 206
Kiesinger, Kurt Georg, 56
Kinder, Kirche, Küche, 197

Kindergärten, 145, 157
Klein, Hans, 7
Kohl, Helmut, 2−8, 59, 97, 103, 106, 113, 163, 174
  Marshall Plan speech, 3
Kombinate (state-owned combines), 10
Kommanditgesellschaft (KG) (limited partnership), 47
Kommanditist (limited partner), 47
Komplementär (general partner), 47
Kreditanstalt für Wiederaufbau (KfW), 5, 188
Krenz, Egon, 11
Krüger, Wolfgang (case study), 190
Kunst (performing and fine arts), 203

Labour costs, 29
Labour courts, *see* **Arbeitsgerichte** (labour courts)
Labour offices, 53
Landesstellen (state bodies), 138
Landesverband der Sächsischen Industrie (LSI) (State Association of Saxon Industry), 139
Landesverbände (state associations), 130
Landgerichte (regional courts), 40
Landkreis (rural district), 54
Langer Samstag (Long Saturday), 32
Language, German business, 31
Language barriers, 103
Law on the Chambers of Industry and Commerce, Provisional Regulation, 142
Law personnel, 42−5
Law-support officer, *see* **Rechtsbeistand** (law-support officer)
Lawn-mowers, noise levels, 171
Lawyer, professional *see* **Rechtsanwalt** (professional lawyer)
Lay assessors, 42
Legal fees, 44
Legal reserve, 83
Lehrlinge (apprentices), 147, 162−3, 196
Leicht, Robert, 17
Leipzig, 192
Leistungsgesellschaft (high-performance society), 26, 119, 165
Leisure society, *see*

Freizeitgesellschaft (leisure society)
Leitender Angestellte (senior manager), 116
Leuna, AG, 24
Liabilities, disclosure of, 83
Lifelong learning, 156–7
Limited liability, 48
Local courts, *see* **Amtsgerichte** (local courts)
Lockouts, 133–5
Lohn- und Gehaltstarifvertrag (wages and salaries agreement), 112
Lohn- und Tarifpolitischer Ausschuß (Wages and Collective Bargaining), 132
Lohntarifverträge (wage agreements), 133
Luftfahrt Bundesamt (Federal Aviation Office), 210
Lufthansa, 3, 5, 7, 15

Management board, 51
  report, 78
Management buyouts in east, 192–3
Management development:
  in east, 160, 162
  in west, 155–6
Managers:
  in east:
    female, 203
    male, 199–203
  in west:
    female, 196–9
    male, 195–6
Managing director, *see* **Geschäftsführer** (managing director)
Manteltarifverträge (framework agreements), 113, 133
Manufacturing industries, 19–31
Master of Business Administration (MBA), 153–5
Mechanical engineering industry, 23–4
Mechaniker (mechanic), 205
Mediation procedure, voluntary, *see* **Schlichtungsverfahren** (voluntary mediation procedure)
Mercedes-Benz, 23, 29–30, 122, 180, 214
Messe (trade fair), 214–16

Messe-Müdigkeit (trade-fair fatigue), 215
Metal Trades Employers' Federation, 132
Metal-Workers' Union, *see* **IG Metall** (Metal-Workers' Union)
Middle managers, 200–1
Ministry for Labour and Social Affairs, 131
Mioba (case study), 192
Mitbestimmung (worker co-determination), 108
Mitbestimmungsgesetz (Co-determination Act) 1976, 116–17
Mittelstand (small and medium-sized companies), 22, 68, 182, 185–7
  takeovers, 219–21
Mittlerer Abschluß (intermediate school leaving certificate), 146
Modrow, Hans, 11
Montanmitbestimmungsgesetz, 131
Motorway network, 35
Mülder & Partner (research survey), 202–3
Müllologen (rubbishologists), 105
Murmann, Klaus, 132

Nationally-owned enterprises, *see* **Volkseigene Betriebe** (VEBs) (nationally-owned enterprises)
Neo-Nazis, 102, 105–6
Neptun Shipyard, 193
Neue Bundesländer (new federal states), 11
Neue Heimat, 111–12
New federal states, *see* **Neue Bundesländer** (new federal states)
Newspapers, business, 207
Nichtsozialistischer Reisekader, 200
Nitrogen oxide emissions, 174
Nord–Süd Gefälle (north–south divide), 26
North–south divide, *see* **Nord–Süd Gefälle** (north-south divide)
Notar (notary), 45

Oberlandesgerichte (appeal courts), 40
Oder-Neisse Line, 103, 104
Offene Handelsgesellschaft (OHG) (general unlimited partnership), 46–7

Öffentliche Dienste, Transport und Verkehr (ÖTV) (Union of Public Service and Transport Workers), 113, 114

Oil prices, 6

Old-age transition payments, *see* **Altersübergangsgeld** (old-age transition payments)

Opel, 23, 121, 180

Options and Futures Exchange, 69

Ossi (eastern German), 16

Ost–West Gefälle (east–west divide), 26–7

Ozone-layer hole, *see* **Ozonloch** (ozone-layer hole)

Ozonloch (ozone-layer hole), 174

Packaging laws, 105

Packaging Ordinance, *see* **Verpackungs-Verordnung** (Packaging Ordinance)

Paper manufacture, 179

Partner:
   general, *see* **Komplementär** (general partner)
   limited, *see* **Kommanditist** (limited partner)

Partnership:
   civil law, *see* **Gesellschaft des bürgerlichen Rechts** (GbR) (civil law partnership)
   general unlimited, *see* **Offene Handelsgesellschaft** (OHG)
   limited, *see* **Kommanditgesellschaft** (KG) (limited partnership)
   silent, *see* **Stille Gesellschaft** (SG) (silent partnership)
   special limited, *see* **GmbH & Co KG** (special limited partnership)

Patentgerichte (patents courts), 42

Patents courts, *see* **Patentgerichte** (patents courts)

Pay freeze, 114

Peace obligation, *see* **Friedenspflicht** (peace obligation)

Penetration, business, 208

People's capitalism, *see* **Volkskapitalismus** (people's capitalism)

Personnel director/manager, *see* **Arbeitsdirektor** (personnel director)

Pfeifer, Hans-Wolfgang, 17

Pieroth, Elmar, 194

Place strategy, 212–13

Planned economy, 10–11, 13

Pöhl, Karl Otto, 59, 60, 61, 70

Police Trade Union, *see* **Gewerkschaft der Polizei** (GdP) (Police Trade Union)

Polish relations, 103

Political organization, 15–17

Polytechnic school, *see* **Polytechnische Oberschule** (polytechnic school)

Polytechnics, 150, 151–2

Polytechnische Oberschule (polytechnic school), 158

Population, 165

Postal and telecommunications industry, 32

PREUSSAG, 7

Pricing strategy, 212

Print-Workers' Union, *see* **IG Medien** (Print-Workers' Union)

Printing Employers' Federation, *see* **Bundesverband Druck** (Printing Employers' Federation)

Privatization, 3, 5, 7, 9
   eastern German, 13–14

Product strategy, 209–11

Productivity levels, 29

Profit appropriations, 87

Profit and loss account, 79–80

Prokurist, 52–3, 196

Promotion strategy, 214–16
   promotion weeks, *see* **Werbewochen** (promotion weeks)

Proportionality, principle of, *see* **Verhältnismäßigkeitsprinzip** (principle of proportionality)

Prudence principle, 81

Public finances, eastern German, 13

Public prosecutor, *see* **Staatsanwalt** (public prosecutor)

Public sector borrowing, 71

Public Service and Transport Workers, *see* **Öffentliche Dienste, Transport und Verkehr** (ÖTV)

Racism, 106

Rahmentarifvertrag (framework agreement), 113

Railway systems, 35

Rasenmäherlärm-Verordung
(Ordinance on lawn-mower
noise), 171
Realschulabschluß (intermediate
school leaving certificate), 146
Realschule (intermediate school), 146
Rechtsanwalt (professional lawyer),
43–5
Rechtsbeistand (law-support officer),
45
Recycling, waste, 176
Red Army Faction, *see* **Rote Armee
Fraktion** (RAF) (Red Army
Faction)
Reformhäuser (health-food shops),
180
Refugees, *see* **Übersiedler** (refugees)
Refuse disposal, 167
Regional courts, *see* **Landgerichte**
(regional courts)
Reichsmark (RM), 57
Reifezeugnis (A-level certificate), 147
Reineke, Hendrikus, 192
Rentnerquotient (dependency ratio),
93
Research and Development (R & D),
15, 19, 30
Retail industry, 180–1
trade restrictions, 32–3
Returnees, *see* **Aussiedler**
Rhine–Main–Danube Canal, 36
Richter, Hans, 55
Richter (judges), 42
Ricke, Helmut, 32
Ridder, Wulf, 33
Robotron, 14
Rohwedder, Detlev, 13, 207
Romanians, 106
Rote Armee Fraktion (RAF) (Red
Army Faction), 207
Rotkäppchen (case study), 192–3
Rühe, Volker, 16
Rural district, *see* **Landkreis**

Sachbearbeiter (specialists/experts),
196
Safety standards, 210
Salzgitter, 7
Satzung (statutes), 49
Saxony, 16
BDI in, 139
Schenker, 3, 5

Schlepper (sherpas), 104
Schlesinger, Helmut, 9, 60, 62
Schleyer, Hanns-Martin, 207
Schlichtungsverfahren (voluntary
mediation procedure), 118
Schmidt, Helmut, 56, 106
Schools, *see* Education
Schuldscheine (borrowers'
promissory notes), 71
Schumpeter, 95
Schwerpunktstreiks (selective
strikes), 133
Science Council, *see* **Wissenschaftsrat**
(Science Council)
Service sector, 31–3
strategy, 209–11
Settlement procedures, industrial,
117–18
Sex discrimination, 197–9, 203
Shareholders, 49, 50–2, 69–70, 218
Shop Opening Hours Act 1956, 32–3
Sickness rate, 120
Siemens, 24, 29, 121
Simon, Hermann, 185–7
Single European Market (SEM), 33,
100, 107, 126, 210
Skilled workers, 149–50
Small companies:
in east, 191–2
finance for, 187–8
Social courts, *see* **Sozialgerichte**
(social courts)
Social Democrats (SPD), 2, 6, 9
Social market economy, *see* **soziale
Marktwirtschaft** (social market
economy)
Social welfare, 131
Sole trader, *see* **Einzelkaufmann** (sole
trader)
Solidarity pact, *see* **Solidarpakt**
(solidarity pact)
Solidarpakt (solidarity pact), 17,
97–8, 114
Soziale Marktwirtschaft (social
market economy), 1–2, 11–12,
13–15
Sozialgerichte (social courts), 42
**Sozialistische Einheitspartei
Deutschlands** (SED) (Communist
Party), 10, 199
Sozialpartner (social partners), 115
Späth, Lothar, 15, 26
Staatsanwalt (public prosecutor), 43

Staatssicherheitsdienst (Stasi, state security service), 38
Stadtkreis (urban district), 54
Standards:
  safety, 210
  technical, 210
State Association of Saxon Industry, 139
State bodies, *see* **Landesstellen** (state bodies)
State co-operatives, eastern Germany, 34
State pensions, 6
State-owned combines, *see* **Kombinate** (state-owned combines)
State-twinning system, 17
Statistisches Bundesamt (Federal Statistical Office), 189
Statutes, *see* **Satzung** (statutes)
Steuerberater (tax adviser), 88, 90
Steuerlüge (tax lie), 9, 113
Stewards, *see* **Vertrauensleute** (stewards)
Stiftung Industrieforschung (Industry Research Foundation), 202
Stihl, Hans Peter (entrepreneur case study), 183–4
Stille Gesellschaft (SG) (silent partnership), 48
Stock corporation, *see* **Aktiengesellschaft** (AG)
Stock Corporations Act 1965, 50
Stock exchange, 68–71
Stock Exchange Act, 217, 218
Stock Exchange Committee of Experts, 217
Stoltenberg, Gerhard, 3, 5, 7
Strategy:
  distribution, 212–13
  export marketing, 208–16
  place, 212–13
  pricing, 212
  product/service, 209–11
  promotion, 214–16
Strauss, Franz Josef, 5, 15, 26
Strike action, 117
  selective, 133
Structural adjustment, eastern German, 13
Stumpfer, Werner, 122
Stuttgart valuation technique, 221

Sulphur dioxide emissions, 173
Supervisory board, report, 78

Takeovers, 216
  negotiated, 219–21
  public, 217–19
Tarifautonomie (bargaining autonomy), 112
Tarifgebiet (bargaining area), 133
Tarifgemeinschaft Deutscher Länder, 131
Tarifpolitischer Ausschuß (Collective Bargaining Policy Committee), 133
Tarifunion (harmonization of conditions), 123
Tarifvertragsgesetz (Collective Agreements Act), 112
Tax lie, *see* **Steuerlüge** (tax lie)
Taxation, 4–5, 29, 91–2
Taxpayers' Association, *see* **Bund der Steuerzahler** (BdSt) (Taxpayers' Association)
Technical school, *see* **Fachschule** (technical school)
Technical standards, 210
Technik (art and science of making useful artefacts), 203–4, 214
Techniker (technician), 204
Technische Überwachungsvereine (TÜVs) (Industrial Safety Surveillance Associations), 210
Telecommunications industry, 32
Textile manufacture, 179–80
Thümmel, Dieter, 91
Thuringia, BDI in, 139–40
Tietmeyer, Hans, 60
Töpfer, Klaus, 176
Tourism, 36
Trade associations, *see* **Fachverbände**
Trade fair, *see* **Messe** (trade fair)
Trade tax, *see* **Gewerbesteuer** (trade tax)
Trade unions, 108–11
  in east, 123–4
  medium-term concerns, 125–7
Trading economy, *see* **Gewerbliche Wirtschaft** (trading economy)
Trading Regulations, *see* **Gewerbeordnung** (Trading Regulations)
Training Schemes, 96
Transport infrastructure, 35–6

Treibhauseffekt (greenhouse effect), 174

Treuhandanstalt (Trust Agency), 1, 13−16, 27, 54, 191

Treuhandgesetz (Trust Agency Law), 13, 54

Trunk road system, 35

Trust Agency, *see* **Treuhandanstalt** (Trust Agency)

Trust Agency Law, *see* **Treuhandgesetz** (Trust Agency Law)

Tutzing Declaration, 178

Überfremdung von Volk und Heimat (over-foreignization of people and homeland), 106

Übersiedler (refugees), 93, 103−4

Umweltbundesamt (UBA) (Federal Environment Agency), 171

Unemployment, 2, 6, 93, 107
in east, 95−8
graduates, 99
guest workers, 100−2
in west, 94−5
young people, 99

Ungeregelter Freiverkehr (unregulated free market), 69

Unification, 8, 11, 113, 163
funding costs of, 9

Unification Treaty, 39, 53, 123

Union of Salaried Employees, *see* **Deutsche Angestellten- Gewerkschaft** (DAG)

United Kingdom, Community Charter rejection, 126

Universities, 99−100, 147, 150, 152−5, 159−60

Urban district, 54

Valuation calculations, takeover, 219−21

Value equalization, 54

VEBA, 3, 5, 6, 27

Verband der Chemischen Industrie (VCI) (Association of the Chemical Industry), 24

Verband der Wirtschaft Thüringens (VWT), 139−40

Verband Deutscher Elektrotechniker e.V. (VDE) (Association of German Electrical Technicians), 210

Verbände Die (The Associations), 128−9

Verbaucher-Initiative (Consumer Initiative), 181

Vereidigter Buchprüfer (sworn accountant), 91

Verein Deutscher Ingenieure e.V. (VDI) (Association of German Engineers), 205, 210

Verein Deutscher Maschinenbau- Anstalten (VDMA) (Association of German Machinery Manufacturers), 23−4

Vereinigung der Deutschen Arbeitgeberverbände (VBA) (Confederation of German Employers' Assns.), 128

Vereinigung der Kommunalen Arbeitgeberverbände, 130−1

Vereinigung Technischer Überwachungsvereine e.V. (VTÜV) (Fedn. of Industrial Safety Assns.), 210

Vereinigungen Volkseigener Betriebe der DER, 130

Verhältnismäßigkeitsprinzip (principle of proportionality), 117

Verpackungs-Verordnung (Packaging Ordinance), 168, 176, 178

Versprochen ist versprochen (a promise is a promise), 124

Vertrauenskörper (body of stewards), 115

Vertrauensleute (stewards), 115

Verwaltungsgerichte (administrative courts), 42.

VIAG, 5, 7

Vocational training, 30
in east, 158−9, 162
in west, 147−9
higher, 149−51

Vofa, 97

Volga Republic, 103

Volkseigene Betriebe (VEBs) (nationally-owned enterprises), 10, 13

Volkskapitalismus (people's capitalism), 5

Volkswagen, 3, 5, 6−7, 15, 23, 27, 180

Volkswirtschaftslehre (VWL) (economics), 147

Vorsprung durch Technik (in the lead through engineering), 203

Vorstandsmitglieder (management board members), 51
Vorstandsvorsitzender (management board chairman), 51
Vredeling Initiative, 126

Wage negotiations, 95, 113, 114, 132−3
Wages and Collective Bargaining Policy Committee, 132
Wages and salaries agreement, *see* **Lohn- und Gehaltstarifvertrag** (wages and salaries agreement)
Währungsreform (currency reform), 57
Waigel, Theo, 7, 72
Waldsterben (dying forests), 166
Walter Raymond Foundation, *see* **Walter-Raymond-Stiftung**
Walter-Raymond-Stiftung (Walter Raymond Foundation), 135
Waste disposal, 167, 176
Waste Water Technology Association, *see* **Abwassertechnische Vereinigung e.V.** (ATV)
Water contamination, 166−7 treatment for, 174−6
Waterways network, 35−6
Wealth, redistribution of, 5
Weiss, Heinrich, 136
Weiter so (more of the same), 6
Weiterbildung (management training), 155−6
Weltanschauung (view of the world), 203
Werbewochen (promotion weeks), 214
Wertausgleich (value equalization), 54
Wessi (western German), 16
White-collar workers, *see* **Angestellte** (white-collar workers)
Wildlife, harm to, 167−8
Wirtschaftliche Wende (economic turnround), 2, 4
Wirtschafts- und Sozialwissenschaftliches Institut (WSI), 130
Wirtschaftsausschuß (economics committee), 125

Wirtschaftsprüfer (WP) (accountant/auditor), 88−9
Wirtschaftsprüferkammer (Chamber of Accountants/Auditors), 91
Wirtschaftsverbände (business associations), 129
Wirtschaftswunder (economic miracle), 2, 26, 165, 182
Wissenschaft (knowledge, science, some arts), 203
Wissenschaftsrat (Science Council), 163
Wohlstandsgesellschaft (affluent society), 19, 120, 165
Women, perception of (three Ks), 197
Work ethic, German, 120−2
Working days lost, 119
Working hours, 120
Working week, 121−2
Works Constitution Act 1972, *see* **Betriebsverfassungsgesetz** (Works Constitution Act)
Works' council, *see* **Betriebsrat** (works' council)
Writing off, plant items, 82

Xenophobia, 106

Young people, in west, 99−100

Zentralausschuß der Werbewirtschaft e.V. (ZAW) (Cent. Office of the German Advertising Assn), 214
Zentralbankrat (ZBR) (Central Bank Council), 62
Zentralinstitut für sozialistische Wirtschaftsführung (ZSW) (Central Institute for Socialist Economic Management), 160
Zentralstelle für die Vergabe von Studienplätzen, 147
Zentralverband Elektrotechnik- und Elektronikindustrie e.V. (ZVEI), 137−8
Zentralverbände (business associations), 135
Zukunftsmusik (jam tomorrow), 220
Zweites Wirtschaftswunder (second economic miracle), 18, 37